Space and Play in Japanese Videogame Arcades

This book presents a scholarly investigation of the development and culture of Japanese videogame arcades, both from a historical and contemporary point of view.

Providing an overview of the historical evolution of public amusement spaces from the early rooftop amusement spaces from the early nineteenth century to the modern multi-floor and interconnected arcade complexes that characterize the urban fabric of contemporary Japan, the book argues that arcade videogames and their associated practices must be examined in the context in which they are played, situated in the interrelation between the game software, the cabinets as material conditions of play, and the space of the venue that frames the experience. Including three case studies of distinct and significant game centres located in Tokyo and Kyoto, the book addresses of play in public, including the notion of performance and observation as play practices, spatial appropriation, as well as the compartmentalization of the play experience.

In treating videogames as sets of circumstances, the book identifies the opportunities for ludic practices that videogame arcades provide in Japan. As such, it will appeal to students and scholars of Game Studies and Digital Media Studies, as well as those of Japanese Culture and Society.

Jérémie Pelletier-Gagnon is a Postdoctoral Fellow at the Université du Québec à Montréal, Canada.

Routledge Contemporary Japan Series

110 **Civil Defense in Japan**
Issues and Challenges
Edited by Yasuhiro Takeda, Jun Ito, and Yusuke Kawashima

111 **Mobile Japanese Migrants to the Pacific West and East**
Self-searching, Work, and Identification
Etsuko Kato

112 **Critical Review of the Abe Administration**
Politics of Conservatism and Realism
Edited by Yoichi Funabashi and Koji Nakakita

113 **Lay Zen in Contemporary Japan**
Tradition, Interpretation, and Invention
Erez Joskovich

114 **Japanese Whaling and the People Behind It**
A Look from Within
Nadzeya Shuteva

115 **Dark Heritage in Contemporary Japan**
Relics of an Underground Empire
Jung-Sun Han

116 **Space and Play in Japanese Videogame Arcades**
Jérémie Pelletier-Gagnon

For more information about this series, please visit: www.routledge.com/Routledge-Contemporary-Japan-Series/book-series/SE0002

Space and Play in Japanese Videogame Arcades

Jérémie Pelletier-Gagnon

Routledge
Taylor & Francis Group
LONDON AND NEW YORK

First published 2024
by Routledge
4 Park Square, Milton Park, Abingdon, Oxon OX14 4RN

and by Routledge
605 Third Avenue, New York, NY 10158

Routledge is an imprint of the Taylor & Francis Group, an informa business

British Library Cataloguing-in-Publication Data
A catalogue record for this book is available from the British Library

ISBN: 978-1-032-22685-9 (hbk)
ISBN: 978-1-032-22692-7 (pbk)
ISBN: 978-1-003-27377-6 (ebk)

DOI: 10.4324/9781003273776

Typeset in Times New Roman
by codeMantra

In memory of Masayuki Uemura
who brought new play partners to the world

Contents

Figures

Preface

This book represents the original work of the author, Jérémie Pelletier-Gagnon.

Section I of this dissertation includes material based on the article "Introduction: Geemu, Media Mix, and the State of Japanese Video Game Studies", written with Martin Picard and published in *Kinephanos* (vol. 5, no. 1, 2015). The passages based on this material were written by Jérémie Pelletier-Gagnon. Elements from Chapter 6 were published in *The Journal of Replaying Japan* under the title "Players, Cabinets, and the Space In-between: Case Studies of Non-ludic Negotiation of Video Game Cabinet Spaces in Japanese Game Centers" (vol. 1, 2019).

All pictures featured in this book are, unless otherwise stated, the property of the author. Images belonging to other property holders are used under fair use regulations for research purposes and have been credited to their author(s) accordingly. The games and cabinets featured in the figures remain the respective property of their exclusive owners.

The content of this book has been proofread and copy-edited by Cindy Chopoidalo in accordance with the protocol of The Editors' Association of Canada/Association canadienne des réviseurs.

The floor plans of the case studies featured in Chapters 5 and 6 use the Photoshop "Basic Pattern Element" brushes asset package by Peter Plastic published on Brusheezy.com.

For clarity for an international audience, all Japanese names appear according to the Western order, in which given names precede surnames, except in citations for which the original order is kept.

The transcriptions of Japanese words and names use the modified Hepburn system format, which is the most common romanization system outside of Japan and the closest pronunciation analogue for those who are unfamiliar with Japanese. Macrons are used to express long vowels instead of double vowels when no word-border separates them. For example, the Japanese word for *videogames* is written as *gēmu* as opposed to *geemu.*

In-text references, footnotes, citations, and list of works cited are based on the 9th edition of the Modern Language Association style guide. In cases in which the language of the works cited differs from English, the original language's capitalization rules prevail. In addition, all non-English article and book titles are given in English translations, except when judged unnecessary.

Acknowledgements

This project originated one late evening in 2012 in Japan when my colleague Martin Picard suggested I take my then-burgeoning interest in arcades further in academia as a PhD project. I am very thankful to the many friends and colleagues, both old and new, who accompanied me along the way and supported me in achieving my vision.

The list of people to thank for their involvement in this project and/or in my personal life is too numerous to properly account for here, but I would like to use this space to acknowledge some of the people who helped me in the past few years. Thanks to Toshiya Ueno for taking me under his wing in Japan during my stay at Wako University, and to the entire group of graduate students who accepted a stranger in their ranks for two years. Thanks to Kensuke for showing me the ropes while I was living in Tokyo.

Although this project originated in Tokyo, it is in Edmonton that it took concrete shape. Thanks to Geoffrey Rockwell for introducing me to so many things and so many people. Without your guidance, this project would never have gone anywhere. Thanks to my co-supervisor Massimo Verdicchio for helping me get a hold of the city and for your free spirit. Thanks to the entire department of MLCS and the Office of Interdisciplinary Studies for understanding my (special) situation. These four years in Alberta would have been difficult without the friendship of diverse groups of people who accompanied me at different moments. Thanks to the "dv9" (Andrea, Aiden, Bret, Christina, Dan, John, Lori, and Zach) for the great moments and the fabulous group spirit. Thanks to Lars, Marine, Nicolas, Axel, and Gabi for the awesome company and the great Friday drinks; I could not have hoped for a nicer group of friends with which to share the joy and misery of graduate school. Thanks to all the colleagues I encountered all over the world with whom I share my love of knowledge, Japanese culture, and videogames, but especially Mimi, Sonja, Martin, and Andrew. Of course, thanks to all the Fluffies who mustered up the courage to jump on the ice at every game despite the unforgiving odds.

Thanks to everyone who provided assistance for my field research travel to Japan between January and April 2016. Thanks to my colleagues at Ritsumeikan Center for Game Studies, including Koichi Hosoi, Akinori Nakamura, Mitsuyuki Inaba, Shuji Watanabe, Kazufumi Fukuda, Akito Inoue, and Masayuki Uemura. Thanks to Hiroyasu Katō, Shigeo Tosaki, Yasuo Kawasaki, and Zenshi Ishii for sharing their knowledge of arcades with me, as well as the patrons of the bar 16shots for very insightful conversations and anecdotes during one evening in April 2016. Thanks to Rachael Hutchinson for the inspiration leading to the publication of this manuscript, and to Stephanie Rogers for her infinite patience in coping with the numerous life changes that affected the making of this book.

Thanks also to everyone back home who supported me throughout my academic exile. Merci à ma famille Lise, Bruno, Mathieu et Chloé pour votre soutien et votre présence. Thanks to Daigo and Akané for being there on my return, and thanks to Noémie for appearing in my life just in time for the final sprint. Thanks to Azur for joining the party and for enlightening my days too often spent in front of a computer screen.

I would also like to acknowledge the Social Sciences and Humanities Council of Canada, the GRAND NCE research network, and MEXT for their financial support.

Acronyms and Abbreviations

ANT	Actor-network theory.
AOU	Zen'nihon amyūzumento shisetsu eigyō-sha kyōkai rengō-kai (All Japan Federation of Amusement Facility Operators Association).
AR	Augmented reality.
ASCII	American Standard Code for Information Interchange.
BBCS	*BlazBlue: Continuum Shift.*
Extreme Vs.	*Mobile Suit Gundam: Extreme Vs.*
Fūeihō	Fūzoku eigyōtō no kisei oyobi gyōmu no tekiseikatō ni kansuru hōritsu (Law Regulating Entertainment Businesses).
G.I.	Galvanized iron. Coloquially used to refer to personnel in the US military.
GRAND NCE	Graphics, Animation, and New Media Network of Centres of Excellence.
Gundam Vs.	*Mobile Suit Gundam: Gundam Vs. Gundam.*
IC card	Integrated circuit card.
JAA	Zen'nihon yūen kyōkai (Japan Amusement Association).
JAEPO	Japan Amusement Expo.
JAIA	Nihon amyūzumento sangyō kyōkai (Japan Amusement Industry Association).
JAMMA	Shadanhōjin nihon amusement machine kōgyōkyōkai (Japan Amusement Machinery Manufacturers Association).
MAME	Multiple Arcade Machine Emulator.
MEXT	Ministry of Education, Culture, Sports, Science, and Technology.
MJ5 Evolution	*Sega Network Taisen Mahjoong Evolution 5.*
NAO	Nihon amyūzumento operētā kyōkai (Japan Amusement Operators Association).
NPA	National Police Agency.
Project DIVA Arcade	*Hatsune Miku: Project DIVA Arcade.*

PX	Post exchange.
Senjō no kizuna	*Kidō senshi gundam: senjō no kizuna.*
Shift JIS	Shift Japanese Industrial Standards
TT	Tabletop.
Virtual-On	*Cyber Trooper Virtual-On.*
VR	Virtual reality.
WCCF	*World Club Champion Football.*

Part I

Contextualizing Play in Japanese Amusement Spaces

1 Introduction

Play in Japanese Videogame Arcades as a Culturally Situated Practice

The Fuji TV channel provided an interesting surprise for Tokyo commuters making their way through the Shinjuku train station in the early days of 2015. As part of an advertising campaign publicizing *Psycho-Pass: The Movie* (Shiotani and Motohiro) based on its hit anime series of the same name, 16 60" television screens equipped with motion sensors and digital cameras using Microsoft's Kinetic V2 technology were installed on one long wall of the Tokyo Marunouchi Subway Line Promenade for one week between January 5 and 11 (Akcasu). The screens acted as mirrors, reflecting every one of the hundreds of thousands of commuters walking through that specific hallway of one of the busiest train stations in the world. This seemingly normal monitor, however, had a unique built-in functionality: it would scan the face of every commuter stepping in front of the screen and provide a reading of every individual's mental state and "crime coefficient" expressed in a number based on their facial scan in true *Psycho-Pass* fashion. Based on the resulting number, an Enforcer character of the *Psycho-Pass* universe would be summoned on the screen to either "paralyze" or "eliminate" the guilty commuter with their futuristic Dominator handgun.

Set in the distant future of 2112, the anime series *Psycho-Pass* (Shiotani and Motohiro) takes place in a world in which every citizen's potential for deviancy is routinely scanned by drones in public settings as easily as this installation suggests, to be then calculated by a supercomputer that determines if a citizen should be incarcerated or not. The protagonists of the series are government agents tasked to identify and arrest citizens with a high "crime coefficient", a value determined by a supercomputer based on an analysis of their background and psychological profile, before they engage in any criminal activity. This marketing device plays on the dynamics of the anime series and presents its worldview in a unique interactive fashion that actively involves the public. As a side effect, the installation also creates the potential for serendipitous connections between people who would normally not make eye contact while rushing to secure a seat in the next overcrowded train.

For anyone curious enough to spare a few seconds from his/her busy commute to inspect that unique public interactive interface, the result was often surprising and amusing. People showed different reactions to the information displayed on the screen: some commented on the numbers, others would observe people's scores in silence, and some might even take photographs and share them on their social

DOI: 10.4324/9781003273776-2

media spaces. However, no one involved in this impromptu interactive screen was left completely indifferent to the experience it provided. For a short moment, strangers gathered around a piece of technology that generated a common experience, enabling the potential for interaction and communication in a space that usually encourages anonymity. Commuters were sharing space within a single screen, a disruptive practice for spaces of circulation such as train stations.

If one considers recent arguments denouncing cell phones and other mobile communication devices as threats to the local social fabric and life in its immediacy (Turkle), that gigantic mirror/screen hybrid construct that also provided commuters time to pause to reconsider the space around them demonstrates how interactive digital technology does not necessarily put distance between people, but might also provide a different frame through which other kinds of interactions are possible. The *Psycho-Pass* installation is a testimony to how interactive technologies located in public spaces can propel common engagement with a text and with other individuals sharing the same space. It also indicates that what makes this experience possible is the interinfluences between the materiality of the device (the screen and motion sensors), the software algorithm and themes of the text (the world of *Psycho-Pass*), and the space that supports and influences the experience (a busy train station). Indeed, at the heart of this experience was a specific combination of these three elements that create the successful conditions to draw passersby toward the screen and push them into examining the object along with their surroundings.

Japanese Arcade Videogames and Interactive Digital Entertainment in Public

While these sorts of digital installations might be seen as completely new ways to introduce ludic elements to the public sphere made possible only by the development of high-end digital technology, the presence of public entertainment devices from which the *Psycho-Pass* installation derives has characterized Japanese urban life for decades. TV Tokyo's installation is an example of a broader movement encompassing many forms of interactive amusement equipment that characterize contemporary entertainment in Japan. Its closest counterpart is perhaps the large-scale family amusement parks focusing on digitally enhanced interactive experiences that have existed in Japan since the 1990s. One such example is Sega's Joypolis, a high-technology amusement park in which visitors are invited to interact with one another through simple but innovative digital technologies. Most of Joypolis' open attractions have no instructions, only large touch screens that invite customers to experiment with them and discover their functions. One example amongst many is a wall-mounted screen in which a variety of sea creatures with unique features seem to live. As visitors approach the installation, pictures of their faces are taken and superimposed on the sea creatures that swim across the screen and encounter other creatures and other customers. Many other installations creating serendipitous moments between customers are featured in this space, but certainly the most important inspiration for this type of high-tech urban entertainment are the traditional videogames found in the many arcades in Japan's urban centres.

Arcade videogames constitute an important part of the Japanese urban entertainment cultural background, ever since *Pong* cabinets were first imported to the archipelago at the beginning of the 1970s. By the middle of the same decade, Japanese manufacturers would begin to create their own games, and in 1978, videogames would first break into mainstream culture with the release of *Space Invaders*. In the 1980s, the arrival of home videogame consoles meant that arcade videogame manufacturers would have to create new and innovative experiences that could only be fully appreciated in spaces that came to be called *game centres*. These game centres thus became venues in which children and adults could enjoy interactive experiences that used the latest computation technologies, the most innovative forms of game design, and the most daring interactive devices. Japanese arcade-goers have been sharing screens in public settings since the 1970s, in many different forms.

Pioneers of the public interactive entertainment industry, game centres have displayed many faces over the years, as they have accommodated new trends and regulations that have drastically transformed their architectural structures and social environments. As the cost of high-end technology decreases and the numbers of public digital interactive equipment most likely increases, scholars and designers must develop comprehensive theoretical tools that enable a full understanding of the complex dynamics that govern the experience of playing with digital equipment made for public use. To achieve this goal, it is essential to first examine thoroughly the rich tradition of arcade videogames as a whole, from the perspective of both the games themselves and the material and spatial conditions that are intrinsic parts of the experience that they provide. With their long and diverse history, Japanese game centres provide case studies from which to approach issues and questions related to the dynamics and impact of digital entertainment in public settings. Unpacking the dynamics of play, performance, and intimacy within game centres over a period of approximately 40 years is a first step toward answering larger questions of how interactive technology is put to use in public spaces and how its material conditions either bring its public together or create distance between participants.

The *Psycho-Pass* installation, and the dystopian universe created by famed scenarist Gen Urobuchi for the series, is a reminder of the presence of interactive digital technology in the public sphere, as well as its potential consequences. As such, it brings forward important questions about the negotiation of privacy for individuals engaging with these systems. To a lesser degree, whereas the protagonists of *Psycho-Pass* evolve within a world governed by an "algorithmic tyranny" (Wood 3) that puts the daily lives of citizens under constant surveillance, users of the Shinjuku station also temporarily exposed themselves to the public eye when facing the screen, similarly to how game centre patrons must negotiate the presence of other players and observers within an arcade. This book seeks to uncover new objects, texts, and contexts that will provide new questions and perspectives to the scholarly study of videogames and our relationship to ludic interactive technology in public spaces.

The objective of this book is to provide an understanding of public videogame playing from a holistic perspective, one that accounts for the materiality of the machine, the affordances of the software, and the space as the context of the play activity. At its core, this project considers videogames primarily as the purveyor of a play activity and as a practice, and thus it aims to interrogate how these practices play out in the context of Japanese videogame arcades while considering in equal part the influence of its texts, material conditions, and spatial context.

There has been much academic study of the medium of videogames, but keeping in line with contemporary trends, arcade videogaming has been somewhat relegated to the domain of history and retro-gaming culture. By shifting our gaze onto contemporary Japanese game centre culture via a series of field studies, I want to bring attention to a form of play rarely studied in academia, as well as objects and cultural practices whose presence is often limited to the boundaries of Japanese studies. Most importantly, the objective of this study is to reconsider the practice and theoretical ideas behind play as a primarily situated activity, both spatially and culturally. This book seeks to examine play as it occurs in Japanese game centres from a historical perspective. It includes thorough on-site investigations of the fundamental dynamics of the practice and case studies that serve as reference material for future studies. Practices of play in public settings, and in other settings in general, are in a state of constant evolution, which partly explains why the historical study of play can be challenging.

Situated Gaming: Between Software, Materiality, and Spatial Contexts

The guiding principles of this project's approach to the question of gaming in public are listed below:

1 Arcade gaming operates around the axis of gregariousness. The act of play in public settings is discussed according to how the presence or absence of bystanders or observers, and to whether one is part of a group or not, is being negotiated;
2 This axis of gregariousness affects the play of a specific game. How the act of play is conducted affects how bystanders act, and thus affects play as a whole. The experience of a game played in a situation where one is aware of others' presence and gaze is different from one where players feel isolated from the crowd. The same game may thus be approached in different ways and provide different experiences.

This project considers videogames as devices composed of three different axes which, when combined into a single assemblage, allow us to place the notion of play at the centre of the activity. Just as Newman invites us to consider play as a "socially and culturally situated practice" (Newman 153), the goal of this project is to regard games as sets of circumstances in which certain objects encounter an audience in a specific time and space. The first element of this assemblage is software, the basis of all videogames, which provides the rules and the virtual world that players negotiate. The software is then packaged and presented to players in a set of material conditions, most commonly the arcade cabinet made up of different parts ranging from the screen to the joystick and buttons. This element comprises the input methods through which the player's actions are mediated, and the physical play conditions that the game imposes on the player. The third layer of this assemblage examined in this study is the space in which the activity takes place. Arcade gaming, as opposed to other forms of digital entertainment, is firmly rooted in a space that is specifically structured to provide a particular play experience. As such, it is difficult to read the arcade game experience without considering the context in which it takes place. I will demonstrate how the combination of these three elements generate both ludic and social conditions that greatly influence how arcade games are used, how communities form around them, and how they come to influence the nature of the space in which they are played. Arcade games are meant to be observed as much as to be played; a player who decides to interact with a machine automatically agrees to become a ludic performer and the object of the gaze of other players in the vicinity.

To account for this phenomenon, this project introduces and develops the notion of *ludo-egregore* as a theoretical concept that brings attention to the relationship between people and technology present in the space of the videogame arcade. This concept takes its inspiration from the notion of egregore, as developed by the situationist movement to characterize the group spirit between participants in a specific gregarious activity. The concept of ludo-egregore considers videogames as the catalytic collective activity of play that involves both active and non-active participants, and both human and non-human agents. This concept seeks to unpack the phenomenon surrounding the act of gaming in public settings, where players are exposed to specific material and spatial conditions. It adopts a microcosmic perspective on the influence of egregores, created by the act of play and the object of the game, on the course and form of the play activity, and their own influence on the generation of other egregores. The ludo-egregoric perspective enables a more complex understanding of digital entertainment and allows us to consider a videogame as a profoundly situated experience rather than a pure textual object dissociated from its context.

Why have I chosen to study specifically video arcade games? The North American arcade scene almost completely disappeared in the brutal recession of the game industry in the mid-1980s and is no longer a driving force in Western videogame culture. On the other hand, the Japanese arcade industry not only survived but has also retained an important cultural presence in the country, although the emergence of home consoles and mobile gaming, the ageing population, and the concentration of capital in the game industry has influenced the types of games manufactured and the number of venues being operated. According to the National Police Agency (NPA), 4,381 operating game centres were registered in Japan in 2017 (Keisatsuchō seikatsu 1), a far cry from the 44,386 venues reported in 1987 (Ippan shadanhōjin). The decline in the operation of small neighbourhood game centres explains this sharp drop in terms of total venue numbers, but the game centres currently operating in Japan are now much bigger, more concentrated, and more financially stable than they were in previous decades. Although the 1980s saw tremendous pressure

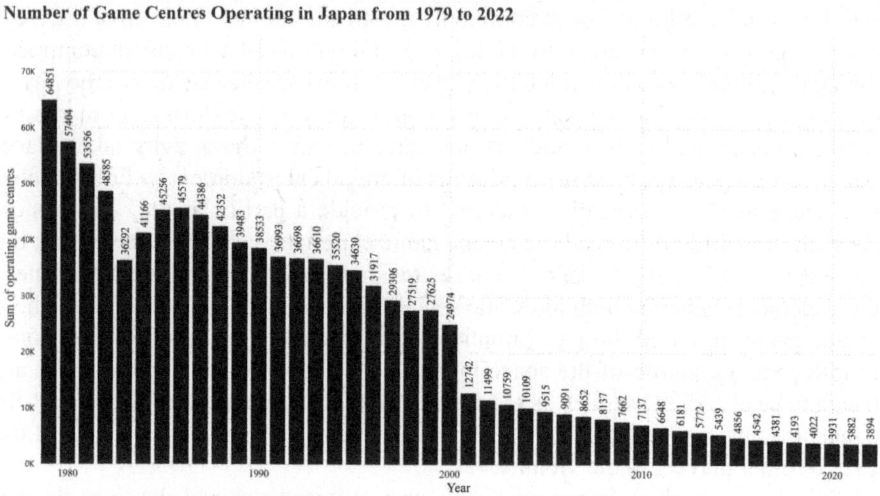

Figure 1.1 A chart compiling the number of game centres in Japan based on data collected by the National Police Agency. Though changes in the data acquisition and compilation accounts for the steep decline in 1982 and 2002, the chart clearly indicates a constant decrease of the number of videogame arcades in Japan (chart compiled by the author).

Source: This chart is based on data published by the National Police Agency in yearly white papers between 1979 and 2022. The calculation method varies significantly over the years as categorization changed from calculating the total number of game centres to compiling those which obtain accreditation from the agency, and eventually establishing a distinction between venues that operate mainly as game centres and those whose floor space is only partly dedicated to videogames. The chart represents the total number of game centres identified for each year.

put on the business, game centres did not close with the democratization of player culture that home consoles provided, but evolved into different venues, housing different machines providing different experiences.

As of 2023, the industry is mainly represented by a singular business association, the Nihon amyūzumento sangyō kyōkai (Japan Amusement Industry Association, or JAIA)[1] and publishes its own industry journal, *Amyūzumento sangyō* (*Amusement Industry*).[2] It also has had various consumer magazines covering events and new products over the years such as *Gekkan arukadia* (*Monthly Arcadia*), published by Enterbrain until 2015, and *Dengeki ākēdo* (*Dengeki Arcade*), published by ASCII Media Works.[3] In addition, the industry sponsors an annual showcase, the Japan Amusement Expo (JAEPO), which introduces customers to the new games they will be experiencing throughout the year in one of the country's numerous arcade parlours.

Innovative game design and attention to consumer interaction with machines and spaces are essential for the game industry, which makes Japanese game centres an important case study for the examination of ludic human-machine interactions and their social affordances. This project focuses on Japanese game centres because, although arcade culture is a ubiquitous element of digital urban entertainment in

Japan that caters to all ages, it is largely non-existent in the West and thus virtually absent from Western game studies. The Anglophone literature in the field acknowledges the importance of studying play as a situated practice and as a performance, but most of these studies are theoretical and call for more work to be done in this area (Bayliss; Fernández-Vara; Kort et al.; Mäyrä). Although Western game scholars are aware of the need to study arcades, such studies remain scarce perhaps due to the lack of an influential space-dependent game culture in the West. The innovations in the domains of technology and design that could redefine our understanding of digital entertainment are therefore understudied in Western scholarship, and one of the objectives of this project is to bring to light such ludic objects, both those that provide public performances and those that focus on providing quiet spaces for more private interactions with technology.

"What Are Kids Looking for in the Spaces of These 'Game Centres'?": Game Centres as a Third Place

The question that is most often asked in discussions of Japanese game centres in the Western world is why arcades still exist in Japan. Though the simple presence of public gaming venues is surprising for many contemporary foreign observers, we should acknowledge that the idea of leaving the comfort of one's home to go to often disreputable parts of town to play videogames with strangers puzzled many social critics and media personalities at the turn of the century as well. In a 2001 article from which the heading of this section is taken, child psychologist Hiroyuki Aihara adopts an open mindset to examine these spaces that, until that time, had often been denounced in similar publications as nothing more than hotbeds of criminality (100). Aihara states that videogame arcades are socialization spaces located outside of the common surveillance grid of the dominant disciplinary regimes to which Japanese children are subjected: the family and the school. Game centres are among the few places that offer a "real" sense of social mixing whose encounters are unbounded by class, education, or age. This space and its collection of players and observers, which themselves form a microcosm of society, also becomes a place in which youth can develop self-confidence and a freer sense of self-expression in an alternative regime of value, based on gaming prowess rather than on social status, interpersonal relationships or academic success.

Although game centres are not urban utopias of perfect social mixing and harmony because the act of playing is inseparable from non-ludic spheres of life, Aihara's reading of these spaces echoes some of Ray Oldenburg's concerns with the concept of the *third place*. Embodied in urban venues such as coffee houses, bistros, or *piazzas* in Europe, third places function as public gathering spaces allowing social life to flourish outside of home and work (XVIII). These spaces, in which participants can share their ideas and values, enable individuals to meet and happily exchange ideas in a positive, egalitarian, comfortable, and playful setting with other people belonging to the same community, and thus develop a vital basis for the development of connections with the social body (42).

The idea of the arcade as a third place has been explored in relation to venues in the West, especially in its function as a forum for players to meet, interact, share tips, and structure normative practices, all around a common ludic and playful setting (Harper 138–39).[4] However, the dynamics of game centres, as well as of the broader Japanese videogame culture in general, remain different enough to warrant an extended interpretation of the concept. Though the third place was born from the archetype of the coffee house venue, discussions with friends or acquaintances are no longer the primary appeal of these spaces. Patterns of socialization and communication still occur, but take on different forms. They host a range of different types of digital and non-digital entertainment activities, each providing its own materiality to a place designed to maximize customer interest. The aforementioned apparatus of the communication notebook is one of them, but so is also, as we will see in the following chapters, both distant and active observation, as well as communication through online platforms.

Even though, as Aihara suggests, youths may be seeking genuine and unsupervised social connections and, through these, lay the foundation for positive personal growth, any serious concrete answer to his original question lacks the approach of empirically investigating arcade game machines in action, or a focus on what is concretely happening in game centres between users, machines, and spaces. What types of games create new social connections? How are cabinets mapped within game centre spaces, and how does this mapping influence the activity occurring within? How does space affect machine design and, subsequently, the behaviour of players? If game machines are at the heart of imagining the social world in game centres, more attention must be paid to the types of social practices that they afford. By analyzing real instances of physical and ludic encounters between players and machines and reading them through the concept of ludo-egregore, we can answer these questions and begin to comprehend the reasons for the presence of arcades in contemporary urban Japan in a world in which videogames are just a finger swipe away on smartphones. Observing these encounters through field study in different types of settings is essential for such an analysis.

As previously discussed, game centres are venues whose functions and spatial structures have changed tremendously as they adapted to evolving sociocultural paradigms. But as game centres metamorphose over the decades, they are also subject to the needs, peculiarities, and cultures of their direct locales, whether on a busy commercial street or in a residential district. One of the major elements in establishing local urban specificities is the Japanese zoning system, which is decided at the national level, unlike North American standards in which municipal legislatures directly exercise power over zoning. As such, all cities in Japan[5] are under the authority of a broad national zoning system that emphasizes height, volume limitations, and uses of structures to "prevent a mixture of buildings used for different purposes in one area" (City Planning). Japan's zoning system, composed of 12 different classifications, allows for considerable flexibility in the design of urban landscape as it operates on an inclusion basis. Relevant for the case at hand, zones designated as residential areas may host small shops and offices, but these are limited according to height and floor space, rather than according to their individual uses. Game centres are subjected to these rules under the amusement facility category, and as such are allowed in residential areas, but are limited in terms of floor space. Alternatively, game centres opening in commercial zones are not limited by floor space and may span multiple floors. Thus, game centres are featured in a variety of urban districts, and although the nature of the use remains the same with regard to zoning policies, their structures and functions differ significantly depending on their location in the city.

A field study of arcade gaming in Japan, therefore, must consider the different types of venues serving different districts and publics. Though zoning laws are a major influence on the structure that any venue may adopt, most game centres are also fluid entities whose internal physical organization and, most importantly, player base fluctuate depending on the season, day of the week, and hour of the day. On the one hand, following the release of new products, certain games are displaced somewhere else within the venue while others disappear entirely. On the other hand, the customer base of game centres also varies greatly in terms of number and occupation over the course of a single day; students and young people tend to play games outside of school hours, while it is rare to see children beyond afternoon hours. Thus, encompassing the entire culture of a specific game centre, or of game centres in general, is not a realistic expectation for this project. Any empirical study of a location should instead be considered as discrete snapshots of time-specific windows of observation. By taking diverse and relevant samples of these snapshots, we can begin to account for the diversity of public play and the many functions of game centres as urban sites of play.

Culturally Situated Game Studies

Japanese videogames have been studied since the establishment of the field of game studies, but they have been examined mainly from the perspective of the various localized forms into which they are adapted for the Western market and their reception abroad, and are discussed more in terms of elements of an interconnected global market than as cultural products of a specific time and place. As Martin Picard states, "it is as if the only manifestation of the Japanese videogame industry had been made on a global level, while the specific development of the industry on the Japanese territory had never existed" ("The Foundation of Geemu"). Since the beginning of the twenty-first century, the subject has been explored with reference to transcultural change and transformation, and the genres that are unique or distinctive to Japanese games (Consalvo, "Console Video Games"; "Convergence and Globalization"; Picard, "Haunting Backgrounds"). In more recent years, however, scholars around the world have accounted for the global diversity of context in which games are produced and consumed (Apperley; Jin; Liboriussen and Martin; Penix-Tadsen; Wolf). As the study of Japanese videogames has decentralized and moved away from the North American and European spheres, scholars of game culture in Japan have acknowledged the need to consider the broader media ecology from which these games originate, and have approached games as examples of localized products making their way out of Japan and to the global public (Navarro-Remesal and Loriguillo-López; Pelletier-Gagnon; Picard, "The Foundation of Geemu"). The establishment of a substantial body of works culturally centred around the local Japanese videogame market, supported by a stronger understanding of its ties to a media environment specific to Japan and its connections to the complex processes of circulation and negotiation in overseas markets, indicates the development of Japanese videogame studies as a subfield of its own. The creation of international forums for Japanese game studies, such as the annual Replaying Japan conference series that began in 2012 and its sister journal published at Ritsumeikan University, has contributed to the formation of intellectual spaces for interdisciplinary approaches that combine game studies, Japanese studies, and other research fields.

However, despite the evolution of the field, the topic of Japanese arcade videogames has remained a marginal subject in the Anglophone world, aside from a few isolated but important academic works (Eickhorst; Hjorth and Chan) and journalistic studies (Ashcraft and Snow). However, it is also important to mention that, despite providing rough sketches of the history of game centres, none of these projects has been built firmly upon the tradition of scholarly literature on arcade videogames developed in Japan itself. Western literature often views arcade games through the prism of nostalgia, with discussion of retro-gaming practices and issues regarding game preservation (Guins) comprising the majority of the work. Such an oversight emphasizes the strong ties between the field of game studies and certain privileged strata of Western society, who can afford high-end game consoles or computers.

As a result, Western game studies tend to emphasize privileged narratives of videogame production and consumption. In Africa, Asia, and South America, where economic conditions have long prevented the broad spread of domestic entertainment technology, or in places in which urban dwelling space is scarce, arcade parlours are very much part of the social fabric of life. Thus, to study arcade games and public gaming in general is an entrance point into issues pertaining to the study of digital entertainment production and consumption on a global level, and particularly in economically marginal markets. It leads us to challenge our understanding of games as commodities and fluctuating functions during their lifespan. For example, even as the Super Nintendo home console became obsolete in the northern hemisphere at the beginning of the 2000s, consoles find reimagined purposes in different contexts. In 2004, I had the chance to personally witness the repurposing of one such console into a coin-operated arcade machine that attracted children to a convenience store in the remote mountain village of Valle de Los Angeles in Honduras. As the forms of play that these games generate evolve, so must our interpretation of these games in their redefined context. Although I do acknowledge the importance of these global issues, this project focuses solely on how the games present in the game centres in Japan enable us to consider the region of Japan in terms of videogame consumption (Liboriussen and Martin) from another, more culturally situated angle.

Observations and Lines: Methodology

Between January and April 2016, I conducted field studies in three distinct Japanese game centres, each belonging to different urban locales spanning the two major cities of Tokyo and Kyoto, in order to shed light on the gaming practices that take place in those locations and evaluate the interinfluences of spatial and machine design on the play experience. With the aforementioned elements in mind, I concentrated my observations of these game centres over a period of a few days, during which I visited the venues over long stretches of time and at different periods to observe and take notes on a variety of customers and ludic trajectories.

The primary data-collecting method for this field study was participant observation, which lent itself well to the context of game centres. I immersed myself in the culture of three separate venues and observed their rhythms by analyzing the general behaviour of players and observers engaged with game machines, both in groups and on an individual basis. I did not make contact with participants nor conduct interviews, but took notes after witnessing specific behaviours or noticing relevant phenomena. Categories of publics (groups, individuals, male, female, …) and numbers of individuals were recorded on certain days. The advantages of this methodology are numerous: in addition to permitting a greater focus on recording non-verbal behaviour, it also ensures that my presence as a researcher was not noticed and that venue-goers' behaviour was not influenced. One of the unwritten rules of game centres is that players typically do not acknowledge each other's presence, especially in large venues. Game centres exhibit a certain culture of anonymity and interpersonal distance, in which customers rarely interact directly with people with whom they are previously acquainted, and taking pictures of machines and people is usually frowned upon.

This cultural climate facilitated the data-gathering process and minimized my impact in the space. Some of the photographs I took over the course of this study are used as visual evidence of machine placement and spatial design; however, any faces of individuals that do appear in these photos are blurred to comply with these customs and to respect privacy. My methodological choice of restricting any contact with patrons had certain disadvantages, such as a resulting inability to connect gaming behaviour with the personal situations that characterize the participants' lives beyond the arcade through follow-up discussions; even so, it is well suited to capture players' and observers' behaviour at a micro- and macro-level and remain unbiased by the incentive of subsequent rationalizations of actions by the individuals themselves. The sociological aspect of this type of research leads to different types of inquiries and research directions outside of this project, some of which have been examined by other scholars in the past (Katō).

In order to acquire new types of data on the practices associated with game centres, which is a main objective of this project, it was essential to establish the methodology upon the principle of avoiding direct interaction between myself as researcher and the populations of the game centre studied. Taken in the context of the broader scientific literature on arcades and their players, this choice requires further clarification. Both academic projects and industry-led player studies generally involve a certain level of input gathered directly from players, ranging from in-depth interviews to generic profiling surveys, in order to base practices within the background of sample individuals from which broader tendencies are extrapolated. However, this project emphasizes shifting the focus towards the basic structures that frame the arcade-going experience, an alternative perspective that would enable uncovering the political stakes within. Therefore, a methodology based on observation rather than on direct interaction in the form of interviews or surveys was deemed more appropriate to accomplish these objectives. Specifically, the benefits of this choice of methodology were twofold: it ensured the acquisition of data that fit the project's needs, and also maximized the quality of the data itself.

On a fundamental level, this investigation focuses primarily on the role of software design, machine affordances, and spatial conditions, understood as a mixture of both architectural elements and the layout of the various machines on the floors, in structuring and suggesting patterns of interactions with games, as well as with other venue goers. The various types of behaviours in which participants engage around the machines are not necessarily the results of a conscious decision-making processes and would be challenging for individuals to rationalize as specific micro-practices. Asking players and observers directly about the reasons behind specific gestures or actions taken within the venue cannot be expected to provide the necessary information to answer the questions raised here. Similarly, it is possible that the answers provided to such questions might be influenced by interviewees' expectations and assumptions about what would be considered proper answers in the context of the interview. Considering the objectives stated above, the limited time available, and the low probability of useful returns in designing and conducting interviews and surveys, I decided to adapt my approach to participant observation to maintain distance between myself and the observed groups and individuals.

Additionally, although the choice to keep a low profile over the course of the observation period would seem counterintuitive within the context of a participant observation data-gathering method, it contributed to ensuring that the natural flow of the gaming behaviour I witnessed would remain undisturbed. In the context of the observation of phenomena occurring as part of casual game playing experiences, this aspect was deemed a priority in order to ensure the behaviour observed would be unaltered by my presence as researcher. As interaction between venue-goers is generally very low and customers tend to keep to themselves, this type of observation was appropriate to accomplish this objective. While it is not possible to guarantee that the presence of a foreign researcher would remain for the most part unnoticed in these spaces beyond any doubts, as the theme of this very project even suggests, we can reasonably assert that my presence exerted minimal influence on the activities and behaviours I observed. Only on two occasions would this rule be broken, both of which occurred at the game centre Tsujishōten, where I took the initiative to ask basic background information about the venue to the owner, and when a player noticed my presence and offered a seat at a specific game cabinet, probably assuming that I was waiting in line patiently for it. Both situations are taken into account in the subsequent case study analysis.

The objective behind the use of this method was to capture empirical examples of players' and observers' interaction with specific game machines in real-life conditions. The information acquired from these observations would then be used as the basis for a comparative analysis between games and venues, whose anticipated results could help to highlight the different ludo-egregores generated by certain games through the social affordances of their software, machines, and spatial conditions. This project was partly inspired by Tom Apperley's 2010 study of gaming rhythms, but differs because of its related focus on the formation of gaming cultures at a micro-level, which is informed directly by the social affordances of the material conditions of specific games and, in so doing, more appropriately acknowledging the extent of their agency as non-human social actors.

As established previously, this project adopts the stance developed by Doreen Massey that space is a fundamentally multilayered entity whose individual layers, in their plurality, add different dimensions to a place that itself is the result of the different interactions occurring between these layers. Scratching the ludo-centric surface of the different game centres investigated in this section reveals the venues as architectural spaces, as spaces of circulation of people, goods, and games, and as spaces connected both to national media circuits and to smaller local cultural networks. In the venues where they were present, this spatial investigation also involved the study of a variety of paratextual sources found amongst the game machines, and which, taken as a whole, provide additional clues as to the dynamic of the place housing them.

A detailed presentation of all activities taking place in all game centres examined and an analysis of all the machines being played there is beyond the scope of this project. However, not all game centres feature a wide range of game genres, and certain venues prefer to mark their presence in a city by specializing in certain types of games and attracting a specific sort of crowd. The architectural condition of game centres is often challenging for venue operators; sonic information from some games easily travels through their often-tight spaces, and thus becomes a distraction for other players. For this reason and others, some genres of games cannot be easily installed right next to other types of games without affecting the overall game experience. This creates situations in which the presence of certain types of games prevail over others, and explains why certain genres are segregated from the most centralized locations of a space. Taking this aspect into account, this investigation focuses on a few significant elements that define the social space of each venue; most importantly, the games or genres that define the social space of each game centre will be objects of more thorough analysis to identify the most visible type of ludo-egregore occurring in this space.

Echoing our previously stated interest in the situated aspect of the play activity, the observations conducted as part of this close reading process are contextualized in the physical space of the venues. The ways in which machines are installed, isolated, or exposed to facilitate performance play all come to influence their function and how players interact with them. Additional amenities often present in game centres and corridors of circulation also allow and structure customers' navigation of the space. In order to account for this, I have drawn up maps of the venues that are the subjects of the first two case studies. These maps not only provide information as to the placement of the machines in these spaces but also, and perhaps more ambitiously, demonstrate the extent of the connections of the different machines and services present in the spaces, thus arguing for a holistic reading of these spaces.

Inspired by the work of Tim Ingold, these visual representations of the spaces under discussion attempt to highlight common patterns of circulation, as informed by empirical observations, in the form of lines connecting the game machines to each other so as to turn game centres into complex ludic networks. Ingold establishes a clear difference and preference for lines over nodes as significant and more dynamic objects of analysis, something that has largely been lost in the modern development of utilitarian mapping and transportation systems, and which affects contemporary urban life: “To an ever-increasing extent, people in modern metropolitan societies find themselves in environments built as assemblies of connected elements. Yet in practice they continue to thread their own ways through these environments, tracing paths as they go” (75). Similarly, videogame enthusiasts who wander player centres in search of ludic encounters also trace and retrace paths as so many navigators of these spaces, establishing ever-changing connections and rhythms before deciding on engaging with machines or not. Game centres are constituted of multiple types of official and informal “lines”, anywhere from the waiting line bordered by webbing barriers to automatic staircases directing player traffic. Thus, parts of this analysis seek to relocate the nature of game centres into the relationship between players themselves and the space by reading their circulation into the space of game centres as a creative process in itself (Lee and LiPuma). This discussion includes many different elements and objects of analysis: the physical place of the arcade on an architectural level, the social space of the arcade situated around the play space of the machines and elsewhere in the venue, the material presence of the game cabinet as an agent structuring the social and ludic sphere, and the virtual space of the games themselves. In addition, my analysis also focuses on the intersections of these elements, where one aspect of the game centre will directly affect others; specific case studies of practices witnessed during the field research process are used to illuminate these intersections and the “lines” that they in turn help to generate.

Each game centre will be discussed in relation to individual areas of interest identified over the course of the field study. For each venue examined, the analysis will focus on a limited number of phenomena, game practices, or structural elements that seem to define the space in relation to the others examined, and that exert important influences on player trajectories and the negotiation of the space. This approach will allow me to emphasize a wider range of elements warranting attention, and in a more meaningful way. While this approach has the downside of restricting a complete parallel comparative analysis of the different venues, this decision also reflects the will to respect the limitations of the data gathered during the field research process, as well as to avoid making speculative claims unsupported by the results obtained.

Diversity and Accessibility: Case Study Selection Process

I began my data-collecting process in the three game centres that are the subjects of this study in 2016. The selection of these specific venues was the result of the evaluation of around ten or so establishments pulled out from the many dozens of game centres, game corners, amusement centres, barcades, and other temporary gaming installations that I visited in different contexts from the moment this project took form in 2012. Of these, three game centres were selected to form the backbone of this research project: A-cho and Tsujishōten, both located in Kyoto, and Sega Ikebukuro GIGO, Sega's flagship arcade, located in the district of the same name in Tokyo. The reasons for these selections are related to two main factors: the diversity of phenomena witnessed within, and the feasibility of the research.

The primary goal of this undertaking is to paint a picture of the Japanese game centre scene that accounts for the diversity of its settings and the wide range of practices found within.[6] This representation comes as an answer to the commonly encountered narratives about game centres as profoundly formatted generic spaces that in turn produce highly standardized patterns of play. Though conglomerate-owned complexes house dynamics of play that need to be addressed as one of the fundamental cores of Japanese public play culture, smaller venues, generally independently owned and only frequented by locals, are often overlooked by commentators, thus, consciously or not, undermining their value as providers of alternative spaces and arrangements of play installations that generate different practices that also come to characterize public gaming. We need to consider these two main types of venues, as well as the myriads of other ones in which play space is structured in ways that can be situated somewhere between these two archetypes, as entities that contribute fully to the creation of the Japanese arcade gaming scene. It is important to point out that large-scale and independent venues are not necessarily mutually exclusive forms of game centres; rather, both contribute to form a network of spaces connected by their offerings of games, but in which said games take on completely different social lives, enable different gaming practices, and sometimes don different textual practices.

The selection of case studies is an attempt to represent these issues. Two of these, Tsujishōten and Sega Ikebukuro GIGO, are located on the most extreme ends of the independent/corporate dichotomy, while A-cho was selected due to its balanced nature between these two archetypes, illustrating the fluidity of such spatial identities. As a result, by putting this question as a central issue within the venue selection process, the samples of game centre activities investigated in this project, while not perfect and still limited in regards to other important issues, provide a picture of arcade gaming in Japan that is as representative as possible of its period considering the objectives and constraints of the current project. This selection also allowed me the opportunity to implement diversity in terms of data acquisition. For example, the size of Tsujishōten made it possible to examine specific examples of player behaviour compared to the conditions of the multi-floor entertainment complex of Sega Ikebukuro GIGO, which made conducting a thorough examination of player trajectory tendencies much more challenging, but which encouraged a shift of perspectives towards its broader media environment and strategies of spatial unification and segmentation.

On a more practical level, since the methodology used in this study required close monitoring of the establishments being observed, I selected venues located in major urban centres and public transit services, which facilitated access to the different locations. The challenge of the field study itself consisted in balancing time spent performing on-site observations in game centres and conducting archival research at the Ritsumeikan Center for Game Studies and the National Diet Library located in Tokyo. Therefore, the venues needed to be in the vicinity of these institutions, or easily accessible by public transportation or a short bike ride, so that I could investigate them easily and frequently. I visited and took notes in each of the three game centres up to three times a day, almost every day of the week, while keeping in mind the need to visit the locations during different periods of the day (morning, afternoon, evening, night), and for various lengths of time.

Considering these parameters, arcades located in the suburbs, in the countryside, or too far away from public transit could not be considered for this project. However, that is not to say that these venues do not deserve critical attention; the impact of the circumstances and potential challenges of arcades in rural areas on the social life of their space and the ludo-egregores identifiable within would certainly be worthy of investigation in a future study and would bring to light yet other aspects of public gaming in Japan. However, due to the industry's reliance on elements of urban life such as a high population density, important foot traffic, and ease of access, it is still important to characterize public gaming as a predominantly urban phenomenon, which supports the selection of venues located in urban centres for analysis in this project.

What This Book Is Not

Arcade gaming and game centre culture are a vast subject area that invite a variety of approaches. However, this book is not a social or anthropological study of arcade players. Rather, this project is rooted in a historical, empirical, and comparative approach toward the design of arcade videogames in relation to the evolution of the space of game centres themselves. This study is comparative at its core, examining different assemblages of arcade videogame devices that could be found in Japan at different periods, informed by the sometimes-inevitable comparison with the arcade culture developed in the United States at similar moments. This book is both a theoretical inquiry of situated gaming and a cultural study of Japanese game centres based on research that incorporates both archival work and empirical observations in field examinations of specific sites. However, due to the nature of its methodology, this project is not a sociological study of Japanese arcade gaming spaces and does not attempt to answer questions that only a framework influenced by sociological methods could answer. It features reflections based on observations rather than participant interviews or longitudinal participant study cases; its objective is to examine and unpack the broader social, cultural, and political implications of the structures of arcades as technological urban playgrounds as opposed to investigating specific practices in relation to factors external to the arcade space itself. No data resulting from participant interviews or any other sort of direct contact with arcade-goers are used in this project.

Because it is my intention to explore the dynamics of Japanese game centre spaces as independent phenomena situated in a specific locale, this book does not directly address the development of Western arcade spaces, except when such discussion helps to clarify issues related to Japanese game centres. Similarly, environments like those of Western arcade spaces, such as penny arcades, casinos, eSports bars, or venues that provide situated instances of augmented reality (AR) and virtual reality (VR) experiences, are not covered in this project. Although AR/VR spaces are of interest as new manifestations of digital technology for ludic purposes tied to the space of the urban sphere, they are too recent of developments to be included in this study, and their effects and influence remain to be observed. Already, academic work unpacking the use of these new technologies in the Japanese cultural context has emerged to challenge our expectations of their potential (Giard).

While this study aims to account for the diversity of instances of public gaming in Japan, it cannot hope to fully account for the diversity of game centres across the country or the practices they host. Thus, this project is not an extensive study of all game centres and other gaming parlours in Japan, but is limited to the presence of arcade games within the major urban centres of the Tokyo metropolitan region and the city of Kyoto, where the field study for this project was mainly conducted. However, the discrepancy in these case studies between spatial conditions and cultural practices demonstrates that each individual venue creates its own play conditions that are as meaningful and worthy of examination as the games themselves. Although this project can only hint at the myriad situated play cultures in Japan, it introduces and establishes a framework for the further examination of these spaces and practices in relation to their structures and material conditions.

Book Outline

This book is divided into two sections that, respectively, cover a historical and a contemporary perspective of Japanese arcade videogame spaces. Part I provides an overview of the initial development and evolution of the industries of arcade game development and game centre operation, from the creation of the first urban amusement centres in the early twentieth century to present-day network-connected digital game centres, as well as the theoretical framework that informs my case study analysis.

Chapter 2 argues that the analysis of game centres and other forms of Japanese urban amusement establishments must be grounded in specific periods and sociocultural realities. It starts by initiating a discussion of the representation of Japanese videogame arcades in Western media as imaginary canvases upon which its fears and fascination about human-machine interactions are projected. In representing game centres as disorienting spaces and play practices as trace-like behaviour, outsider perspectives from the West articulate a techno-Orientalist discourse that contributes to the Othering of the Japanese subject through its relation to technology. This is followed by an account of the development of spaces associated to public play in Japan from the early nineteenth century to the late 1970s, including amusement rooftops, cabarets, and medal game parlours. Providing an overview of early forms of electromechanical machines and medal games, this section situates early forms of arcade games in their material and spatial contexts as a necessary preamble to the emergence of the first spaces dedicated to videogame play in urban settings; independent coffee houses.

The following chapter examines the evolution of videogame-related spaces in Japan from the 1970s to the 2010s while identifying key events and technologies that act as significant paradigm shifts in this process, alongside the social frictions and struggles to which they were exposed. An overview of the reform of the Law Regulating Entertainment Businesses of 1984 leads us to trace its impact on the standardization of arcade spaces and the subsequent consolidation of the game centre operation scene as the place of online technology and network connectivity. This discussion is contextualized in prominent academic discourses that permeated scientific narratives around game centres broken down into several waves: the personality psychology focused on the positive and negative influences of videogame playing, anthropology, and the symbolic repurposing of videogames as texts, as well as social studies centred on the arcade as a site of communication.

Chapter 4 provides the theoretical perspective and an overview of the main ideas forming the framework of this project. This section discusses works from across many disciplines that touch on the concepts of software, hardware, and space, as part of the formation of a transdisciplinary framework for the study of the act of play in public. Different sets of ideas related to research on design theory and ecological perception, such as Gibson's theory of affordance and Latour's actor-network theory, help to account for the functions of game cabinets as the main anchors of the game experience. In addition, Deleuze and Guattari's work on spatiality, de Certeau and Lefebvre's work on the structure of space, and the situationists' subversive interpretation of the potential of urban spaces contribute to a discussion of the notion of space, a central element to our analysis (Debord). Taken together, these ideas allow us to consider arcade games as assemblages that generate specific ludic and social affordances that players negotiate as they interact with the machines. This section ends with a definition of the framework of ludo-egregore, a concept that takes play into account both as a situated activity in which agents of different natures influence the course of play, and as a fluid activity that is made and constantly reformed through the participation of active and non-active agents.

Section II applies the framework of ludo-egregore to different case studies in order to examine contemporary arcade videogames in their context, specifically from the perspective of the conditions built into their spatial structure and the ludic trajectories adopted venue-goers. Chapter 5 takes us into our first case study, the game centre A-cho, located on Teramachi-dori in Kyoto, through which we focus on examining performance play and observant play as two interrelated types of ludic engagements. This dynamic is afforded by the spatial structure of the space, which generates specific locations and moments to direct attention towards a specific play session, as well as distanced engagement. This is followed by a discussion of A-cho's involvement in the digital communication and service industry, which opens the possibility of questioning the idea of the videogame arcade as a space bound by physicality, and of the type of labour on which operators rely on to actualize the space. This first case study provides an account of an organized fighting game event that demonstrates the dynamics of the contraction and dissipation of venue-goers' attention in context as a result of the interplay between the human and non-human agents involved.

Still in Kyoto, just a few streets south of the eponymous JR train station, is the case study of the following chapter, Tsujishōten, a modestly-sized game centre that offers a different perspective on play practices: the tactics venue-goers use to appropriate the arcade and turn it into a homely space. Within, small groups of players converge and, afforded by the spatial formation of more intimate ambiences, occupy the cabinet space through objects, symbols, and practices, which sometimes extend past the ludic purposes of the space. Observations of gregarious play sessions of the game *Mobile Suit Gundam: Extreme Vs.* provide us with an opportunity to analyze this phenomenon as co-constructed by players' behaviours and by the spatial and play conditions made available by the operator. Tsujishōten also allows us to think of videogame arcades in terms of the long-range transformation of the space itself; it explores the idea of the game centre as a palimpsestic surface in relation both to its architecture and to the practices observed within, and also gives us a platform from which to consider the broader issue of videogame arcades as sites of opposition to capitalist incentives and as sites of cultural formation within the city.

Chapter 7 takes us to Tokyo, where Sega Ikebukuro GIGO, our final case study, is located. This large-scale industrial game centre, once Japan's largest in the 1990s, invites us to approach the interrelation between the spatial structures and play dynamics in terms of the compartmentalization of players and experiences. It discusses how the spatial structure and the media mix become tools to both unify and segment the space of the arcade, especially in relation to sonic ambiance and interpretation of gendered game interests. This leads into an analysis of cabinet side panels, prevalent on most game machines but examined specifically in the context of the case of the game *Hatsune Miku: Project DIVA Arcade*, as cultural interfaces that afford and cultivate certain methods of engagement and social behaviour. Drawing on the works of Habermas on the public sphere and Anderson on the concept of imagined communities, the chapter concludes with a reflection of the individualizing effects of the emergence of national networks in the context of the increasing interconnectivity of games and venues uniting, but limiting their audience to, Japan.

These last three chapters demonstrate that the experience of arcade gaming is not a static phenomenon, but is, rather, in perpetual motion and transformation due to the constant negotiation between the ludic trajectories of players, the affordances of certain games, the subversion of these affordances in practice, and the spatial structure that enforces certain paths for players to take and certain activities in which to engage. The concluding chapter summarizes the concept of ludo-egregore in the context of the findings of this study, as well as potential other research contexts that touch, in various degrees, the study of situated gaming or play in public, such as videogame preservation and the game centre as a heterotopia in the urban imaginary.

Notes

1 JAIA was formed with the merger of two major business associations in 2018: the Shadanhōjin nihon amusement machine kōgyōkyōkai [Japan Amusement Machinery Manufacturers Association or JAMMA] and the Zen'nihon amyūzumento shisetsu eigyō-sha kyōkai rengō-kai [All Japan Federation of Amusement Facility Operators Association or AOU], effectively uniting two segments of the industry that had mostly operated independently until then.

2 To this, we can add the industry journal *Amyūzumento jānaru* (*Amusement Journal*), formerly *Koin jānaru* (*Coin Journal*), which publishes industry performance data and new product information.

3 Initially issued as *Dengeki ākēdo kārdo gēmu* (*Dengeki Arcade Card Game*), the renamed magazine published its last issue in February 2017.

4 Todd Harper uses the term "third space" to describe a specific case study analyzed in his work, but his analysis remains in line with Oldenburg's concept.

5 Certain locations, such as the city of Tokyo and Kyoto are designed as national strategic special zones. A council consisting of national, local, and private entities is allowed to suggest strategic plans to reach certain cultural or economic targets.

6 The axis of venue diversity of this project does not account for many other types of venues such as game centres operating in malls or arcade videogame spaces oriented towards children, which deserve their own studies. On the latter, see the work of Yasuo Kawasaki ("Kodomo-muke gēmukōnā"; "The History of 'Game Centre' in Japan").

Works Cited

Aihara, Hiroyuki. "Gēmu sentā to iu kūkan ni kodomo wa nani o motomeru ka? [What Are Kids Looking for in the Spaces of Game Centres?]." *Jidō shinri* [*Child Psychology*], vol. 55, no. 11, 2001, pp. 1108–13.

Akcasu, Audrey. "Check Your Psychopass Levels at Shinjuku Station." *Japan Today*, 4 Jan. 2015, https://japantoday.com/category/entertainment/check-your-psycho-pass-levels-at-shinjuku-station.

Apperley, Tom. *Gaming Rhythms: Play and Counterplay from the Situated to the Global*. Institute of Network Cultures, 2010.

Ashcraft, Brian, and Jean Snow. *Arcade Mania! The Turbo-Charged World of Japan's Game Centers*. Kodansha International, 2008.

Bayliss, Peter. "Notes Towards a Sense of Embodied Gameplay." *Proceedings of the 2007 DiGRA International Conference: Situated Play*, 2007, http://www.digra.org/wp-content/uploads/digital-library/07312.19059.pdf.

Certeau, Michel de. *L'Invention du quotidien Vol. 1, Arts de faire'* [*The Invention of the Quotidian: Vol. 1, The Art of Doing*]. Union générale d'éditions, 1980.

City Planning Division. *Introduction of Urban Land Use Planning System in Japan*. Japanese Ministry of Land Infrastructure and Transport, 2003, https://www.mlit.go.jp/common/001050453.pdf.

Consalvo, Mia. "Console Video Games and Global Corporations." *New Media & Society*, vol. 8, no. 1, 2006, pp. 117–37.

———. "Convergence and Globalization in the Japanese Videogame Industry." *Cinema Journal*, vol. 48, no. 3, 2009, pp. 135–41.

Debord, Guy-Ernest. "Théorie de la dérive [Theory of the Derive]." *Les Lèvres nues*, no. 9, 1956.

Deleuze, Gilles, and Félix Guattari. *Capitalisme et schizophrénie 2 : Mille plateaux* [*Capitalism and Schizophrenia: A Thousand Plateaus*]. Éditions de minuit, 1980.

Eickhorst, Eric. *Game Centers: A Historical and Cultural Analysis of Japan's Video Amusement Establishments*. U of Kansas, MA Thesis, 2006.

Fernández-Vara, Clara. "Play's the Thing: A Framework to Study Videogames as Performance." *DiGRA '09 - Proceedings of the 2009 DiGRA International Conference: Breaking New Ground: Innovation in Games, Play, Practice and Theory*. Brunel University, vol. 5, 2009, pp. 1–9.

Giard, Agnès. "Frapper un mur pour dire « Je t'aime » ? Les stratégies fatales au Japon [Hit a Wall to Say 'I Love You' ? Fatal Strategies in Japan]." *Rusca*, vol. 10, no. 1, 2018, http://www.msh-m.fr/le-numerique/edition-en-ligne/rusca/rusca-territoires-temps-societes/les-numeros-108/numero-10-le-mur-un-phenomene-616/.

Gibson, James J. *The Ecological Approach to Visual Perception*. Houghton Mifflin, 1979.

Goffman, Erving. *Frame Analysis: An Essay on the Organization of Experience*. Northeastern UP, 1986.

Guins, Raiford. *Game After: A Cultural Study of Video Game Afterlife*. MIT P, 2014.

Harper, Todd. *The Culture of Digital Fighting Games: Performance and Practice*. Routledge, Taylor & Francis Group, 2014.

Hjorth, Larissa, and Dean Chan. *Gaming Cultures and Place in Asia-Pacific*. Routledge, 2009.

Ingold, Tim. *Lines: A Brief History*. Routledge, 2007.

Ippan shadanhōjin nihon kurēngēmu kyōkai, [Institute of Japanese Crane Game Associations]. "Kyōkai ni tsuite [About the Association]." *Kuretatsu Japan*, https://web.archive.org/web/20181205050818/http://kuretatsu.com/association.html. Accessed 6 Sept. 2018.

Jin, Dal Yong. *Korea's Online Gaming Empire*. MIT P, 2010.

Katō, Hiroyasu. *Gēmu sentā bunkaron: media shakai no comyunikēshon* [*Theory of Game Centre Culture: Communication in the Media Society*]. Shinsensha, 2011.

Kawasaki, Yasuo. *The History of "Game Centers" in Japan: Historical Changing and Social Positioning as Entertainment Facilities*. Fukumura shuppan, 2022.

———. "Kodomo-muke gēmukōnā no hensen [The Transition of Game Corners for Children]." *Contents bunkashi kenkyû*, vol. 10, no. 11, 2017, pp. 57–76.

Keisatsuchō seikatsu anzen-kyoku [National Police Agency Security Division]. *Heisei nijūkyū-nen ni okeru fūzoku kankyō no genjō to fūzoku kankei jihan no torishimari jōkyō-tō ni tsuite* [*On the current situation of the fūzoku industry environment and crimes related to the fūzoku industry in 2017*]. Keisatsu-chō, Mar. 2018, pp. 1–28, https://web.archive.org/web/20180308232241/https://www.npa.go.jp/publications/statistics/safetylife/hoan/h29_fuzoku_jihan.pdf.

Kort, Yvonne A. W. de, Wijinand A. IJsselsteijn, and Brian J. Gajadhar. "People, Places, and Play: A Research Framework for Digital Game Experience in a Socio-Spatial Context" in *DiGRA '07 – Proceedings of the 2007 DiGRA International Conference: Situated Play*. The University of Tokyo, vol. 4, 2007, pp. 823–830.

Latour, Bruno. *Reassembling the Social: An Introduction to Actor-Network-Theory*. Oxford UP, 2005.

Lee, Benjamin, and Edward LiPuma. "Cultures of Circulation: The Imaginations of Modernity." *Public Culture*, vol. 14, no. 1, 2002, pp. 191–213.

Lefebvre, Henri. *La Production de l'espace* [*The Production of Space*]. Éditions Anthropos, 1974.

Liboriussen, Bjarke, and Paul Martin. "Regional Game Studies." *Game Studies: The International Journal of Computer Game Research*, vol. 16, no. 1, 2016, http://gamestudies.org/1601/articles/liboriussen.

Massey, Doreen B. *For Space*. SAGE, 2005.

Mäyrä, Frans. "The Contextual Game Experience: On the Socio-Cultural Contexts for Meaning in Digital Play." *Proceedings of the 2007 DiGRA International Conference: Situated Play*, 2007, http://www.digra.org/wp-content/uploads/digital-library/07311.12595.pdf.

Miller, Roy Andrew. *Japan's Modern Myth: The Language and Beyond*. Weatherhill, 1982.

Navarro-Remesal, Victor, and Antonio Loriguillo-López. "What Makes Gêmu Different? A Look at the Distinctive Design Traits of Japanese Video Games and Their Place in the Japanese Media Mix." *Journal of Games Criticism*, vol. 2, no. 1, 2015, pp. 1–17.

Newman, James. *Best Before: Videogames, Supersession and Obsolescence*. Routledge, 2012.

Oldenburg, Ray. *The Great Good Place: Cafés, Coffee Shops, Community Centers, Beauty Parlors, General Stores, Bars, Hangouts, and How They Get You Through the Day*. Paragon House, 1989.

Pelletier-Gagnon, Jérémie. *Video Games and Japaneseness: An Analysis of Localization and Circulation of Japanese Video Games in North America*. McGill U, MA Thesis, 2011.

Penix-Tadsen, Phillip. *Cultural Code: Video Games and Latin America*. MIT P, 2016.

Picard, Martin. "The Foundation of Geemu: A Brief History of Early Japanese Video Games." *Game Studies: The International Journal of Computer Game Research*, vol. 13, no. 2, 2013, http://gamestudies.org/1302/articles/picard.

———. "Haunting Backgrounds: Transnationality and Intermediality in Japanese Survival Horror Video Games." *Horror Video Games: Essays on the Fusion of Fear and Play*, edited by Bernard Perron, McFarland, 2009, pp. 95–120.

Pong. Arcade videogame cabinet, Atari, 1972.

Space Invaders. Arcade videogame cabinet, Taito, 1978.

Shiotani, Naoyoshi, and Katsuyuki Motohiro, directors. *Psycho-Pass*. Production I.G., 2013.

———. *Psycho-Pass: The Movie*. Production I.G., 2015.

Turkle, Sherry. *Alone Together: Why We Expect More from Technology and Less from Each Other*. Basic Books, 2011.

Wolf, Mark J. P., editor. *Video Games Around the World*. MIT P, 2015.

Wood, Mark A. "Algorithmic Tyranny: Psycho-Pass, Science Fiction and the Criminological Imagination." *Crime, Media, Culture*, vol. 15, no. 2, 2019, pp. 323–39.

2 Balls, Medals, and the Other

Techno-Orientalism in Videogame Arcades and the Early Amusement Spaces in Japan (1903–1978)

Situating Game Centres

What Are Game Centres?

While Japanese arcades arguably house the most technically advanced play equipment in the videogame industry, their significance reaches far beyond simple urban entertainment spots where customers engage in ludic activities. At their simplest level, game centres are service industry commercial operations in which, in exchange for a small amount of money inserted directly into the desired machine, players can play a variety of videogames for a relatively short amount of time. But, at a deeper level, game centres are socioeconomically significant urban spaces in which different demographics and different types of emerging technologies encounter one another in interactions that are constantly negotiated.

Indeed, the acts of entering, observing, and playing in game centres are always, consciously or unconsciously, acts that force players to mediate themselves in public through machine interactions. Players conciliate aspects such as performance versus intimacy, public space versus private venue, and the immediate social interactions occurring in the space versus the broad national reach through which machines facilitate communication patterns. The structure and existence of game centres in Japan derive from a rich history of technological public play, and their presence in contemporary urban cityscapes is the result of negotiations and compromises between technological breakthroughs, socioeconomic circumstances, and broader ideological principles that regulate the presence of play in the public sphere. Indeed, these spaces are not neutral; everything from the architectural frameworks of these venues to the careful arrangement of the cabinets redirects to these elements, which structure the play experience at its core.

Considering all these elements is essential to understanding what game centres are and to realizing that their essence is the result of such negotiations, to which a single fixed interpretation cannot truly do justice. This is not to say that game centres or arcades resist interpretation, but that such interpretation must be grounded in a specific timeframe and a specific sociocultural reality.

DOI: 10.4324/9781003273776-3

Western Representations of Japanese Videogame Arcades

Since the turn of the millennium, the curious electronic playgrounds of game centres have been attracting attention from overseas. In Western media, Japanese videogame arcades have often been represented as exotic play sites that defy comprehension: as futuristic playgrounds of blinding lights and deafening sounds, in which Japanese players willingly put themselves into a trance-like mental state using ludic machines and become oblivious to their surroundings.

In a scene from the 2003 film *Lost in Translation* (Coppola), Charlotte, a recent Yale graduate accompanying her husband on a business trip to Tokyo, visits an arcade and witnesses several singular snapshot moments of players engaging in ludic activities: a man slowly beating the drums of a *Taiko no tetsujin* cabinet, a very focused *Guitar Freaks* player dressed in punk-style clothes, and another young man frantically dancing and hitting the buttons of a *Pop'n Music* game station. Charlotte is initially amused by these singular forms of gaming, and presumably also by the colourful and childish presentation of the play equipment, but her smile quickly fades when she realizes the seriousness of these players' focus and their isolation during the play process. Here, arcades are represented as spaces that exemplify, and potentially amplify, urban solitude, in which, despite the public nature of these spaces, players engage in self-reclusion through videogames, echoing the psychic state of the movie's protagonist. The 2001 French action movie *Wasabi* (Krawczyk), in which the protagonists become involved in a gun fight in the middle of a game centre, represents the arcade space as a disorienting maze of electric devices, a nightclub in which dancing itself is replaced by the playing of *Dance Dance Revolution* and rhythm games. Similarly, the 2012 documentary *100 Yen: The Japanese Game Center Experience* (Crawford) strives to provide Western gamers with a look at the Japanese arcade scene, but emphasizes its culture of high achievements, competitiveness, and performance play by examining only a handful of select games, which ends up presenting arcades through a gendered male-dominated narrative and downplaying the casual side of the experience.

Other types of myths and narratives about the Japanese game centre industry and culture also endure. For example, the story that the popularity of *Space Invaders* (Taito, 1978) in 1978 single-handedly caused a 100-yen coin shortage nationwide, the only type of change that was accepted to operate the arcade cabinet, is one that often accompanies discussion of the emergence of Japanese arcades (Ashcraft 74). This narrative, whose veracity is now considered doubtful but is thoroughly ingrained in videogame culture and often repeated outside of Japan,[1] is symptomatic of the fascination of the Western public and press with Japanese game culture and its status as an imaginary canvas onto which extraordinary stories can be imposed and which betray an underlying fascination for the perceived relationship between Japan and high technology.

All of these narratives draw on some of the stereotypes of techno-orientalism, depicting a hyper-technologized Japanese society with a deep affinity for innovative technology, and seemingly more at ease with machine interactions than with interpersonal relationships. As a side effect, they also depict arcade gaming as monolithic extensions of this worldview, as sites for hectic engagement with borderline-incomprehensible technology via expert player narratives of high achievement and performance play. Indeed, in Western discourse, game centres often become privileged sites that represent Japan as a futuristic technological Other and as a "screen on which the West has projected its technological fantasies" (Roh et al. 4). Decontextualized online videos sneakily capturing the enthralling performances of *Dance Dance Revolution* virtuosos, describing the execution as "machine-like" and often interpreted as representative of the entirety of the Japanese public gaming scene are abundant on *YouTube* and other video-hosting websites. To some extent, by pointing out extreme skill levels and attributing those skills to the players' ethnicity, these narratives fall within the greater trend of othering Japanese through the practice of video gaming by downplaying the dedication and passion of these individuals as mere ethnic attributes. These interpretations favour the techno-orientalist metaphor of the technological Asian body, inspired by the current place of Japan in the global economic system, which infuses the traditional mystique of the Orient with that of our awe and fears of high-end technology (Lozano-Méndez 184–85).[2]

In the context of the emergence of globalization characterized by information capitalism and the acceleration of media circulation, Toshiya Ueno suggests that the techno-orientalist stereotype of the Japanese subject, which he broadly names "Japanoid", is the "interface of control" through which power is exerted on the Japanese subject through representation (95). This stereotype of the "automated Other", more machinic than human, can be interpreted as embodying the "envy and hate" (96) of the West's own relation to technology. Indeed, behind these representations lie a fascination with technology as a source of awe to be harnessed for efficiency, as well as the fear of the loss of control to the machine and the cyborgization of the self through play. In their role as sites of everydayness that cross the line between public performance and intimate leisure activities, videogame arcades are particularly sensitive to these representations as the stereotype of the Japanoid as the automated Other becomes an attractive interpretive schema for the foreign observer. A *YouTube Shorts* video titled "Unbelievable Japan Drum Game Skills" from user @AurorasJapanLife exemplifies this larger trend explicitly by adding a dramatic textual overlay reading "Taiko Drum Master Level: Japan" over a footage of a young man playing *Taiko no tetsujin* blindfolded at a cabinet by a sidewalk of a busy street.[3] The control of the gaze towards Japanese videogame arcades has shifted from that of Charlotte's, and director Sofia Coppola's, cinematic stroll of the early aughts towards the tourists and expatriates eager to document and broadcast their experience of Japan to the world, but little has changed in terms of the interpretation they provide.

The fact that arcade culture has not been as prominent in Anglophone Western societies since the middle of the 1980s also contributes, from a comparative perspective, to the establishment of Japan as a place in which arcades still exist, by extension nurturing the perspective that Japan is a country that values its videogame cultural heritage. As such, it romanticizes the image of game centres as consensual spaces, devoid of frictions with rulemakers, industry players, and the broader Japanese society. Although this image is relatively positive, it is important to keep in mind that, as Thomas Lamarre reminds us by reformulating Said's work, these statements contribute to "posit a putative unity in the interest of stabilizing an object of knowledge" (6), such as, in this case, Japanese videogames and videogame arcades.

Although these narratives present awe-inspiring examples of game centre culture, they fail to account for the multiplicity of experiences that permeate these spaces. Despite what the narratives that are usually taken for granted indicate, there is no single game centre experience, but rather multiple ones that coexist in the cityscape and sometimes alongside one another within single establishments. To properly come to understand the state of game centres in Japan and grasp the dynamics of videogame play in public settings, it is essential to first debunk Western discourses about Japanese arcades, which can only be done by revisiting the history of Japanese public amusement spaces in relation to the gradual emergence of the diverse forms of play conducted therein. Such examination must also consider the socioeconomic and political developments that greatly influence the evolution not only of arcade videogames but also of the venues themselves and how they structure the experience, preventing certain forms of interactions and enabling others.

Game centres are contested sites in which users, stakeholders, and the broader public do not share the same interests, which often creates conflicts and tensions. These frictions are often tainted by the dominant ideologies governing the cultural value of work, leisure, and political agency within the context of a fluctuating neoliberal economy, resulting in the establishment of different venue styles and ludic norms that succeed themselves chronologically and sometimes come in conflict with each other. From the rooftop amusement parks of the 1930s to the contemporary large-scale game centres, certain configurations of play favoured within certain establishments at certain periods make certain ideas about social class, citizenship and, to a certain degree, nation-building visible.

To sketch a history of digital public amusement in Japan is to trace the multiple forms of synergies between machines, social norms, and spaces, while also avoiding looking at the evolution of arcade game technologies from a teleological perspective. One should indeed avoid establishing a narrow narrative that privileges the agents and events that generated the most dominant forms of public play in contemporary Japan. This chapter thus introduces a history of early amusement and game centre evolution presented in conjunction with historical events and conditions that triggered the development of new sites of public gaming, and the new experiences they enabled, regardless of whether these forms of play can still be found today. In addition, this process is informed by an overview of the media and academic discourses that surrounded the establishment of these spaces within the Japanese context.

Japanese Amusement Spaces from the Meiji Era to the Post-war Period

The first large-scale entertainment machine was showcased in Japan during the fifth National Industrial Exposition of 1903 in Osaka, with the installation of a massive carousel for public amusement imported from Germany. The demonstration successfully captured the imagination of the Japanese market, and entrepreneurs soon started to import small-scale amusement equipment such as mechanical rocking horses (Nakafuji 66–67).While these machines were at first scattered in different shops around the city, it was the Takarazuka Shin'onsen, a hot spring resort located at the outskirts of Kyoto and home of the famous Takarazuka dancing revue, that became the first entertainment complex of importance to dedicate an entire space to these machines (Akagi, "Shakōjō ni okareta kōka de ugoku gorakuki" 53). In 1928, the venue introduced some of the first electric rocking horses produced in Japan, along with other equipment such as *omikuji* (fortune paper) vending machines, all installed in the same pavilion.

These devices were created by Kaiichi Endo, a visionary inventor and businessman who was in the process of making vending machines, automatic signs, and rocking horses in the aftermath of the Great Kanto earthquake in 1923 (Eickhorst 16). Through his company Nihon gorakuki seisakusho, he sold various pieces of amusement equipment of his own design to department stores across the country. Virtually the only provider of such products in Japan at the time and facing almost no competition from other manufacturers, he was able to keep a low volume of production and mostly focused on creating new types of machines and new forms of play (Akagi, *Sore wa "pong"* 33). Later, Endo successfully convinced the owners of the Mitsuya department store in the Asakusa quarter of Tokyo to join him in a new business venture inspired by American amusement parks: the creation of an amusement space that would be located on the roof of one of Japan's most prestigious department stores, a first in the country (Nakafuji 67).

In 1931, Sports Land, the first urban space dedicated to amusement machines of all sorts, opened its doors. It was meant to attract families in a district that otherwise catered more to the interests of an adult demographic in its entertainment and shopping options (Kamiya). These types of establishments housed a variety of attractions such as miniature trains, rocking horses, vending machines, Ferris wheels, shooting ranges, strength testing machines, and a few early electromagnetic games. Pictures of some of these early amusement machines, including Endo's famous walking mechanical elephant, can be seen in the 1936 marketing pamphlet *Nihongorakushōhō,* which was distributed by Endo's company to showcase available products (Nihon gorakuki seisakusho 3).

Some of the machines depicted in the marketing pamphlet can be interpreted as having been deliberately designed in accord with the imagery of the Japanese pan-Asian empire project that was being put into motion during this period. Indeed, Endo's walking elephant, a piece of original mechanical play equipment with no parallel in the West, and some of the designs of his strength testing machines made in the form of tigers and elephants whose tails and trunks can be moved left and right, can be interpreted as representations of the domestication of exotic animals and, by association, the absorption of the East Asian countries from which they originate. Other machines more overtly promote nationalistic narratives. Amongst them, the shooting range installations advertised in the pamphlet sport large paintings of the Japanese naval fleet sailing forward (Nihon gorakuki seisakusho 4), and some early pachinko machines are built around scenic views of Mount Fuji (Nihon gorakuki seisakusho 9). These elements demonstrate the direct influence of wartime ideologies on family-friendly urban entertainment, which was no different than many other aspects of urban life at the time, and which most likely helped legitimize their presence in the eyes of the authorities. In addition to embodying these sociopolitical ideas and, to some extent, familiarizing them by making them playable, other devices such as the *omikuji* vending machines (Nihon gorakuki seisakusho 13), for their part, demonstrated the embracing of new demographic technological innovations in order to breathe new life into traditional practices and rituals.

The concept of rooftop entertainment flourished until the turbulent era of the Second World War. As Japan turned its gaze towards the conquest of East Asia, public campaigns demonizing the purchase and use of luxury products gradually discouraged people from using disposable income for unproductive activities. This trend culminated in the Ministry of Commerce and Industry's adoption of the "Regulation Limiting the Production and Sale of Luxury Products and Others" (Shashihintō seizō hanbai seigen kisoku) in July 1940 as part of the greater National Mobilization Law (Kokkasōdōinhō) to centralize the economy and direct national resources towards the production of war material. Amongst other things, the policy severely restricted the production of goods that were considered superfluous to the war effort, including amusement machines and other play equipment. This policy also forced the termination of rooftop amusement space operations throughout the country (Akagi, *Sore wa "pong"* 33). Operations finally resumed during the American occupation and peaked during the 1950s and 1960s, providing inexpensive entertainment options for the urban working class. The Mitsuya department store building housing Sports Land itself miraculously survived Tokyo's firebombing while most other structures around it burned to the ground; its rooftop amusement space reopened in 1946.

With the fast expansion of entertainment choices in the post-war era and the birth of a middle class with access to more disposable income, the urban entertainment world shifted towards new types of entertainment and new forms of thrills. However, unlike in the pre-war period, these would not be original products born of local creativity, but rather imported goods, usually discarded products from overseas as a collateral effect of the technological race that characterized the amusement industry and the inevitable obsolescence of its products over the years. This second wave of public amusement machines is intimately tied to the opening of Japan to external influences in the aftermath of the war; the American occupation of the archipelago exposed Japanese people, and people in Tokyo particularly, to the pop culture entertainment preferred by the American G.I.s (military personnel). Electromechanical machines such as pinball games and jukeboxes made by foreign companies were imported to Japan and distributed in venues in which American personnel, and the Japanese staff and occasional guest, would gather to spend their free time, such as bars and cabarets (Endō et al. 13).

As the occupation came to an end, these machines made their way out of American post exchanges (PX) and canteens towards the broader population in other types of public spaces. Since most machines from the pre-war period had disappeared as a result of the extended conflict and this new entertainment equipment was radically different, the broader population was not accustomed to these new coin-operated machines and were at first baffled. There is an apocryphal story that some people mistook jukeboxes for stoves when they first started appearing in food and liquor establishments (Nakafuji 67). During this period, the word *kogatayūgikai* (small-scale amusement equipment) gave way to the more English-sounding *gēmu mashin* (game machine) (67). Service Games, a jukebox distribution and maintenance company founded in Honolulu in 1940, was the first enterprise to spearhead that movement by exporting amusement machines to Japan as early as 1945 (Akagi, *Sore wa "pong"* 36). In 1952, Service Games moved its headquarters to Tokyo directly due to the unfavourable policies concerning gambling machines in the United States. However, with the adoption of import restrictions and the limited number of machines available to purchase from the occupation forces, it soon became clear that continuing this type of business with the Japanese public would require the establishment of local manufacturers. Nihon kikai seizō, a manufacturing company formed after the dissolution of Service Games in 1960, then developed and commercialized the *SEGA-1000* in 1960, the first jukebox made in Japan.

Once brought into the Japanese context, these imported machines embodied an aura of exclusivity born from a nascent culture of metropolitan cultural circulation, a phenomenon that was limited to a privileged few in the context of the foreign occupation. In an era of steep income inequalities and flourishing black markets, enjoying a game of pinball or a song from a jukebox was not universally affordable. Initially, only professionals with ties to the GI culture or people in administrative positions were allowed access to American culture, representing the slowly strengthening political and cultural bonds between Japan and the United States that would continue to develop during subsequent decades.

When trade regulations were relaxed at the end of the American occupation, other trading companies, which would later become major players in the game industry, joined the competition, dramatically increasing innovation in this still-young field. Created in 1954 in Tokyo, the trading company Rosen Enterprises, named after its founder David Rosen, successfully launched a semi-automatic photo booth operation called *Photorama*, which spread throughout Japan thanks to a franchise system that was then unknown there. In a country in which job applications required an official identity photo, the high speed and low cost of this method were definite advantages over the competing traditional photo studios (Akagi, *Sore wa "pong"* 39–40). Later, Rosen Enterprises would import electromagnetic games, and collaborated with the Tōhō and Shochiku movie theatre complexes to introduce them to the public. This collaboration inspired the creation of the "Hibiya Gun Corner" in 1960, the first example of urban game complex housing gun and electromagnetic games that started a new trend in major cities (Akagi, *Sore wa "pong"* 40; Eickhorst 20). Around the same period, bowling ranges, which had grown in popularity through the 1950s, also began to house electromagnetic games of all kinds to help their customers endure the long waiting queue, which sometimes stretched to two hours, to secure a bowling line (Sono 47). Over the years, the popularity of these games turned bowling alleys, which at first were open 24 hours and then reduced to

22 hours, into something closer to multipurpose amusement spaces, which greatly benefited emerging game manufacturers.

In 1965, the arcade machine import company Nihon goraku bussan, after its unification with Nihon kikai seizō, merged with Rosen Enterprises to become SEGA Enterprises Ltd. The newly-formed company began in-house production of electromagnetic games and released *Periscope* (1966), the company's first original amusement machine, whose versatile size and innovative audio-visual design became the first success in the industry to be made in Japan (Akagi, *Sore wa "pong"* 42, Eickhorst 20).[4] Two other important companies also contributed to the new urban entertainment environment: the Taito Trading Company and Nakamura seisakusho (later to be known as Namco). Russian expatriate Michael Kogan, whose family had fled Russia for China in the 1920s due to the rise of anti-Jewish sentiments in Europe, funded the Taito Trading Company in 1953. The company's initial focus was the local production of vodka and the distribution of peanut vending machines, and Taito would approach bars and other watering holes to distribute both products. To expand their business in similar venues, the company then imported, distributed, and ultimately produced jukeboxes and various types of electromechanical game machines to be installed in the ever-growing number of urban entertainment venues in Japan. On the other hand, Nakamura seisakusho, funded in 1955 to supply and operate rooftop amusement parks, adopted a more family-friendly perspective and soon expanded its business to the production of game machines, especially video racing games such as the 1970 hit *Racer*.

Other independent distributors such as Kansai seiki seisakusho also produced and distributed arcade games for bowling alleys, movie theatres, and other "gun corners", but the three main players of the industry, SEGA Enterprises, Taito Trading, and Nakamura seisakusho, would reap greater benefits by combining machine production and direct involvement with venue operations (Akagi, *Sore wa "pong"* 52–54).

Medal In, Medal Out: The Sigma Method and Medal Games in the 1960s and 1970s

The booming motion picture industry of the 1960s and the popularity of bowling alleys in the 1970s had the effect of establishing specific hotspots throughout the cities where electromagnetic machines and videogames could be installed and turn a profit, such as movie theatres or department stores. However, these machines were never considered the main attraction of these locations (Nakafuji 68); when venues closed down, electromagnetic gun games and driving games had to leave as well and find new homes. Permanent spaces for arcade machines would not appear until the beginning of the 1970s, setting the stage for videogames to make their debut and extend the play potential of coin-operated games beyond shooting and driving simulations.

The second innovation of the post-war period was the development of "medal games", modified gambling machines that used token coins called "medals" without market value, instead of regular coins. Gambling is technically illegal in Japan;

operating or taking part in gambling activities is considered a crime, which made gambling machines previously imported for the use of G.I.s stationed in the country unusable on the secondary market. However, in 1969, a businessman named Katsunori Manabe developed a way to refurbish these machines to use medals, a technical and marketing innovation then known as the *Sigma method,* after the name of Manabe's company (Nakafuji 70).[5] The repurposing of these machines was probably most likely inspired by a previous business venture led by the Taito Trading Company. In 1964, Taito was granted a permit to produce the *Olympia*, the first medal-operated slot machine of its kind to be released in Japan (Akagi, *Sore wa "pong"* 48). Released in the year of the Tokyo Olympics from which it took its name, the machine was received favourably by the public. In the years following its release, numerous "Olympia Halls" opened across the country, but the fad predictably died off some time later. However, this set the stage for the very profitable Pachislot business that often accompanied medal games in game parlours.

Manabe understood that medals could effectively harness the excitement generated by real gambling machines, but without the legal implications and consequences that come with manipulating real money. Strong from the early success of this method, Sigma opened the first medal parlour of its kind in 1971, the Shinjuku Game Fantasia Milano, established in the same building as a movie theatre. Sigma's medal game amusement centres, an early example of spaces entirely dedicated to public amusement machines, were meant to give an impression of glamorous otherworldliness; the venues were richly decorated to contrast with everyday life and help patrons forget about the worries of daily life (Eickhorst 21). Manabe's vision was that twentieth-century urban entertainment should not be exclusively based on the enjoyment of material goods, but also, and for the most part, on "abstract" experiences provided by machines and other sorts of electronic technologies that could be enjoyed in their own right. Manabe wished to create "halls of encounters" between people and game machines (Nakafuji 71). Further investing in this venture, Sigma continued to experiment with more medal game concepts, and ultimately released its first horseracing simulator, *The Derby,* in 1975, immediately following SEGA's *Harness Race*, which had hit game centres the year before. The company is still operating at the time of publishing, albeit under the name of Adores, and caters to an ever-wider urban demographic with regular new medal-based game offerings.

Although Manabe insisted on creating spaces that transported users away from daily life and created a unique sense of wonder for its medal games parlours, the very act of playing these types of machines reflected and, to some extent, reinforced the actual socioeconomic conditions that Japan had reached as a result of the 30-year-long "economic miracle" from the beginning of the occupation to the mid-1970s. The transformation of gambling machines into, essentially, "spending machines" was not neutral, but was inspired by the act of "spending" located at the heart of the nascent consumer society into which Japan itself was slowly transforming. Similarly, Michael Oppitz insisted upon this aspect in his discussion of pinball machines as multifaceted social agents that remediated ideological statements into everyday life (81). Medal games were a form of mass entertainment that, amongst many others, participated in the transformation of a certain part of the Japanese public into consumers by familiarizing them with the daily act of consumption, which could be enjoyed as entertainment in its own right. From the outset, what medal games offer is the joy of spending coins by putting them into a complex machine, which itself remains static until the player's input. As they circulate through the machine, medals activate a variety of devices that provide pleasurable and exciting audio-visual output and, sometimes, grant medals back to the user in greater number for him/her to extend his/her playtime. Since nothing can be officially gained from exchanging medals and no clear goal is presented to the player, the pleasure of playing these games was essentially derived from the very act of spending, even if framed in a controlled environment, and without any serious consequences beyond that of the initial purchase of medals at a set price. Medal game parlours were spaces in which the pure pleasure of spending was both encouraged and carefully staged.

Sigma not only established the foundation of the medal game industry but also created the basic template for the first venues that would come to be called game centres in Japan, years before the arrival of videogames. Throughout the 1970s, the dark spaces of game centres and their glamorous atmosphere attracted a diversified clientele by emulating the principles of casinos found in the United States (Eickhorst 21). However, the association between medal games and gambling, and therefore the association of game centres with illegal activities, was easy to make, and this association tarnished the public image of game centres over time. By 1974, concerns became serious enough to warrant Sigma, the leader of the industry, to start a public relations campaign to promote medal game playing as a healthy hobby that involves no money or prize exchange ("Gēmu kōnā no imēji" 2). Nevertheless, medal games provided a boon for the amusement industry in solidifying its bases: they provided a new type of machine that proved more reliable than the high-maintenance electromechanical game machines, allowed more flexibility and innovation in their game design and target clientele, and secured amusement machine venues as mainstays in the fabric of urban environments.

From the mid-1970s onward, electronic videogames would be slowly introduced into the spaces of game centres amongst other venues such as bowling alleys, gun corners, and department stores. Game centres welcomed early videogames such as Atari's *Pong*, first imported by Nakamura seisakusho, as well as its locally produced variants such as *Elepong* and *Pong-Tron*. These machines featured original *Pong* electronic boards purchased from Atari and other manufacturers in the United States (Gorges, *Space Invaders* 62–63), installed in cabinets that, despite being designed entirely in Japan, were built according to the American upright cabinet standard. This cabinet style was repurposed by most amusement machine manufacturers throughout the early years of the introduction of videogames in Japan. The first original videogame produced in Japan, Taito's *Soccer,* created by Tomohiro Nishikado, was released in November 1973 (Akagi, *Ākēdo TV gēmu* 77; Gorges, *Space Invaders* 68).

Kissaten and the Emergence of Early Videogame Arcades

During the mid-1970s, in the heyday of medal game popularity, game centre operators did not prioritize the installation of videogame cabinets. The industry invested its creative efforts into innovating the medal game concept in order to keep the thrills fresh and customers interested. If anything, the first videogames featured in these spaces were simply interesting additions meant to distract customers between sessions on medal game machines. Videogames would make a much more significant impact in other types of venues, such as coffee houses, before game centres would start truly diversifying their business.

In the 1970s, Japan was enjoying the repercussions of a high-growth economic period that began some time after the end of the American occupation. This "economic miracle" was the result of a constellation of favourable factors such as the success of trading ventures and the emergence of a highly educated workforce, but also, and in no small part, the tireless dedication of white-collar employees, called *salarymen,* to their companies. Although the promise of lifetime employment and superior salaries were much sought-after staples of success in the post-war Showa era, being a *salaryman* also meant sacrificing one's health and personal time for the sake of the company, at the risk of becoming a stranger to one's own family (Brinckmann and Rogge 25). Throughout the decade, it became clear to some of these workers, as well as to prospective students, activists, or eccentric personalities, that tying oneself down to one company to do what sometimes amounted to alienating work for the rest of one's life was not an exciting prospect. As a result, some of these disillusioned people refused corporate life and instead opened individually owned coffee houses called *kissaten* as alternatives (White 74). Shops established during the *kissaten* boom were structured and decorated according to the personalities and quirks of their owners, as spaces in which individual and nonconforming self-expression was allowed, attracting like-minded customers into a micro-society based on similar niche interests in an atmosphere that encouraged discussion. The number of coffee houses, which served all manner of hot and cold drinks and simple dishes, increased exponentially in cities, becoming relaxation spaces for workers on their lunch breaks. They became spaces of respite in which white-collar employees could indulge in some personal time undisturbed by the demands of the rapidly developing high-speed capitalist system. These venues often offered various distractions, such as manga or newspapers to read, but the one innovation that drastically altered the evolution of these venues was the replacement of standard coffee tables with videogame cabinets.

Amidst the efforts to bring more novelty to the ball-and-paddle-based concept upon which videogames had relied since the release of *Pong*, Atari and Kee Games produced *Breakout* in 1976, a game initially conceived by Nolan Bushnell himself (Kent 71). By that year, Atari and Nakamura seisakusho, which would become Namco the following year, had developed a strong business relationship through the importation and publication of the former's arcade products, and the company was approached to distribute the arcade game in Japan on behalf of Atari through a licensing partnership. As Akagi explains, the initial reception of *Breakout* was lukewarm; the games that attracted the most attention at trade shows in 1977 were *Ball Park* and *Blockade*, but *Breakout*, which was shipped in a regular stand-up cabinet at the time, was only distributed in limited quantities and in select venues (Akagi, *Sore wa "pong"* 111). This situation opened the door for other Japanese manufacturers to start releasing clones of the game as early as February 1977.

The first company to start what would later be called the *burokku kuzushi* genre was Universal, with the release of an upright game machine called *Scratch*. Over the following years, a plethora of other *Breakout* copies from approximately ten different manufacturers (Akagi, "Bideo gēmuki no yakushin" 64) would see the light of day, much to the discontent of Atari and, more importantly, Namco, which expected to hold a monopoly over the *Breakout* market as the only company with an official distribution licence. However, that situation allowed many Japanese manufacturers to take risks and experiment with alternative ways to deliver the successful *Breakout* experience to Japanese gamers, ones not necessarily tied down to Atari's initial machine design. One such design innovation came from the Taito Trading Company with the release of *Table Block*.

Also called by the nickname *TT Block* (TT for "tabletop"), *Table Block*'s innovative aspect was not related to game play enhancements, but the redesign of the machine to fit a broader range of venues, which in turn could reach a bigger consumer pool. Table-type cabinets (*tēburukei kyotai*) were placed in many kinds of venues, from bars and watering holes to bowling alleys and gun corners, but it was in the *kissaten* of the late 1970s that they would find the most receptive crowd and where their designs would best fit. *Table Block* was the fourth game in the *TT* series, and premiered the same year as a cocktail table version of *Western Gun*. While cocktail table-type arcade machines had been circulating in the United States since 1973 (Akagi, *Sore wa "pong"* 112), they were not as widely used as the stand-up cabinet type. However, the size of Japanese venues mandated that arcade cabinets should be smaller and be used for different purposes, for which the cocktail cabinet type was well adapted. 1977 marked an important milestone in the amusement industry as, for the first time, the industry's focus shifted from medal games and the traditional game centre venue model to the concept of table-type videogame machines and the café as the quintessential space for playing videogames, either alone or with company. Café operators welcomed this new source of income with open arms as they were able to fully integrate these games into the dynamics of their establishments; the creator of *Double Dragon*, Yoshihisa Kishimoto, through his biographer Florent Gorges, recalls that, during this period, patrons would sometimes offer free drinks or various types of gratuities when a customer reached a certain threshold as a play incentive (Gorges, *Yoshihisa Kishimoto* 56).

From then on, most videogames released in Japan would be brought to the public in the form of table cabinet videogames. However, the arrival of a specific game, *Space Invaders*, would bind early arcade videogames to *kissaten*. From its release in the summer of 1978 to October of 1979, *Space Invaders* caught the attention of Japanese people in all major cities. The phenomenon reached its peak when a total of over 280,000 machines were installed around cities in virtually any type of venue that would take them (Ishikawa et al. 169). However, machines would mostly be concentrated in one specific type of venue, the invader houses: coffee houses in which table-type arcade machines replaced all traditional coffee house tables and in which *Space Invaders* and other copies created by other manufacturers were constantly being played. While many coffee houses were completely repurposed as invader houses, many more establishments opened specifically for the purpose of becoming invader houses during this period. For the first time, videogames had a permanent place of their own in these cafés, which slowly became videogaming dens due to the large amount of revenue that this activity generated. Groups of customers would flock in to these new spaces to try to establish new high scores on the machines while sipping their favourite drink.

Hundreds of invader houses were opened in 1978 and 1979, which established the essential network that allowed other videogames to reach a broader demographic in the following years. Emerging into the space of marginality and eccentricity of the *kissaten*, in contrast to electromechanical and medal games that were more influenced by the commercial imperatives of their early environments, they could be seen as more easily leaning toward the potential for dissension from major tenets of social ideologies. While nothing suggests that invader houses saw the emergence of well-defined subcultures, which would be seen later, voices contesting their now unmistakable presence in the public sphere would soon emerge and lead to transformations in their relationship with urban space.

Notes

1 Charles Paradis's article in the magazine *Numismatic* indicates that, according to numismatist Mark Fox, "the Japanese mint increased production of copper-nickel 100-yen coin in the late 1970s to counterbalance the hoarding and melting of the 60-percent-silver 100 yen struck in 1957–66" (47).

2 In his 2014 work on videogame arcade culture in the United States, Todd Harper also encounters this archetype of the "Asian background as a marker of skills" (114). Through his discussion with players from the community, the idea of having "Asian hands" emerges as a way to describe a particularly talented player whose skills and reflexes are natural, something seen only in players of Asian origins (114–15). Harper associates this expression with the tradition of Orientalism, compartmentalizing and limiting the Other in terms of body parts, expressing both longing and fear for the Asian subject.

3 The original video can be accessed at https://www.youtube.com/shorts/pw1jFjPfPGM. No additional details are available in the description, leaving the viewers to speculate on whether the video is staged or consent was obtained from the participant before filming.

4 Nakamura seisakusho produced and put to market a game also named *Periscope* prior to SEGA's release (Akagi, *Sore wa "pong"* 50). As was common at a time when game design concepts were limited, both games shared many similarities, but where Nakamura seisakusho's game consisted of a giant cabinet that could accommodate three customers at a time, in 1968, SEGA redesigned it into a smaller single-player design that could accommodate a variety of venues (Modified 'Periscope' Unit 99).

5 This system was also known as the "medal in, medal out method."

Works Cited

Akagi, Masumi, editor. *Ākēdo TV gēmu risuto – kokunai – kaigaihen (1971–2005)* [*The List of Arcade Video Games – Domestic and Foreign Compilations (1971–2005)*]. Amyūzumento tsūshinsha, 2006.

———. "Bideo gēmuki no yakushin, kaze no inbē kyōsō [The Progress of Video Game Machines, The Wind of the Invader Mania]." *20 Seiki* [*Century*] *Youth Culture Clip Magazine*, 2016, pp. 64–65.

———. "Shakōba ni okareta kōka de ugoku gorakuki no tanjō [The Birth of Coin-Operated Amusement Machines Put in Social Meeting Places]." *20 seiki (20th Century) Youth Culture Clip Magazine*, 2016, pp. 52–53.

———. *Sore wa "pong" kara hajimatta – ākēdo TV gēmu no naritachi* [*This All Started with "Pong" – The Birth of Videogames*]. Amyūzumento tsūshinsha, 2005.

Ashcraft, Brian, and Jean Snow. *Arcade Mania! The Turbo-Charged World of Japan's Game Centers*. Kodansha International, 2008.

Ball Park. Arcade videogame cabinet, Taito, 1979.

Blockade. Arcade videogame cabinet, Gremlin and Nakamura seisakusho, 1977.

Breakout. Arcade videogame cabinet, Atari and Kee Games, 1976.

Brinckmann, Hans, and Ysbrand Rogge. *Showa Japan: The Post-War Golden Age and Its Troubled Legacy*. Tuttle, 2008.

Coppola, Sofia. *Lost in Translation*. Focus Features, 2003.

Crawford, Brad. *100 Yen: The Japanese Game Center Experience*. Strata Studios, 2012.

Dance Dance Revolution. Arcade videogame cabinet, Konami, 1998.

Derby, The. Medal game, Sigma, 1975.

Double Dragon. Arcade videogame cabinet, Technōs Japan, 1987.

Eickhorst, Eric. *Game Centers: A Historical and Cultural Analysis of Japan's Video Amusement Establishments*. U of Kansas, MA Thesis, 2006.

Elepong. Arcade videogame cabinet, Taito, 1973.

Endō, Masanobu, Toru Iwatani, Tomohiro Nishikado, Shigeichi Ishimura, and Yusuke Koyama. "Nihon degitaru gēmu gakkai 2010 nenji taikai kichō kōen 'nihon degitaru gēmu no reimei' zenhen [Annual Convention Keynotespeech of the 2010 Japanese Digital Game Research Association 'The Dawn of Japanese Video Games,' First Part]." *Journal of Digital Games Research*, vol. 5, no. 2, 2011, pp. 13–30.

"Gēmu kōnā no imēji appu ippan muke kyanpain [Public Campaign for the Improvement of the Image of Game Corners]." *Gēmu mashin*, 30 Oct. 1974, p. 2.

Gorges, Florent. *Space Invaders: Comment Tomohiro Nishikado a donné naissance au jeu vidéo japonais* [*Space Invaders: How Tomohiro Nishikado Gave Birth to Japanese Videogames*]. Omaké Books, 2017.

———. *Yoshihisa Kishimoto: Enter the Double Dragon*. Editions Pix'n Love, 2012.

Guitar Freaks. Arcade videogame cabinet, Konami, 1999.

Harness Race. Medal game, Sega, 1974.

Ishikawa, Hiroyoshi, Akira Fujitake, and Kosē Ono. *Nihon fūzoku jiten* [*Japanese Entertainment Dictionary*], *American Culture 3 70's*, edited by Hiroyoshi Ishikawa, Sansēdo, 1981.

Kamiya, Setsuko. "Top-Floor Tokyo." *The Japan Times Online*, 18 May 2015.

Kawasaki, Yasuo. *The History of "Game Centers" in Japan: Historical Changing and Social Positioning as Entertainment Facilities*. Fukumura Shuppan, 2022.

Kent, Steve L. *The Ultimate History of Video Games – From Pong to Pokémon and Beyond : The Story Behind the Craze That Touched Our Lives and Changed the World*. Three Rivers P, 2001.

Krawczyk, Gérard. *Wasabi*. TF1 Film Productions, EuropaCorp Distribution, 2001.

Lamarre, Thomas. "What Is a Techno-Region?" *The Newsletter: International Institute of Asian Studies*, no. 50, 2009, pp. 6–9.

Lozano-Méndez, Artur. "Techno-Orientalism in East-Asian Contexts: Reiteration, Diversification, Adaptation." *Counterpoints: Edward Said's Legacy*, edited by Mayy Talmisānī and Stephanie Tara Schwartz, Cambridge Scholars, 2010, pp. 185–2010.

"Modified 'Periscope' Unit Released by SEGA Ent." *Cash Box*, Mar. 1968, p. 99. https://archive.org/details/cashbox29unse_32/page/n185/mode/2up, Accessed 29 June 2023.

Nakafuji, Yasunori. "The Expansion of the Amusement Industry in Japan." *Bulletin of Shinshu Junior College*, vol. 9, no. 1, July 1997, pp. 66–76.

Nihon gorakuki seisakusho [Japan Amusement Machine Works]. *Nihongorakushōhō* [*Japan Amusement Product Information*]. 1936.

Olympia. Medal game, Sigma, 1964.

Oppitz, Michael. "Shangri-La, Le Panneau de Marque d'un Flipper. Analyse Sémiologique d'un Mythe Visuel [Shangri-La, A Pinball Machine Marquee. Semiotic Analysis of a Visual Myth]." *L'Homme*, vol. 14, no. 3–4, 1974, pp. 59–83.

Paradis, Charles. "Insert Coin to Play: Space *Invaders* and the 100-Yen Myth." *The Numismatist*, Mar. 2014, pp. 46–48.

Periscope. Arcade electromechanical cabinet, Sega, 1966.

Pong. Arcade videogame cabinet, Atari, 1972.

Pong-Tron. Arcade videogame cabinet, Sega, 1973.

Pop'n Music. Arcade videogame cabinet, Konami, 1998.

Racer. Arcade electromechanical cabinet, Nakamura seisakusho, Sega, 1970.

Roh, David S., Betsy Huang, and Greta A. Niu. "Technologizing Orientalism." *Techno-Orientalism: Imagining Asia in Speculative Fiction, History, and Media*, edited by David S. Roh, Betsy Huang, and Greta A. Niu, Rutgers UP, 2015, pp. 1–20.

Scratch. Arcade videogame cabinet, Universal, 1977.

Soccer. Arcade videogame cabinet, Taito, 1973.

Space Invaders. Arcade videogame cabinet, Taito, 1978.

Table Block. Arcade videogame cabinet, Taito, 1977.

Taiko no tetsujin. Arcade videogame cabinet, Namco, 2001.

Ueno, Toshiya. "Japanimation and Techno-Orientalism." *Proceedings of the Seventh International Symposium on Electronic Art*, 1996, pp. 94–96.

Unbelievable Arcade Drum Game Skills. Directed by @AurorasJapanLife, *YouTube* Shorts video, https://www.youtube.com/shorts/pw1jFjPfPGM. Accessed 8 July 2023.

Western Gun. Arcade videogame cabinet, Taito, 1977.

White, Merry. *Coffee Life in Japan*. U of California P, 2012.

3 Policing and Centralization

Game Centre Spaces from the *Shinfūeihō* Reform to the Interconnected Arcade (1976–2016)

What Should Game Centres Be?

The 1970s was the golden age of independently owned videogame arcades in Japan. The earliest data showing the number of *kissaten* housing videogames in Japan indicate that, in 1979, around 35,000 venues were operating. By 1982, this number would dwindle to around 23,300, a steep decline that would persist over the years while the number of game centres structured around medal games was also decreasing ("Shōwa 58 nenpan shiyakusho" chart 1–7). Indeed, after the initial *Space Invaders* boom, game centres and cafés would have a difficult time retaining their customer base; the love affair between Japan's mainstream crowd and videogames lasted only as long as they kept their novelty appeal, which was firmly grounded in the zeitgeist of the end of the 1970s. However, a form of media panic that complicated the manufacturer-operator business relationship also contributed to the decline of videogame-related venues.

The arrival of videogames on the urban entertainment scene led to important structural reforms intended to define the nature of this new form of play, police its effects more effectively, and regulate its overall presence in the societal fabric. Fractures opened between different stakeholders. Industry associations and corporations negotiated software innovation against regulations of their content, while governments sought to define and classify game machines, and corporations sought to invest and rethink the spatial design of game centres, pushing away independent operators. Rifts also opened between different agents: parents and teachers against industry, mainstream media, arcade videogames technology and home consoles, as well as between opposing scientific perspectives. Within this evolutionary process that saw the game centre operation business consolidate into a full-fledged industry, the space of game machines, both within the boundary of a venue and invested by game centres in the city, remains a site of rapid transformation.

Protect the Children: Media Panic and Industry Self-regulation

Playing arcade videogames was originally an entertainment activity that mostly targeted adults as prospective consumers due to the nature of the spaces in which they were played such as game centres and coffee houses. However, the number of

DOI: 10.4324/9781003273776-4

children and teenagers attracted to the thrills of arcades steadily increased, often replacing the adult population who gave up the hobby after the *Space Invaders* boom came to pass. Children and teenagers were now frequenting coffee houses and other venues to play videogames themselves. However, after the 1978 popular craze, invader houses and game centres were seen as unproductive and addictive; thus, both videogames and the spaces in which they were played were put under great scrutiny by the mainstream population.

Across all major media newspapers, such as the *Asashi Shimbun*, the *Mainichi Shimbun*, and the *Yomiuri Shimbun*, most news coverage and opinion pieces published about arcades explored the potential negative effects of videogames on children due to their seemingly addictive nature and their ties to criminal activities. Some of the articles that propagated such negative discourse about videogames included "The Things that Consume Youth's 'Dream' – Television Game Advertisement, Money Transfer, and Indifference" ("Shōnen no yume wo kui mono" 9), "The Overheating Invader Games – Succession of Children's Delinquency Cases: Theft and Fake Coins" ("Kanetsu inbēdā gēmu" 15), or "Not Building any Game Centers – Complete Plan Withdrawal: Tokyū's Subsidiary Parent Teacher Association in Strong Opposition" ("Gēmu sentā tsukurimasen" 20). Game centres had already been featured in the crime reporting sections of newspapers throughout the 1970s; between 1973 and 1978, all media coverage included stories about police arrest reports for gambling, theft, murders, or other criminal activities. All of this negative media coverage would establish the base of a media and academic discourse known as *bideo gēmu akueikyōron*, or the "videogames' negative influence" discourse.

Some of those anxieties were justified: gambling was the greatest problem that kept game centres and invader houses from enjoying the status of legitimate entertainment. Between the start of the videogame boom in the late 1970s and 1983, yearly police arrests of individuals involved in gambling activities in game centres had reached 8,482 individuals over 1,671 cases, accounting for over 50 percent of all gambling-related offences in Japan (Kinefuchi and Murase 94). In addition, the same sources pointed out that 10 percent of all game centres in Japan had a link in some way or another with violent criminal groups (94). For these reasons, the idea that game centres and other videogame-related venues were hotbeds of criminality that could potentially lead children towards delinquent behaviour was gaining more ground within the Japanese public. In the same vein, individuals fond of playing videogames post-*Space Invaders* boom were dismissed as unproductive and anti-social people. It is reasonable to think that this discourse was also, in some way, a self-fulfilling prophecy; as frequenting videogame arcades became a socially disapproved activity and the general public slowly started to abandon them, the concentration of ill-intended individuals increased.

To counter this bad image and reassure the public and the authorities as to the social accountability of the industry, the *Zen'nihon yūen kyōkai* (Japan Amusement Association, or JAA)[1] released the *Invader Games Self-Control Declaration* (Inbēdā gēmu jishuku sengen) to its members and the public on June 2, 1979.

This document detailed a self-regulation plan that addressed most of the public criticism of videogames in four concrete points: videogame cabinets were not to be installed in venues unsupervised by a manager; non-accompanied children under the age of 15 would not to be allowed to play; children under the age of 18 were not to be granted access to videogame venues after 11:00 PM;[2] and the practice of granting prizes or rewards based on the result of a videogame session should be forbidden ("Inbēdā gēmu jishuku sengen" 1). This document was devised when a growing number of prefectures, cities, and venues themselves were acknowledging the issues that the media were pointing out about videogames and were starting to enact policies to address the two issues at the heart of the public's concerns: the links between videogames and gambling, and the negative effect of frequenting arcades on young people ("Zenkoku kakuchi de mondaika" 1).

As a result, schools would forbid students to go to invader houses and venues would also severely restrict access. The media, including print media, would also reach children directly. For instance, the first issues of the popular videogame manga *Gēmu sentā arashi* featured an appendix explaining to the reader how to play certain videogames and, especially, how to achieve great scores by explaining secret techniques. At the end of the chapter *Kessen! Gyarakushi wōzu* (*Bloody Battle! Galaxy Wars*), the first compilation volume of the series included an appendix that, instead of sharing secret play techniques for *Space Invaders*, explained some of the regulations that children should observe with regard to playing videogames in game centres. Arashi Ishino, the series' protagonist, instructed readers to respect the will of venue owners that do not allow school children on their premises, and reminded them that they should be accompanied by an adult when they do play games and be mindful of spending too much of their allowance in one sitting (Sugaya 206). While videogames were played by very diverse demographics, the issue of social acceptance of the media mostly centred on the effects of videogames on children's development.

This specific embodiment of the videogame media panic shares some of the characteristics of its American equivalent that occurred at the beginning of the 1980s while still showing some paths of divergence. As Carly A. Kocurek explains, the media panic surrounding videogame culture in the United States emphasized violence in videogames as a potential negative influence on the minds of young players (68), and also partly because of the potential for triggering delinquent behaviour due to the nature of the space in which games were located (59), similarly to the Japanese discourse at the turn of the 1980s. The Japanese rhetoric does not emphasize violence as inherent to the games, but focuses instead on preventing players from becoming involved in gambling activities, being abused by other customers, or, most importantly, losing sight of their studies. Thus, what is at stake in the *akueikyōron* rhetoric is mostly the influence of the spaces and venues on children's broader socialization patterns and the development of a good work ethic in their schooling, rather than any problematic content in the games themselves. Criticism and calls for reforms mostly targeted game centres, not the games.

Titillating Pixels: Policing Eroticism in Videogame Arcades

The *Invader Games Self-Control Declaration* represents an early attempt to change the nature of the structure of videogame arcades to be more accommodating to social demands and norms, despite the impossibility of being able to control the highly heterogeneous structure of the arcade scene directly. There are many other examples of similar self-regulation mechanisms implemented within the Japanese videogame industry during the 1990s, notably amongst erotic PC game developers (Pelletier-Gagnon and Picard 37). However, one instance of business association self-regulation originating from the amusement industry affected game centres directly.

During the years following the introduction of *Space Invaders* to cafés, as videogames began to lose their novelty, manufacturers created video mahjong arcade machines made to entertain salarymen on their lunch breaks. These types of games filled an important role by replacing lost revenues caused by the end of the *Space Invaders* craze, and enabled venue owners to stay in business (Kawasaki 6). Mahjong is a board game originating from China, played with a variety of painted tiles that players combine to outscore their opponents. The game has been an integral part of Japanese social pastimes, and mahjong parlours have been common social venues in urban Japan throughout the twentieth century. With the arrival of early electronic mahjong games, and especially with the release of the epoch-making *Janpyūta* in 1981, not the first game of the genre ever released, but one that for the first time offered both a simplified set of controls and a single-player mode facing the computer (5), fans of the game could now bypass the need for human players and play by themselves at any time.

The popularity of these early machines during much of the 1980s spawned an entire genre that, even after cocktail-type videogame cabinets were discarded in favour of more modern digital play configurations, exploded with the arrival of games inspired by the same concept but each offering its own special feature. One such feature was the emergence, in the second half of the 1980s, of processors capable of generating high-quality graphics, which paved the way for manufacturers to create strip versions of their popular mahjong arcade games. In 1983, Nihon bussan's *Jangō Naito* became the first strip mahjong game to be released in arcades, and manufacturers quickly followed suit.

While it is fair to presume that the presence of erotic videogames in game centres may also have contributed to the estrangement of these venues from broader civil life, it was not until 1990 and the controversy generated by the strip mahjong game *Mājan sūpā maru kinban*, featuring explicit representations of female nudity and a dedicated button to interact with the models, that the Shadanhōjin nihon amusement machine kōgyōkyōkai (Japan Amusement Machinery Manufacturers Association or JAMMA) eventually decided to establish guidelines that, amongst other things, placed limits on the presence of adult content in arcade videogames (Moko; "Kenzenka wo sōgai"). As a result, the visual style of erotic content in arcade games became more cartoonish, as seen in some of the games released during this period, such as the first instalment of the popular *Super Real Mahjong* series, before completely disappearing from manufacturers' new product release lists around the turn of the millennium. Again, in this case, it was policies of self-regulation mandated by a business association, directly concerning the game, that partly triggered important changes in game centres that would ease the public's concerns with the nature of these spaces.

After the Boom: Decline and Competing Technologies

The irreversible decline of game centres' mainstream presence was further accelerated by elements beyond the reach of any regulation. The increase in the number of game development companies resulting from the table cabinet boom meant that more and more games entered the market, and their circuit boards, which became more complex with the technological race for more impressive gaming experiences, commanded increasingly higher prices. Interviews with small game centre operators conducted by the magazine *Koin jānaru* (*Coin Journal)* in 1984 suggest that venues could usually purchase only one or two of the dozen or so new games being released every month ("7-8 Tsukiki" 66). While the growth of the game industry allowed manufacturers to assemble circuit boards for increasingly lower prices, these savings were not reflected on their retail prices themselves, which put additional burdens on venue operators. With the quick arrival of new games on the market, older machines declined in popularity just as quickly, sometimes even before the game started to become profitable after its initial acquisition cost. As a result, venues either had to risk financial stability with the purchase of new games, or find ways to encourage customers to continue playing older games.

Beyond these dynamics that were internal to the arcade game industry, the arrival of home videogame consoles, and especially Nintendo's Family Computer (Famicom) in 1983, signalled a new paradigm to which game centres and manufacturers had to adapt. Indeed, when videogames could be played in the comfort of one's living room, the prospect of having to walk to the nearest café, which often did not have an air-conditioning unit installed, lost much of its appeal. Additionally, games appearing first in arcades would often receive home console ports of varying fidelity only a few months after their initial release. In response, operators often had to lower the machine's price tag for a play session to ¥50, ¥30, or even ¥20 while providing customers with free drinks. Venues would also organize contests with sizeable prices such as bikes, radios, and even personal computers to be won ("7-8 Tsukiki" 67). Operator surveys also indicated that the best-selling games for the months of July and August 1984 were single-player experiences such as *Heiankyō erian* and *Lode Runner*, while sports games and titles compatible with Nintendo's VS System were being played more during May and June ("7-8 Tsukiki" 68–69). This situation demonstrates how arcades had lost much of their lustre and most of their customer base with the rise of affordable home consoles and the drawbacks of the weather, retaining the truly dedicated players: the "videogame freaks".

Shinfūeihō: Defining and Regulating Game Centers on a National Level

Game centres continued to develop in an unsteady economic climate for both manufacturers and operators; even as the number of venues slowly diminished, the videogame industry kept growing steadily. Improvised venue operators originating from the *kissaten* businesses either closed their businesses or fully embraced the videogame revolution by turning their establishments into small-scale game centres. No regulatory system prevented operators from maximizing their revenues by running their establishments 24/7 or compensating players for high scores and winning competitions, which often had the side effect of attracting ill-intended customers and leading to the presence of gambling-related activities. These venues were registered as food-and-drink establishments, as amusement centres were in the 1950s, but they made local populations anxious due to their popularity and their apparent shady reputations. In 1984, the Japanese government decided to legislate the status of arcade videogame operations in a fashion that profoundly transformed the industry while also offering a legal definition of videogames that would shed light on their status as a device occupying a legal grey zone in Japanese society, which emphasizes the importance of reading these machines in their immediate and broader context.

The set of regulations affecting food, drinks, and entertainment businesses in Japan is known as *Fūzoku eigyōtō no kisei oyobi gyōmu no tekiseikatō ni kansuru hōritsu*, often shortened to Fūeihō, or *Law Regulating Entertainment Businesses*, which was first established during the occupation period in 1948. It was created to establish greater surveillance and control over restaurants, bars, and other establishments catering to the nightlife demographic by imposing a system of venue registration. As the urban entertainment landscape changed over the years, the core principles of Fūeihō were subjected to several reforms and amendments every time a major trend or new medium was introduced. Notable milestones of these laws include amendments to include pachinko parlours in 1954, billiards clubs in 1955, and "soap lands", or Turkish baths, which offered bathing and massage services coupled with various types of sexual interactions, in 1966 (Haye 172). However, with the arrival of videogames and of new forms of urban entertainment during the 1980s, the Fūeihō underwent one of the most significant reforms of its history, nicknamed the Shinfūeihō or the *New Law Regulating Entertainment Businesses*. This set of legislations required the registration of most businesses housing arcade machines at their local prefectural office and limited the operating hours of game centres to midnight.

The legislation, which was voted on in 1984 and effectively implemented in 1985, involved many months of negotiation between police forces and the industry, during which the legal definition of videogames was sketched. At the time, many videogames featured in game centres consisted of electronic mahjong and poker games, two types of games associated with gambling problems in other spheres of the entertainment industry. During the negotiations, representatives of the Nihon amyūzumento operētā kyōkai (Japan Amusement Operators Association, or NAO[3]) attempted to convince members of the House of Councillors in charge of deliberating on the final form of the bill that, instead of regarding all videogames as equivalent machines without considering their individual nature, a distinction should be made between machines simulating gambling activities and other types of videogames unrelated to gambling principles (Akagi 319–22). This could have allowed operators to simply remove problematic machines to escape regulation while reducing the risk of illegal activities surrounding certain types of games.

However, during the hearing, representatives of the NPA challenged this proposal by demonstrating that systems, specifically Nintendo's VS System and Data East's Deco Cassette arcade cabinets, allowed operators to interchange the content of machines by switching boards. Therefore, there was no efficient way to regulate the content of the games being offered in game centres since operators could switch their content very easily, and thus change how the machines were used. The National Police Agency insisted that differentiating games according to their themes would not be efficient in reducing gambling activities since machines could be used in different ways and for different purposes (Akagi 320). This interpretation takes into account the nature of cabinets themselves and indicates how these, not the games themselves, should be the focus of regulations, while at the same time reinforcing that the problem was not that certain games were themed around real-life gambling activities (like poker or mahjong), but the way in which the games could be used. As a result of this decisive demonstration, emphasis was put on regulating the potential of videogames to inspire and facilitate gambling activities. Thus, videogames were associated with a specific legal category: "machines that could potentially be used as part of gambling activities" ("Fūzoku eigyōtō").

The point of this process was to determine a definition of videogames as a legal entity, and its result was to establish that cabinets were complex compounds of different elements, and that these specific assemblages and not simply the software itself was at the heart of gaming activities. It was understood that, due to their board-switching feature, arcade videogames, which comprised mostly table cabinets, were not simply restricted to a single form of experience, but multiple purposes that were difficult to predict and legislate. Acknowledging the potential functions of the machines beyond their existence as simply ludic objects granted authorities the legitimacy to establish greater control over public videogame activities.

Moreover, this point also raises questions about the definition of arcade videogames and game centres, shifting focus from game software toward the material object existing within a specific context. The argument that the legal liability of a machine is dependent on its use, and thus that the network consists of the people, space, and atmosphere around it, as opposed to a stable, formal nature that emphasizes its software, opens perspectives on videogames as objects that constitute more than their primary ludic aspect. Samuel Tobin calls this bias "ludic essentialism", or the overemphasis of the ludic aspect at the expense of all others in critical readings of videogames ("Cocktail Cabinets"). As Tobin explains in the case of arcade games, the arcade game itself can be used for many more purposes than simply as a ludic machine, and each type of arcade machine provides material conditions that come to define their use, such as socializing, gambling, or even simply holding coats.

This interpretation is reminiscent of the principles of object-oriented ontology, which characterizes ideas related to the intellectual movement called the speculative turn. This large and diversified school of thought and body of works strives to disentangle objects and Cartesian subjects and examine the world beyond the limitations of human cognition and categorization (Srnicek et al. 3). From this perspective, an arcade videogame is much more than its phenomenological subject, more than its software and the text it provides. The material reality of the device itself and its connections to the surrounding agents of its environment also matter. While it is true that an arcade game cabinet can be used as a videogame platform, it is also a device around which people can socialize while sipping a drink, doing homework, reading, or, indeed, gambling, and this fact should not be overlooked. In the field of game studies, and specifically in a discussion of the afterlife of discarded arcade games, Rayford Guins speaks of the need to stop exclusively looking *at* games and start looking *around* them as well in order to expand our understanding (7). If anything, the definition of videogames brought forward as a result of *fūeihō* legislation points at the challenge of defining what arcade games are, and hints at the importance of looking at arcade games contextually and not uniquely as machines with a clear and limited purpose.

The changes that the *fūeihō* renewal brought forward only affected venues of which 10 percent or more floor space was occupied by videogames. Therefore, spaces such as grocery stores and department stores were exempted from complying with the new regulations as long as they operated a small number of machines. Dedicated venues such as game centres, invader houses, or medal parlours had to apply to and secure permission from the prefectural office allowing them to continue business, effectively registering them at a governmental facility intended to track the number of venues operating in the country. Additionally, all game centres were required to observe the mandatory 12:00 AM closing time across Japan. In order to prevent children from playing in game centres at the same time as adults, a time restriction was imposed on underage customers, past which they were not allowed to frequent game centres. In the case of game centres located in the greater Tokyo metropolitan area, children under the age of 16 were refused entry at 18:00, while people under the age of 18 could enter the premises past 22:00 (Nobuoka et al. 7).

These regulations had concrete effects in reducing gambling and other criminal offences occurring in game centres (Kinefuchi and Murase), but in return made it more difficult for small-scale game centres to continue operating effectively. Over the next few years, many game centres closed down in urban centres, while the surviving ones consolidated their businesses to run bigger operations that could generate enough revenues during the shorter time window that the law allowed. But the post-*shinfūeihō* era signalled a period of transition in the game centre business that saw the emergence of other types of game centres that were much larger in scale and operated on the basis of rationalized financial plans supported by strong sources of capital.

Industry Consolidation, Media Convergence, and the Standardization of Game Centre Operations

At the beginning of the 1990s, the industry attempted to expand its market share and target new demographics to make up for the absence of young customers who could no longer play in game centres. To do so, game manufacturers became involved in the operation business directly and built large-scale venues that addressed the issues known as the "three Ks": *kurai* (dark), *kitanai* (dirty), and *kowai* (scary) (Nobuoka et al. 4). Where past game centres were often small and crowded places shrouded in dim lights that were meant to create a nightlife atmosphere, the new type of game centres that Sega, Taito, and Namco built reimagined these spaces as large, spacious, and brightly lit family-friendly multi-floor complexes. They spared no expense providing customers with lavish dreamlike décor in what were often some of the most expensive districts in the country. During this boom, it was not uncommon to see decorations in game centres that were inspired by, for example, kitsch reinterpretations of ancient Egyptian pyramids or Easter Island's giant Moai statues; certain game centres were structured around foreign themes and sported outlandish art pieces. Where medal game parlours designed spaces that exuded wealth and abundance in a context of high economic growth, these game centres associated amusement with spaces that exuded a sense of exoticism and otherness often present in the fictional and narrative aspects of videogames, and in which we can find traces of the influence of the then-nascent phenomenon of globalization.

The major land and real estate acquisition necessary for the establishment of such venues would probably also not have been possible without the financial climate brought forward by the economic crisis that hit Japan at around the same time. The value of real estate in major urban centres plunged at the beginning of the decade, never to recover again, which helped lower exploitation costs. In 1992, Sega opened the Pasela, a 1,730 square-metre game centre in Ueno, while Taito opened a comparable-sized game centre, Taito in Game World, located in Shinjuku. At approximately the same time, Sigma opened Trail One Games in Yokohama (Nobuoka et al. 31). The following year, Sega would open Ikebukuro GIGO in the district of the same name, adding a formidable 3,899 square-metre game centre complex to the company's assets that stretched over eight floors (33). These types of establishments could also be found in the suburbs and the countryside, attracting families on the weekends. Over the decade, the concept of the "game centre" and its negative connotations would slowly develop into the idea of "amusement centres", convivial spaces deeply connected to the fluctuations of real estate capitalism.

The diversity of entertainment options provided by these spaces helped consolidate game centres' revenues and industry growth; between 1989 and 1994, industry profits doubled while attendance increased steadily (Nobuoka et al. 23). In addition to karaoke booths, children's rides, and other play equipment such as air hockey tables, large-scale game centres normalized the use of crane games, a type of machine reinvented with Sega's 1985 release *UFO Catcher*, which swapped cigarettes, lighters, and other adult-oriented prizes for stuffed characters, fashion goods, and collectible straps. On the same note, the restrictions imposed on younger demographics also allowed the integration of medal game corners in venues targeting salarymen and couples in the later hours of the day. Both innovations dramatically increased revenues generated by game centres despite the financial crisis of the 1990s. This was due to effective monetization schemes, and to the appeal of game centres to a larger demographic, most notably women, who had seldom visited arcades before that time. Even as the high-end entertainment options of the previous decade such as resorts and golf memberships declined, demand for "cheap, close and amusing" options increased as the nation was now breaking historical records in terms of available leisure time while, at the same time, wages started to fall (Tokuyoshi Nakazawa 12–13). These elements, coupled with efficient profit maximization methods, led industry analysts to declare that the amusement industry was very much "crisis-proof", which presumably led to further investment (Tokuyoshi Nakazawa 1; Nobuoka et al. 1).

Having access to more space and, to a certain extent, control over games that were placed in venues enabled manufacturers to innovate in terms of game design and provide compelling alternatives to the competing home console market. In 1985, Sega released *Hang On*, the first game of a genre that would come to be known as "taikan games" (body feel games, or immersive games). Unlike traditional videogame machines, *Hang On* invited players to directly sit on a replica bike on which they would perform leaning motions to steer the cabinet left and right.[4] Sega quickly followed suit with other "taikan" experiences such as *Space Harrier* and *After Burner*, bulkier machines that tracked players' joystick manipulation and moved according to their input. These machines drew new crowds who were not necessarily familiar with videogames, but were immediately attracted by the prospect of both haptic feedback and engaging in an activity that mimicked motorbike racing.

By the 1990s, powerful manufacturers and venue operators such as Sega planned to build large-scale simulation installations that bridged reality and gaming in some of their biggest venues, further developing the "taikan" concept. Perhaps the ultimate embodiment of this genre was Sega's *Super Circuit*, an eight-player game in which players raced remote controlled karts against each other through modified cabinets of standard racing games. It was only possible to install such devices in the largest game centres, leaving smaller venues to focus on more traditional videogame experiences. Here, the change in space considerably influenced the direction in which certain genres of videogames would evolve, while dramatically improving the image and reputation of game centres across the country. Frequenting amusement centres was now considered a legitimate activity.

The large-scale game centre spaces that emerged as a result of the legislation around videogame arcades in the mid-1980s enabled the introduction of new forms of arcade videogames, as well as the renewal of older devices found in previous forms of arcade spaces, such as children's rides and crane games. In a way, these large-scale entertainment centres integrated the principles of the earlier rooftop amusement spaces, medal game parlours and invader houses in a single venue, thus, in a way, turning the space into a panorama of the history of Japanese public gaming in which each individual floor is dedicated to a type of play. This sort of assemblage generally constitutes the arcade game experience that is typically referred to in Western media. In these spaces, fighting games were often found on the first floor, and medal games were usually located on the second or third floor, just below the shooting game floor. Pachinko machines were also sometimes integrated into this structure, further diversifying the business model, narrative, and social dynamics specific to each venue. With the slow decline of small, independently owned venues, this structure would become the template of most game centres both in densely populated urban centres and on the outskirts of cities.

Spaces of Communication: Academic Discourse on Game Centres

Beginning with the unanticipated success of *Space Invaders*, it quickly became impossible for the Japanese mass media to ignore videogames as a national hobby, or their dedicated players; both quickly attracted suspicion from commentators and the public. Videogames, both in arcades and on home consoles, necessitate a high level of concentration from their players, who sometimes seem to be completely absorbed by the game and cut off from the rest of the world. Media observers would raise questions about the potential harmful side effects of this activity.

The first wave of Japanese scholars interested in the subject examined the medium from a personality-psychology perspective, asking whether playing videogames truly had any negative effects on young people's interpersonal development. An early study conducted in Sapporo compared the bodily effect of playing videogames to that of jogging on various subjects and discovered that, after a gaming session, these individuals had more difficulty concentrating and their blood pressure and heart rate increased, but these results were only observed in certain individuals with the added nuance of significant variations that resulted only from playing specific genres of games (An'ei 858). The notion that videogames could impact children on a psychological level and negatively affect the development of healthy personal and social lives spread and influenced discourse about games. This phenomenon peaked with the release of *The Famicom Syndrome*, which, amongst other things, criticized the effects of videogames on children (Fukaya and Fukaya). Researchers such as Akira Sakamoto worked for many years testing and nuancing the hypothesis that videogames necessarily lead to increased aggressive behaviour and social isolation, while others demonstrated that the representational field in videogames is set on a metaphorical plane, and posited that violence enacted in the realm of videogames does not hold the same affective value and psychological impact that it does in the real world ("Bideo gēmu no akueikyōron ha"; "Terebi gēmu asobi ha").

Another important voice during that debate was that of Rika Kayama, whose book *Bideo gēmu to iyashi* (*Videogames and Healing*) acknowledged the positive effects of videogames on some children, demonstrating that games could nurture positive self-esteem and help children develop skills to overcome various challenges in their lives. Despite this positive contribution, neuroscientist Akio Mori claimed in *Bideo gēmu no kyofu* (*Fear of the Game Brain*) that, based on electroencephalography experiments, playing videogames could physically damage children's brains and trigger violent behaviour, a condition that he called the "game brain". Although Mori's claims were widely criticized, the book continued to inform debate about the social legitimacy of games into the early 2000s, and forced scholars to address the issue.

This debate eventually covered the issue of young people playing in game centres, but the perception of game centres as hotbeds of criminality drove this discussion more toward questions of security and socialization. At the beginning of the 1990s, game centres had begun a normalization process based on the new regulations dictated by the *fūeihō* reforms, which made it easier to gather data relative to the types of activities taking place in these venues and their physical structures. Such data were presumably used to strengthen industry standards for safer customer use. At least two studies in 1993 and 1994 focused on such issues. The former was an analysis of the sound level in game centres that suggested that regulating the decibel output in these venues (Mirbod et al.), and the latter was a population density analysis conducted with the intent of finding the best methods to implement evacuation procedures in case of hazard, whose results indicated a vast difference in attendance rates between urban (with high attendance on weekdays) and suburban venues (with high attendance on weekends) (Nakaya et al.).

Interest in players themselves, the reasons why they choose to play in public venues instead of at home, and the effects of this activity on them, dominated academic attention, most likely due to the climate of the field of videogame studies as described above, and the conclusions of these studies were mostly negative. In 1994, Shin Nakamura published the results of a survey of players attending a specific game centre around Kabukicho in Shinjuku, which claimed that youths who played videogames in large amounts showed signs of deficient interpersonal skills. Although the 1985 regulations of game centres significantly decreased crime rates in game centres, spaces that were not technically game centres but still housed a few cabinets attracted young people and provided them with unregulated spaces in which they could misbehave (Kinefuchi and Murase 102). In the 2000s, researchers found links between game centre attendance and the so-called "snapping behaviour" (*kireru kōdō*) in youth, a syndrome characterized by spontaneous anti-social conduct often taking the form of sudden rushes of anger (Kimura et al., "Gendai shōnen no 'kireru'"). While causal relationship between asocial behaviour and the practice of videogame playing in general remained difficult to firmly establish ("Gendai shōnen no 'kireru'" 331), such research nevertheless contributed to the overall intellectual environment that vilified nightlife youth activities including videogame playing and spending time around convenience stores in urban areas, and a tendency to approach certain youth behaviour as a clinical condition. Reinforcing these connections, another study focusing on regional differences between game centre uses by middle school children and their display of snapping behaviour was conducted by the same core members of this research team (Kimura et al., "Gendaichugaku no futekiō" 623). This second study indicated not only that the types of uses in regards to companionship and time spent in game centres differed between urban, semi-urban and rural areas but also that certain connections could be made between geographical contexts and the display of snapping behaviour amongst children, with semi-urban areas demonstrating the highest level. Scholars stated that such discrepancy warranted further research in order to confirm these connections.

Until this point, studies of game centres took pragmatic approaches focusing on understanding the structures of these spaces and the experiences of the players, but this research was mainly driven by a negative bias toward videogames and players. The study of game centres was centred on a limited group of players (youths, mostly males) and was highly critical. Most scholars approached game centres as an urban problem that lured youths into unproductive activities, rather than seeing them as cultural hubs. Game centres were perceived as institutions that made it difficult for young people to integrate into the mainstream social sphere and fulfil their social duty of studying to eventually become "productive" members of society by joining the corporate world. Such interpretations came at the expense of the study of the games themselves, the devices used to play them, and the culture that developed around the arcades.

Fortunately, several scholars turned their eyes toward these elements and contributed to providing a more nuanced understanding of early situated videogame culture. One of these was Shin'ichi Nakazawa, whose close reading of *Xevious* in 1983 regarded the game as a mythopoetic narrative determined by the creative interaction between the author/designer and the players. Nakazawa identified the same characteristics in videogames that define mythological texts: the power to arouse readers' narrative curiosity and motivate them to extend the text through sustained engagement beyond the confines of the screen ("Game Freaks Play with Bugs"). Nakazawa's methodology, inspired by structural anthropology, involved exploring the games and, more importantly, the derivative works created by fans; in this case, the collection of *dōjinshi* published by GameFreak. Nakazawa's fairer method gave more credit to players, and, as a result, proved that videogames, as engaging texts, need to be examined from a broader perspective in order to make sense of them, and that behind the surface of the stereotypical asocial player is in fact a deep level of player communication in which the meanings of games and methods of interacting with them, such as secret techniques and controller manipulation tricks, are negotiated. Following this work, Nakazawa later published *Poketto no naka no yasei* (*The Wilderness in the Pocket*), a psychoanalytical essay that positions *Poketto monsutā aka - midori* as an object that enables children to engage in deep levels of communication with their peers and help them develop a healthy and independent psyche beyond the influence of the commercial interests and marketing messages to which they are exposed. Studies such as Nakazawa's drew attention to the agency of players in their relationship with digital play technology.

However, humanists tended to ignore this methodology in favour of clinical experiments and personality-psychology research. With the emergence of game culture as a field of study in the mid-2000s, and a new wave of academics that grew up alongside videogames, interest in games as texts and gaming as a legitimate activity was reignited. Similarly, a new energy, leading to new perspectives, appeared in the study of arcade gaming and game centres. During the 2000s, Hiroyasu Katō produced extensive studies of game centre culture, culminating in the publication of the monograph *Gēmu sentā bunkaron.* Katō introduced the idea of studying game centres as singular social spheres by drawing on the methodology of social studies in order to examine youth subculture surrounding arcade venues at a precise moment during the 1990s. His book strongly rejected the popular conception of game centres as nothing more than hotbeds of criminality and spaces that prevented the healthy development of socialization skills, seeing them instead as places in which teenagers could reinvent themselves outside of the very constraining family unit and the highly structured school system in Japan. Katō introduced "communication notebooks" (communication nōto), small books in which game centre regulars engaged in long-term conversations or shared their artistic creations amongst each other using pen names and without ever meeting in person, as communication tools enabling positive socialization patterns. Originally created to keep track of high scores and secret techniques amongst players in the 1980s, they eventually evolved into anonymized, full-fledged communication devices that users appropriated for themselves.

Katō contextualizes communication notebooks in the broader history of the development of a non-competitive gaming subculture centred on arcade videogames in Japan, which evolved concurrently to major innovations in cabinet design and space development. He identifies the critical moment at which the culture of videogames began to acquire a life of its own: when the "L shaped" cabinets, often called the *candy cabinet* in English, first appeared during the mid-1980s and allowed players to better observe other people's game sessions, players would come to game centres alone and interact with other customers (Katō, *Gēmu sentā bunkaron* 84). Often, players would first know each other by their handle names featured on the score screen of cabinets, rather than their real names (*Gēmu sentā bunkaron* 91). Here, playing acts as a form of public performance and handle names as a textual device that, according to Katō, gave rise to this subculture, which, despite not openly contesting normative social conventions, often finds itself having to negotiate between the desire to use arcades as safe and comfortable cultural hubs (exemplified by writing graffiti or profanities in notebooks), and the reality of navigating a privately owned space which can impose its own regulations (such as addressing complaints coming from other clients and banning certain types of expression) (*Gēmu sentā bunkaron* 218).

Inspired in large part by Erving Goffman's metaphor of the theatrical performance to unpack the phenomenon of human face-to-face social interactions, Katō acknowledges that social interactions are influenced by the atmosphere of game centres in which players behave according to the unstated social code of the venue imposes. However, Katō never fully explores how these social behaviours might potentially be influenced by the design of videogame machines themselves, and how the space, which is often carefully constructed and presented, influences players' interaction with the machines. His work points to the idea that elements such as handle names and the performance/audience relationships that develop in these venues are constituted by social etiquette that, although not plainly stated, influence how players "play out" their social roles as players and venue-goers. However, it is legitimate to consider that the face-to-face "conversations" that players engage with the games themselves by playing them is governed not only by the same social standards permeating the space of game centres but also by what the machine commands players to do through its software and interface design.

Katō's conclusion generates some questions about the nature of the agents shaping the arcade play experience, and these questions stand as points of departure for the critical enquiry conducted in later chapters of this thesis. Before addressing these questions, we must still discern the nature of game centres in the twenty-first century, as well as the structures and issues that are at the heart of game centres and the arcade game industry today, in a changing context in which game playing in the public sphere has now been strongly integrated into mainstream culture.

The Centralization of Arcade Videogame Play

Because of the innovations and trends of the amusement industry in Japan, the state of contemporary game centres in Japan in the second decade of the twenty-first century is radically different from that of the 1990s, when arcades experienced a second revival. Comparing data on the number of game centres located within the district of Shinjuku between 2000 and 2016, for example, shows that the number of venues has greatly diminished, replaced by bigger venues tied to companies with a much greater revenue stream. Of the 26 venues listed on a map provided by *Gekkan arukadia* (Sakutarō and Hide 158), at this writing only three still exist under their original names (Shinjuku Sports Land Honkan and two Taito Stations), while the rest were either sold to national chains (Shinjuku Sports Land Nishiguchi became a Sega World branch) or simply closed down. New establishments not featured in the 2000 map belong to the GAO chain. Overall, less than half of the venues have remained in the district.

The continuing phenomenon of videogame arcade concentration into a few key venues that dominate key city hubs explains the transformations of urban amusement structures and demographics. Gone are the days when great amounts of capital were invested into designing new and architecturally unique venues that were not tied to a manufacturer brand name; Sega World, Taito Station, and Namco, all of which have undergone significant changes due to mergers and purchases by other groups, are ruling the increasingly mainstream normative arcade scene with an iron fist.[5] The end of the independent venues established in decrepit buildings and housing older games available to play at a discount price of ¥50 was duly marked when Shibuya's oldest game centre, the Shibuya Kaikan Monaco, which had managed to stay in business since 1978, closed in 2013. A small crowd of players assembled to be part of the somewhat ritualized final moments of the venerable institution, at the end of which they broke into multiple spontaneous "banzai!" cheers, a moment that was immortalized on video and uploaded to *YouTube* ("Gamers gather"; Osada). Two years later, the building became a fashionable clothing store, unrecognizable from the dozen or so around it, and very different from the multi-floor gaming complex, which, according to oral histories of the place, even used to house a fishing pond overlooked by a mezzanine as part of its many business ventures ("Game Over for Shibuya Kaikan"). Finally, the building housing the defunct game centre was demolished in 2016; no traces of the space now remain, except online. The disappearance of these venues also means the definitive withdrawal of spaces that stood for a specific embodiment of game centres and public gaming. For aficionados of retro videogames, there is indeed nothing else to do but show appreciation of times past and seek public gaming experiences elsewhere.

Multiple factors come into play to explain this phenomenon, but many of them can be grouped in the broader issue of the challenges that contemporary games and urban structures pose to the locality of the gaming experience and its attachment to a sense of place as game centre operation has become interconnected and centralized. Multiple developments in arcade game technology slowly contributed to disentangling the player experience and the individual venue. In 1999, Sega introduced the first data retrieval system to be used in conjunction with an arcade videogame; players would purchase and use a magnetic card for the game *Derby Owners Club,* which enabled them to save their progress (Katō, "Online jidai no gēmu sentā" 283). Users could then use the card with any other similar machine in any other game centre in the country to resume their own in-game horse trainer career. Eventually, many other arcade games integrated this system into their games, allowing for the design of long-term arcade gaming experience and more customization options for certain games. In 2001, for the release of *Virtua Fighter 4*, Sega developed VF.net, an online system allowing players to fight each other competitively over the Internet in Japanese arcades and maintaining a ranking system available on either PC or mobile phones (the i-mode). This system was eventually folded into the ALL.net system, which, along with Taito's similar NESYS system and Konami's e-AMUSEMENT system, acts as an online distribution platform allowing online interactions with other players and ensuring a stream of constant system updates.

By 2011, the three great arcade manufacturers, Sega, Konami, and Bandai Namco, would abandon the magnetic card system in favour of slightly different smart card systems that allowed quick player recognition by simply touching cards on a reader panel. These all-encompassing systems are now compatible with a publisher's entire catalogue and act as a single pass document allowing players to track their progress over a variety of games in any game centre connected to the developer network. It is reasonable to say that such a level of online play integration gradually undermined local ranking systems in favour of a national one that is regulated by machine developers directly instead of by venue operators. With the democratization of online play and the establishment of player profiles accessible through the network, gaming cultural capital that was once tied to the local scene tends to erode as national ranking systems are directly embedded into the machine's software, making local scorekeeping obsolete as the publisher's online network fills that role. As players have access to the same cultural capital (essentially, their online identity, consisting of customization and records accessed via a smart card) in any game centres across the country, venues become interchangeable and little incentive encourages players to frequent one over another, which undermines the creation of a local venue-specific culture. Similarly, the development and the rising popularity of internet message boards, social networks, and other web 2.0 interfaces enable socialization between distant players about specific games, and thus supplant the use of communication notebooks in venues as communication methods (Katō, "Online jidai no gēmu sentā" 293), further challenging the stability of local gaming cultures and the social structures within individual venues.

While many socioeconomic factors influence the rate at which players frequent game centres, it is fair to consider that the integration of online connectivity in arcade machines certainly contributed to the major demographic changes that game centres underwent during the 2000s. The consensus was that consumers frequented these venues mostly as part of family outings, in groups of friends, or even as a date environment for couples; however, data gathered by the AOU indicate that by 2013, the demographic of game centres would become much more fractured. Individuals playing arcade videogames by themselves accounted for a third of all venue-goers, as opposed to 12.7 percent in 2004 (Zen'nihon amyūzumentomashin'operētā rengō-kai, "Gēmusentā ni tsuite no ankēto" 2004, 3; "Gēmusentā ni tsuite no ankēto" 2005, 4). Many games released for arcades during the past ten years reflect these changes in demographics, with experiences geared towards solitary gameplay such as the collectible card arcade game genre exemplified by *World Club Champion Football* and *Sengoku taisen*, or the rhythm game genre such as *Hatsune Miku: Project DIVA Arcade* and *Chunithm*. The cabinet design of these types of machines also supports a more individual play style that tends to isolate players from the rest of the venue and makes it difficult to engage play as a purely gregarious activity. As arcade games now connect players from across Japan in both competitive and collaborative options, this comes at great financial expense for individual operators and, to a certain extent, the loss of a sense of local belonging for players.

However, as this chapter demonstrates, game centres are not all built according to the same models and do not follow the same structures or orientations; alongside amusement megaplexes operated by major manufacturers, there are also smaller game centres that cater to specific crowds and support different arcade play experiences. One such example of the latter is the independent game centre Mikado, located in the vicinity of the Takadanobaba train station in Tokyo. Established in 2011, Mikado provides users with the opportunity to play older games from the 1980s and 1990s in an environment mimicking that of the game centres of the same period, a space densely packed with cabinets in a damp light environment. The machines are not connected to any of the nation-wide networks; instead, a schedule indicates special gathering times called *taisenkai* (fight meetings) at which players can meet up to challenge other players and learn techniques from veterans. Tournaments and other such events also help to establish a sense of community around the space itself, and provide a unique play experience.

The contemporary game centre scene is very diverse, characterized by many different types of venues each housing games providing very different play experiences, and as such, it is more accurate to speak of multiple arcade gaming experiences all emphasizing different aspects, rather than a single embodiment, of these types of venues. Japanese arcades are a patchwork of different spaces that mix both the old and the new, the intimate and the public. Some machines enclose players within a plastic cocoon, such as *Kidō senshi gandamu: senjō no kizuna*, while others give them the opportunity to impress the whole venue, such as *Dance Evolution*. However, while new and innovative game designs regularly find their way into game centres, they also share space with older successful "classic" games and medal gambling machines. Certain venues exclusively house retro games installed in cocktail cabinets on which scorelers[6] compete to improve their mastery of classic games; others dedicate their entire floor space to different fighting game franchises. The arcade gaming experience is as diverse as the amount of software, cabinets, and spaces that enable it. The game centre system as a collective of venues all different from one another, but all collectively called "game centres", and the different zones or floors in individual venues, is the sum of all types of public gaming experiences developed over time in urban Japan. These types of spaces do not necessarily replace each other, but coexist for different purposes. This diversity of experiences makes it impossible to point out a model arcade gaming experience, or a model arcade player; rather, studying arcade gaming must involve multiple local empirical analysis.

The evolution of arcade gaming since the invention of videogames is not teleological, and the development of new types of public gaming experiences did not completely erase the presence of those that were already established. In the case of some of the older venues, the architectural space itself is a compromise between pre-existing structures that met the demands of the times in which they were originally constructed and the arrival of new games that challenge these conditions. The content of the space can be erased to make space for other elements, but new space arrangements often bear the traces of previous ones. The genealogy of game centre spaces can be read from the visual or architectural remains present in these spaces, which sometimes betray a will to evoke nostalgic experience that can be traced to previous eras where certain types of games and player fraternity were different.

This overview of game centre development indicates that the play experience is contingent on three main nodes, each of which deserves careful examination: the software, the cabinet, and the structure of the space in which the arcade gaming experience takes place. This inquiry emphasizes that the establishment of a model tailored to the study of situated gaming must involve interdisciplinary theoretical tools adapted to each of these elements.

Notes

1. The JAA was the leading arcade and amusement industry association at the time.
2. There was still no national regulation about the opening times of game centres in 1979; most of them would be open very late; some would even be open 24 hours.
3. The NAO was an arcade industry association that operated during the 1980s.
4. Due to its immersive nature and dedicated cabinet, Sega received a derogation from the National Police Agency allowing them to market the game as a product not bound by regular *fūeihō* regulations. This allowed Sega to install their games in venues other than game centres. The agency would extend this privilege to the industry in general by introducing the category of "driving games without cabinets" (Akagi 325).
5. Sega would sell its entire arcade operation division to the entertainment business holding company Genda in 2022, effectively ending its presence in this segment of the industry (Batchelor).
6. The term *scoreler* refers to individuals dedicated to obtaining high scores in arcade videogames. The scoreler culture first began when high scorers could share their exploits with the publication of various magazines dedicated to videogames in the 1980s, but has now spread to the internet as a means of communication (Szczepaniak 179–81).

Works Cited

"7-8 Tsukiki – Lokēshon betsugyōkyō [Study of the Commercial Conditions of Specific Locations for the Months of July and August]." *Koin jānaru* (*Coin Journal*), 1984, pp. 66–70.

After Burner. Arcade videogame cabinet, Sega, 1987.

Akagi, Masumi. *Sore wa "pong" kara hajimatta – ākēdo TV gēmu no naritachi* [*This All Started with "Pong" – The Birth of videogames*]. Amyūzumento tsūshinsha, 2005.
An'ei, Tetsuo. "Terebi gēmu oyobi kenkō jikyūsō no seitai kinō ni oyobosu eikyō [The Effect of Videogames and Health Marathon Training on Body Functions]." *Nippon eisei-gaku zasshi* [*Japanese Journal of Hygiene*], vol. 35, no. 6, 1981, pp. 858–63.
Batchelor, James. "Sega Exits the Arcade Business after 56 Years." *Gameindustry.biz*, 28 Jan. 2022, https://www.gamesindustry.biz/sega-exits-the-arcade-business-after-56-years#:~:text=Back%20in%20November%202020%2C%20the,rebrand%20all%20of%20its%20locations.
Chunithm. Arcade videogame cabinet, Sega, 2015.
Dance Evolution. Arcade videogame cabinet, Konami, 2010.
Derby Owners Club. Arcade videogame cabinet, Sega, 1999.
Fukaya, Masashi, and Kazuko Fukaya. *Famicom shindorōmu* [*The Famicom Syndrome*]. Dōhōsha shuppan, 1989.
Fūzoku eigyōtō no kisei oyobi gyōmu no tekiseikatō ni kansuru hōritsu [*Law Regulating Entertainment Businesses*]. E-gov.jp, 2016, https://elaws.e-gov.go.jp/document?lawid=323AC0000000122.
"Game Over for Shibuya Kaikan." *The Time Out Tokyo Blog: Your Daily Guide to City Life, News and Culture*. Accessed 13 July 2023, https://web.archive.org/web/20170401105746/http://blogs.timeout.jp:80/en/2013/08/16/game-over-for-shibuya-kaikan/.
Gamers Gather for Final Night at Old School Shibuya Arcade. YouTube, uploaded by *The Japan Times*, 2013, https://www.youtube.com/watch?v=k_cJuBhcwuk&index=3&list=FLgAaYtkWXa1VQv1bg9YvOaA.
"Gēmu sentā tsukurimasen – keikaku wo kanzen tekkai: tokyū no kokaisha PTA no mōhantai de [Not Building Any Game Centres – Complete Plans Withdrawal: Tokyū's Subsidiary Parent Teacher Association in Strong Opposition]." *Yomiuri shinbun*, 2 Sept. 1978, p. 20.
Goffman, Erving. *The Presentation of Self in Everyday Life*. U of Edinburgh, Social Sciences Research Centre, 1956.
Guins, Raiford. *Game After: A Cultural Study of Videogame Afterlife*. MIT P, 2014.
Hang On. Arcade videogame cabinet, Sega, 1985.
Hatsune Miku: Project DIVA Arcade. Arcade videogame cabinet, Sega, 2010.
Haye, Avril. "Prostitution in Japan: Social Management or Regulation?" *Boekifu: Chubu International Review*, vol. 2, 2007, pp. 170–76.
Heiankyo aliens. Arcade videogame cabinet, Denki Onkyō Corporation, 1980.
"Inbēdā gēmu jishuku sengen [Invader Games Self-Control Declaration]." *Gēmu mashin*, 15 June 1979, p. 1.
Jangō naito. Arcade videogame cabinet, Nihon bussan, 1983.
Janpyūta. Arcade videogame cabinet, Alpha Denshi, 1981.
"Kanetsu inbēdā gēmu: shōnen no hikōzokushutsu nusumi ya inchiki kōka [The Overheating Invader Games – Succession of Children's Delinquency Cases: Theft and Fake Coins]." *Asahi shinbun*, 17 May 1979, p. 15.
Katō, Hiroyasu. *Gēmu sentā bunkaron: media shakai no comyunikēshon* [*Theory of Game Centre Culture: Communication in the Media Society*]. Shinsensha, 2011.
———. "Online Yjidai no gēmu sentā [Game Centres in the Online Age]." *Digitaru no wiwa – jōhō to busshitsu ga majiwaru genzaichiten* [*The Digital Moment – Contemporary Mixing of Information and Materiality*], edited by Shigeo Kawashima, Seigakuin daigaku shuppansha, 2014, pp. 267–305.
Kawasaki, Yasuo. "Bideo gēmuki ga tōnyusareta kissaten no yakuwari no minaoshi: gēmuki ga tsukuri dashita tōshikengōkai no aratashii katachi [Reviewing the Role of Cafės that

Introduced Videogame Cabinets: The New Form of Urban Entertainment Created by Game Cabinets]." *Journal of Digital Games Research*, vol. 7, no. 2, 2015, pp. 1–12.

Kayama, Rika. *Telebi gēmu to iyashi – ima koko ni ikiru kodomo* [*Videogames and Healing: The Children Who Live Here and Now*]. Iwanami Shōten, 1996.

Kenzenka wo sōgai suru kikai kijun [*Basic Mechanism That Prevents a Return to Full Health*]. Japan Amusement Machine Manufacturers Association, 2008, http://web.archive.org/web/20101227142414/http://www.jamma.or.jp/2008/04/3513.html.

Kidō senshi gandamu: senjō no kizuna. Arcade videogame cabinet, Sega, 2006.

Kimura, Tomoko, Masazumi Yamaguchi, Tomoko Fuji, Yuyiko Nishida, Sei'ichi Saito, Minoru Harada, and Chiharu Enomoto. "Gendaichugaku no futekiō ni kansuru kisoteki kenkyū (7): chiiki kikaku ni yoru gemu senta riyo to kireru kōdō no kentō [Fundamental Research on Topics Related to the Maladjustment of Contemporary Middle School Students: Research on Regional Comparative Analysis of Game Centre Use and Snapping Behaviour (7)]." *Japanese Association of Educational Psychology*, vol. 43, 2001, p. 623.

Kimura, Tomoko, Tsuyoshi Shimosaka, and Yuyiko Nishida. "Gendai shōnen no 'kireru' to iu koto ni kansuru shinrigakuteki kenkyū (2): gēmu sentā iyobi konbiniensu sutoā no riyō jōken to kire kōdō no kanren [Psychological Research Regarding the Phenomenon Known as 'Snapping' Amongst Youth (2): The Relationship Between the Use Conditions of Game Centre and Convenience Stores with Snapping]." *Bulletin of the Faculty of Human Development*, vol. 8, no. 2, 2001, pp. 327–32.

Kinefuchi, Tomoyuki, and Takahashi Murase. "Gēmu sentā nado eigyō wo meguru shomondai ni tsuite [On the Numerous Problems of Venues Such as Game Centres]." *Keisatsugakuronshū*, vol. 49, no. 2, 1996, pp. 93–103.

Kocurek, Carly A. *Coin-Operated Americans: Rebooting Boyhood at the Videogame Arcade*. U of Minnesota P, 2015.

Lode Runner. Arcade videogame cabinet, Irem, 1984.

Mājan sūpā maru kinban. Arcade videogame cabinet, Capcom and Yuga, 1990.

Mirbod, Seyed Mohammad, Ryoichi Inaba, Hideo Yoshida, Yoko Kawamura, Chiri Nagata, Setsuya Fujita, and Hirotoshi Iwata. "Gēmu sentā ni okeru sōon leberu chōsa [Research on the Noise Level in Game Centres]." *Japanese Journal of Industrial Health*, vol. 35, no. 3, 1993, pp. 208–09.

Moko. "Mājan Sūpā Maru Kinban." *Arcade Fan*, https://web.archive.org/web/20160416061500/http://www.geocities.jp/arcadon765/marukin.html. Accessed 27 Nov. 2023.

Mori, Akio. *Geemu nō no kyofu* [*Fear of the Game-Brain*]. NHK Shuppan, 2002.

Nakamura, Shin. "Gēmu sentā de asobu shōnen no seikatsu to ishiki ni kansuru kenkyū (1): 'telebi' to 'telebi gēmu' wo chūshin ni [Research on the Daily Life and Consciousness of the Youth That Play in Game Centres (1): From 'Television' and 'videogames' Onward]." *Japanese Personality Psychology Society Convention Proceedings*, vol. 3, 1994, p. 25.

Nakaya, Kenji, Shiro Kashiwabara, Eiyu Yoshimura, Takashi Yokota, and Koichi Sakata. "On the Distribution and the Number of People in Game Centers and Their Changes with Time." *Architectural Institute of Japan Kinki Branch Research Report Collection*, no. 34, June 1994, pp. 589–92.

Nakazawa, Shin'ichi. "Game Freaks Play with Bugs: In Praise of the Video Game Xevious." 1984. *Kinephanos*, translated by Jérémie Pelletier-Gagnon and Tsugumi Okabe, vol. 5, no. 1, 2015, https://www.kinephanos.ca/2015/game-freaks-who-play-with-bugs/.

———. *Poketto no naka no yasei: pokemon to kodomo* [*The Wilderness in the Pockets: Pokemon and Children*]. Iwanami Shoten, 1997.

Nakazawa, Tokuyoshi. *Amyūzumento bijinesu no subete ga wakaru hon* [*Comprehensive Book About the Amusement Business*]. Kabushiki gaisha Yamashita shuppan, 1995.

Nobuoka, Yoshikuni, Kazuo Kobayashi, Atsushi Hosokawa, and Yūji Hayami. *Kore kara no gēmu sentā keiei* [*The Future of Game Centre Management*], edited by Yūichi Tadano, Keiei Jōhō Shuppansha, 1994.

Pelletier-Gagnon, Jérémie, and Martin Picard. "Beyond Rapelay: Self-Regulation in the Japanese Erotic Videogame Industry." *Rated M for Mature: Sex and Sexuality in Videogames*, edited by Matthew Wysocki and Evan W. Lauteria, Bloomsbury Publishing, 2015, pp. 28–41.

Poketto monsutā aka – midori. Nintendo Game Boy, Game Freak, 1996.

Sakamoto, Akira. "Bideo gēmu no akueikyōron ha hontō desu ka? Ichikōgekisei, shakaiteki fu tekiō ni kan suru shakaishinrigakuteki kenkyū no gainen [Is the Discourse on the Bad Influence of Videogames True? General Notions from Research on Sociopsychology Related to Aggression and Anti-social Behaviour]." *Gendai no esupuri – jōhōka to taishūbunka*, vol. 312, 1993, pp. 89–96.

———. "Terebi gēmu asobi ha kodomo no shakaiteki hattatsu wo okuraseru ka? Chōsakenkyū no shōtenbō [Does Playing Videogames Delay the Social Development of Children? Small Research Observations]." *Ningen hattatsu kenkyū*, vol. 17, 1992, pp. 21–25.

Sakutarō, and Hide. "Game Center Map." *Gekkan Arcadia*, issue 1, 1999, p. 158.

Sengoku taisen. Arcade videogame cabinet, Sega, 2010.

"Shōnen no yume wo kui mono – TV gēmu tsūshin hanbai hōkinsase shiran kao [The Things That Consume Youth's 'Dream' – Television Game Advertisement, Money Transfer, and Indifference]." *Asahi shinbun*, 8 Feb. 1978, p. 9.

Shōwa 58 nenpan shiyakusho [*1982 White Papers*]. Keisatsuchō [National Police Agency], 1982, https://www.npa.go.jp/hakusyo/s58/s58s0107.html.

Space Harrier. Arcade videogame cabinet, Sega, 1985.

Srnicek, Nick, Levi Bryant, and Graham Harman. "Towards a Speculative Philosophy." *The Speculative Turn: Continental Materialism and Realism*, edited by Bryant Levi, Nick Srnicek, and Graham Harman, Re.Press, 2011, pp. 1–19.

Sugaya, Mitsuru. *Gēmu sentā arashi 1*. Shōgakukan, 1980.

Super Circuit. Arcade videogame cabinet, Sega, 1989.

Super Real Mahjong. Arcade videogame cabinet, SETA Corporation, 1987.

Szczepaniak, John. *The Untold History of Japanese Game Developers: Volume 1*. SMG Szczepaniak, 2014.

Tobin, Samuel. "Cocktail Cabinets: A Critique of Digital and Ludic Essentialism." *Analog Game Studies*, vol. 4, no. 4, 2015.

UFO Catcher. Arcade prize cabinet, Sega, 1985.

Virtua Fighter 4. Arcade videogame cabinet, Sega, 2001.

World Club Champion Football. Arcade videogame cabinet, Sega, 2002.

Xevious. Arcade videogame cabinet, Namco, 1983.

"Zenkoku kakuchi de mondaika [Problematization in All Regions over the Country]." *Gēmu mashin*, 6 June 1979, p. 1.

Zen'nihon amyūzumentomashin'operētā rengō-kai [All Japan Amusement Machine Operators Association]. "Gēmusentā ni tsuite no ankēto shūkei kekka [Aggregate Results of Questionnaires about Game Centres]." *AOU News*, vol. 19, no. 4, May 2004, https://web.archive.org/web/20160806220659/http://aou.or.jp/news/1405/03.pdf.

———. "Gēmusentā ni tsuite no ankēto shūkei kekka [Aggregate Results of Questionnaires about Game Centres]." *AOU News*, vol. 20, no. 3, 16 Mar. 2005, https://web.archive.org/web/20051030185215/https://www.aou.or.jp/news/0503/newa0503-d.pdf.

4 Software, Hardware, and Space

Theoretical Aspects of Public Gaming

Arcade Games as Situated Ludic Assemblages

An examination of the history of the development of public gaming machines, the cultural practices surrounding them, and the venues in which the gaming activity itself takes place in the Japanese context underlines the many instances of negotiation between their constituent parts and the broader media environment. The nature of both venues and machines has changed in reaction to broader sociocultural events that have brought together different users, engagement patterns, and play cultures. While it has become clear that, on a historical level, the notion of playing in public needs to be investigated, this perspective also informs our reading of specific arcade games as non-linear experiences in constant negotiation with venue structures, technological innovations, and politics. The synergy of these different elements can only be observed empirically. Arcade games are machines with distinct social and technological assumptions and purposes, which are constantly being defined and redefined through their relationship with their direct environments.

Approaching arcade machines from the notion of assemblage emphasizes the idea that these machines should be read as the convergence of different and relatively disparate elements, rather than objects with a fixed meaning and place within a regime of value. Deleuze and Guattari define assemblages as a multiplicity of elements, strata, lines, and measures of speed all coming together as a single object or idea in a specific context (*A Thousand Plateaus* 3–4). An assemblage is ephemeral; its parts can be dismantled, reconfigured, and reterritorialized in a new assemblage. As such, assemblages are fluid and reconfigurable, and are not endowed with unique and fixed meanings. The notion of assemblage displaces the focus on meaning towards the functions it occupies within a given context; the study of assemblages necessarily involves a multifaceted approach. Thus, arcade machines, as situated ludic assemblages, cannot be studied in a vacuum, but each of their strata must be examined individually and within a context, in order to understand their role as a catalyst for public play experience.

Arcade game machines are collections of social and technological elements, placed in a specific context. While they might appear stable, with that stability provided by commercial imperatives, the life of an arcade game is a fluid phenomenon that constantly adapts to an evolving environment by changing its elements and

DOI: 10.4324/9781003273776-5

its functions. Arcade games are thus specific assemblages that result from the territorialization of a form of digital play; each machine assembles different elements relative to software, hardware, and space, and unites them into a specific interpretation of public ludic experience. In turn, the machine is subjected to interaction with different types of players who, as important actors in the play phenomenon, recode the machine's assemblage at each encounter, constantly changing the machine's functions and reaffirming their multiplicities.

The objective of this chapter is to develop a methodology to analyze arcade machines as ludic assemblages while acknowledging their nature as constantly changing ludic sites with a multiplicity of functions. Though arcade machines can be explored from a potentially infinite number of aspects, this project focuses on software, hardware, and space. On a historical level, the place of arcade games must be negotiated with their urban settings, political contexts, and broader regime of value. Therefore, the framework of this project establishes the base upon which a closer investigation of arcade game machines can be performed in a situated daily life context. Core elements of this transdisciplinary framework originating from diverse academic literature are then combined into the analytic model that I call the ludo-egregore, a situated model suited to the study of the public digital play phenomenon that emphasizes the fluid, ephemeral and multiple nature of interactions between human (players, observers) and non-human (game, software, space) actors within the public setting of arcades. The concepts and methodology developed in this section will be used to read specific examples of arcade game machines and cultures surrounding the practice of public digital play in Japanese game centres.

In and Out the Magic Circle: Situated Gaming

In his seminal 1938 book *Homo Ludens*, Dutch philosopher Johan Huizinga established play as one of the foundational blocks of civilization. Positing play as a free activity based on the respect of rules within the constrained context of a struggle or a performance (34), Huizinga introduces the notion of a *magic circle* to describe the mental, physical, or representational space that bounds play and allows it to suspend the rules and functions of ordinary life (30). For Huizinga, play is connected to everyday life; it is imbued with social functions and acts as a precursor of cultural formation and a vector of transmission of values.

With contemporary academia turning towards the study of games in general and videogames in particular, Huizinga's concept has been both expanded and contested. Salen and Zimmerman adapted the concept of the magic circle as the basis of game design theory, framing the term as referring to the "distinct boundary" between the real world and the game world, a separation essential for the creation of what Bernard Suits calls the lusory attitude, or the voluntary suspension of rational behaviour in favour of rules imposed by a specific game (Salen and Zimmerman 94; Suits 55–56). In videogames, the magic circle is understood as the interface of the computer within which the game itself is contained and the space in which the user interacts with the game, a self-enclosed space whose dynamics are impervious to outside influences.

However, the simplicity of this model has been heavily scrutinized over the years, and it is now understood that the boundary between play and everyday life is not truly rigid. Recent development in game technology design principles and in the study of users' varying degrees of engagement in play activity have all contributed to the general understanding of play as a pervasive phenomenon that often overflows its own formal boundaries (Montola 46). Focusing on non-normative and often transgressive forms of engagement in certain videogames, such as cheating, Consalvo argues for the contextual study of games as opposed to a strictly structuralist perspective that often overshadows players' involvement as essential agents that embed play itself with meaning ("There is No Magic Circle" 411). The rise of the multiple methodologies of game study has come to problematize the rigid segregation of play and everyday life. In a thorough study, Stenros brings nuance to the debate by dividing the play experience between three aspects of varying degrees of boundaries: the personal *psychological bubble*, the social contract of the *magic circle* that involves shared negotiation of the interpersonal structure, and the *arena* as the physical and temporal structure that fosters play (Stenros 15).

The existence of a boundary surrounding play activities is a critical notion to explore when unpacking the notion of arcade gaming, since the practice is based on the temporary generation of individual or collective ludic spaces. Arcade gaming is usually experienced in commercial venues open to the public, in which players are exposed to a constant stream of patrons who circulate within the space for various purposes. Michael Oppitz's reading of the repurposing of Asian exotic imagery in the design of William and Company's *Shangri-la* pinball machine marquee in 1974, as a therapeutic entertainment device glorifying the notion of competition permeating capitalist society for manual workers, points to the importance of reading pinball machines within their context and their direct environment (81). For Oppitz, a pinball game such as *Shangri-la* only takes on its full meaning when read as a situated social text; Oppitz partly contextualizes the game within an immigrant worker's bistro, suggesting that the game allows workers to reconnect, on a ludic level, with the principle of competition that characterizes the world of the workforce. Oppitz's structuralist perspective provides a limited view of the methods that *Shangri-la* players use when engaged in ludic activity, but points toward a framework that considers the systems of the game, the location of its consumption, and the social values surrounding it as a cohesive whole, thus acknowledging the social life that the machine generates and that is generated by the machine.

In 2007, the Digital Game Research Association (DiGRA) held its annual conference around the theme of situated play, and challenged scholars to examine the effects of the growing ubiquity of digital games on daily life. Papers presented at the conference explored many issues related to the theoretical segregation, or lack thereof, of game spaces and non-ludic spaces. Taken as a whole, the collection of papers from this event further underscored the idea that gaming activities cannot and should not be separated from their direct socioeconomic environments. Holin and Chuen-Tsai pointed out the influence of wealth and the different degree of economic investments of players in online games, arguing that players' different financial situations create an uneven playing field in free-to-play online virtual worlds, creating tension between players adopting different approaches to playing a specific game (342). Gaming requires both disposable income, which is collected in a variety of ways, and time; players must negotiate both of these aspects according to the demands of their daily lives, which creates a disparity between players that mirrors similar disparities outside of the game world. On the topic of MMORPGs and virtual worlds, Lee, Yu, and Lin's interview-based study further explores the connectedness of play with everyday life by tackling the notion of game addiction, when sustained investment in the play activity comes in conflict with personal responsibilities (217). Engagement in the play activity, whether sustained or not, is situated within a certain lifestyle and a certain economic status.

The study of identity politics has highlighted the need to consider the social construction of gaming as a gendered activity. The legitimization of play has, during the early years of the development of a culture around videogames in the United States, leaned on a "clustering of ideas" that included ideas such as "idealized youth, masculinity, violence, violence and digital technology", which Kocurek calls the "technomasculine" (xvii). As a result, the development of the culture, industry, and media representations surrounding videogames were heavily influenced by a socially constructed definition of the media as naturally geared towards boyhood, a bias that still influences mainstream contemporary productions and tends to relegate women to the margins. Taylor, Jenson, and de Castell trace the influences of this phenomenon in situated contexts in which gender construction influences the degree of freedom in engaging the play activity, where the presence of boys tends to neutralize girls' engagement amongst children (306). This particular study demonstrates the idea that the presence of the opposite sex impacts situated play patterns significantly and that, on a broader level, gender discourses are enacted not only in the games as texts but also in their physical context (307).

This notion points out the importance of adopting a holistic perspective toward the study of digital games and acknowledges how many elements of daily life influence play activity. Lammes emphasizes the importance of looking at games not as simple cultural products limited by their own boundaries, but as a collection of "outcomes of gaming practices" (29). This entails accounting for the flexible boundary separating the game and its community (game/agent and community/environment), and supporting self-reflexivity as a viable technique in a game researcher's methodological toolset within a broader re-examination of the subjective proximity between the scholar and the object of study. Indeed, the study of arcade gaming necessarily involves the physical presence of the scholar within the space of the arcade, and encounters with the machines and software, which exposes him/her to the effects of game and machine design and the situated cultural conventions of the play in effect within that space. However, this situation should be embraced rather than repressed within the final analysis, as it provides essential insights as to the more profound dynamics of play at hand. Situatedness also allows the researcher to relate to the "physical locality of playing whilst still relating play to a more global or national context" (25). Underlining the links between this physical locality and the global rhythms of games is essential in the context of studying arcade gaming, and is only possible by encountering these conventions in person.

McGregor echoes the same concerns by stating the importance of the spatial aspects of games, both considering the influence of physical spaces on the game spaces and taking into account how software influences the space in which it is used, such as in augmented reality experiences (538). Mäyrä proposes breaking down the contextual layers at the heart of the gameplay experience and focusing on developing vertical (historical) and horizontal (sociocultural) understandings of the encounter of spaces and play activity in both private and public situations (814). Similarly, Kort, Ijsselsteijn, and Gajadhar note that gaming is intrinsically influenced by the co-presence of other players and spectators in addition to the active player. Individual games enable various engagement patterns based on whether other players take part in the game activity or observe it; such differences in approaching games are key in examining certain aspects of contemporary gaming practices such as online videogame streaming or competitive matches in eSports events (2).

On the same topic, Fernández-Vara developed a model for situated gaming based on the notion of spectatorship as part of a comparison between gaming as performance and theatre studies. Similarly to theatre, gaming can be understood as an activity forcing negotiation between scripted behaviour (the script and the game) and improvisation (delivery and ludic strategies); performing a play, or playing a videogame, requires participants to "restore the behaviours" of a specific text, a process that is necessarily "concretized differently, depending on the socio-cultural setting" in which the play activity occurs (Fernández-Vara 7). From this perspective, a videogame is a device storing a specific range of behaviours for players to unpack through interactions with the machine. From this perspective, players adapt the "script" of the game to their sociocultural conditions, which are defined in part by the co-presence, or absence, of fellow players or a type of audience, and by the space hosting the game activity.

In his monograph *Gaming Rhythms*, Tom Apperley presents a thorough investigation of digital gaming as a situated practice in an intercultural context. Apperley uses Henri Lefevbre's concept of rhythmanalysis to engage in a comparative ethnographic study of the activities of videogame players of internet cafés in Melbourne, Australia and Caracas, Venezuela. This project exposes how gaming as a practice is defined both by the rhythm of the locale and by the global rhythm of gaming embodied in ludic objects and texts. Through observations and interviews, Apperley develops the notion of a "digital game ecology" (14), in which he places the body of the player in the centre of a web of "technological, industrial and global contexts" (14) that are informed by elements that constitute daily routine. The methodology of rhythmanalysis, in the context of situated game studies, broadly proposes to examine how local conditions and regimes of value negotiate and define videogames as a practice and cultural object. It also draws our gaze toward these same objects and practices, born from global regimes of circulation and consumption, subsequently coming to shape their public by introducing a certain rhythm belonging to their modes of consumption and production. As Apperley points out, while games feature elements that invite players to a play in a straightforward fashion, certain contexts might demand that the play activity be structured in unconventional, creative, or marginal ways (87).

This spark of interest in the development of more holistic perspectives toward gaming signals not only the acknowledgement of outside influences on games but also the intrinsic link between games and the contexts in which they are played. Broad questions such as the influence of space on interaction between players of different genders and the impact of social class on game consumption form key aspects of game culture that act as entry points for the study of game centres; public gaming must be examined as an empirical phenomenon open to many outside influences, in which the boundary between the private and the public is under constant negotiation. This project focuses on three key aspects of situated gaming that serve as axes defining the methodological groundings of the empirical analysis of arcade videogames in Japan: software, comprising the fictional and mechanical aspects of games; cabinets as material conditions of the gaming experience; and space as the sociocultural structuring agent that shapes the experience.

Software: Reading Systems and Interfaces

At their core, videogames are, in Espen Aarseth's words, ergodic objects requiring "non-trivial effort" to allow readers to traverse them (1). Digital games use computers to execute various codes and algorithms, and a variety of output devices, such as graphic interfaces and audio devices, to display the image and sound generated by the game's software during a play session. In his book *half-real: Videogames Between Rules and Fictional Worlds*, Jesper Juul defines games as assemblages of rules and fictional elements:

> A game is a rule-based system with a variable and quantifiable outcome, where different outcomes are assigned different values, the player exerts effort in order to influence the outcome, the player feels emotionally attached to the outcome, and the consequences of the activity are negotiable. (36)

When playing a videogame, the user is invited to steer the game's state to a desired outcome, a process that itself implies interacting, to various degrees, with a set of rules that defines the software's mode of interactivity. This definition posits the relationship between code and fiction, which drives the users' purpose, as central to the game experience; the presence of engagement-sustaining elements such as narratives or compelling imagery gives purpose and meaning to a set of rules. Fictional elements give meaning to a set of rules and conditions, and rules allow fictional elements to be used in a meaningful way.

While fiction can also be provided in the form of extra-diegetic elements located in the game's paratext or materiality, the videogame software—understood as the defining element of videogames—comprises these two elements. Software is the foundation upon which the experience of the game is provided to users; through its code, the designer-author embeds the rules and mechanics that will drive the game and, by extension, orient players' actions. Reading and understanding a videogame thus involves employing a critical framework that supports the many singularities of videogames as interactive texts that involve both the pre-established structure designed by its author(s) and the input of the users, without which the game would remain a stale collection of numerical information located on a computer data storage medium. Thus, playing a videogame is an intricate process involving both creative team and players.

Juul argues that most videogames can be categorized according to their individual use of elements based on emergence and progression. Emergence refers to an interactive system that offers a free form of play without strong guidance, similar to a sandbox, offering ludic conditions to be explored and enjoyed. In contrast, progression refers to games in which firm sets of predetermined objectives are supplied within the play experience and constitute its core. Such games are very heavily reliant on a narrative, or the accomplishment of specific tasks in a given order. It is usually difficult to categorize games as belonging exclusively to either one of these categories; videogames will often employ both approaches in a single game, exploiting the potential of both to give directions and purpose to a player, while allowing him/her to exert some degree of freedom in the achievement of an objective. A videogame typically provides an interactive experience that draws on both structures; therefore, examining the system of any given game is as critical as understanding its broader narrative thread. It is through the interaction of these elements that interactive experiences develop their themes and make statements about the world.

To interpret these systems, Bogost focuses on smaller elements that make up the fabric of larger textual systems, which he names "unit operations".[1] This framework constitutes an efficient starting method to engage in critical readings of videogames based on the analysis on their individual elements, and one that is suited to find meaning in arcade videogames, which can easily seem unworthy of such readings because the experiences that they convey may seem, at first glance, too short or simple. For example, the 1986 arcade videogame *Darwin 4078* uses the generic tropes associated with the various types of shooting games released in great numbers during the same decade, such as Namco's *Xevious* or Konami's *Gradius*, but associates its rules and gameplay features with the concept of biological evolution. The user plays as a biotechnological spacecraft that absorbs EVOL resource pallets dropped from a range of flying creatures and other walking lizards, a reference to the Galapagos Islands' marine iguanas. Acquiring resources triggers the metamorphosis of the spaceship to the upper level of its evolution grid, radically transforming its potency and shooting power every time. When hit, the vessel *devolves* to a lower level. Hidden, more powerful evolution states called mutations are also available if the player can discover the evolution/devolution/evolution pattern required to reach them. *Darwin 4078* configures these textual units to form the fabric of the greater gameplay experience around a specific interpretation of the theme of evolution and, on a more self-reflective level, makes a statement about the status of shoot 'em up games in Japanese arcades during the mid-1980s.

Bogost later complements this approach with the notion of "procedural rhetoric".[2] This concept can be seen implemented in the game *September 12* by Gonzalo Frasca in which the user is confronted with the task of exterminating terrorism by means of guided missiles that, while taking down terrorists, also cause collateral damage, which turns more citizens into terrorists (Bogost et al. 6). Ultimately, the message conveyed by the system of this game is simple: there is no real solution, but non-intervention is the least damaging of all. Procedural rhetoric is also useful tool to analyze and critique commercial games that do not necessarily aim at making open sociopolitical claims, but which enforce certain themes, ideas, or patterns of communication by repurposing and adapting generic tropes. The theme of evolution that *Darwin 4078* makes playable using the conventions associated with the vertical shooter genre is conveyed via many elements, such as the interplay of the users' desired outcomes (surviving as long as possible), mechanics at the disposal of the player (shooting enemies, improving armaments) and its fictional elements (constant use of metamorphosis). A player seeking to accumulate the most points would understand that certain evolution states' shooting patterns, firepower, and ship sizes are more useful in certain situations, thus driving the user to learn evolution patterns and adapt his/her ship to its environment. In most shoot 'em ups, players are led to instinctively rush out to acquire all available power-up resources, but what *Darwin 4078*'s system and fiction put forward is the idea of adaptation. While arcade games do not typically feature subversive political content, one can expect any type of software or rule sets can be read as cultural products conveying ideology adapted from or inspired directly by its sociocultural context.

Certain key gameplay elements, or unit operations, that have come to define the arcade gaming experience over the last decades, such as the concept of high scores, versus fighting systems or modern player communication patterns in online games, are located at the software level of these games, and thus reinforces software as the basis for analysis. However, that the game world conditions and parameters with which users interact during the gameplay experience are identical for all players of a specific game regardless of the venue in which the game is being played does not necessarily mean that the experience of the game will be similar. Unlike computer or console home videogames, arcade games rely on distinctively standardized hardware that is often specifically designed for a single title, which is, in turn, installed in venues whose main purpose is to house arcade videogames for commercial exploitation. Since much arcade game software distributed in the form of boards to be plugged into cabinets appears to use deceptively standard material conditions, one can be tempted to shift analytical focus towards the rule-based aspects of arcade games exclusively. The dematerialization and circulation of arcade games on different platforms such as personal computers through emulation, home consoles, do-it-yourself MAME (Multiple Arcade Machine Emulator) arcade machines, and other media favour such an interpretation by sacrificing contextual reading of these games in favour of greater dissemination to the public at large. Though a significant part of their existence and meaning as cultural products is erased in that transfer, these practices contribute greatly to preserving games that otherwise would become lost artefacts of gaming history.

It is precisely the involvement of specific material conditions and the player's constant exposure to the gaze of the public in the space that define the arcade playing experience. The experience provided by an arcade driving game will be different if the user interacts with it depending on the cabinet type, and will also change if the cabinet itself is in a small coffee house or a busy large-scale game centre. The context in which the software is experienced has a tremendous influence on how the software's rules and fictional elements will be read and interpreted. Therefore, any analysis of arcade videogames and practices must take material and social conditions into consideration by examining the material conditions of the game and the space of the game centre.

Hardware: Materiality and Affordance Theory

In *Flow: The Psychology of Optimal Experience*, Mihály Csíkszentmihályi introduces the notion of the state of *flow*, or optimal experience, a state of high engagement in which the sense of time and self-consciousness is effaced (71).[3] There are many points of similarity between the principles of the optimal experience and of videogame design: software creates challenging situations with clear goals and feedback systems for players to navigate through. By making systems flexible or adaptable, and by making good use of a standardized control system, games and their mechanics are more likely to draw and immerse users into their world. However, in the case of arcade videogames, the erasure of self-consciousness also depends on the extent to which users' experience is enhanced, hindered or augmented by the hardware occupying the space of the arcade and the unique control scheme of the game machine, what we shall refer to hereafter as the material conditions of the experience. An important characteristic of arcade games is the nonconformity of most of their control mechanisms to the standards of the game industry, especially of home console videogame controllers, and the design of their hardware from the size, form, and placement of their buttons, down to the size and even the positioning of their screens. Some machines feature standardized formats to maximize approachability for players, while others seek to attract users with unique input mechanisms that separate them from the competition. Whereas flow theory emphasizes the effacement of the interface, Kristine Jørgensen makes the opposite claim that interfaces are not opposed to game worlds, but are rather a part of them, and contribute to the immersion of players by providing a certain layer of familiarity and ludic consistency (as opposed to fictional coherence) to a game by being "unremarkable", that is, by not distracting the user from the experience (24; 37; 57; 103). Jørgensen extends the definition of game worlds to interface, and, as such, prompts us to examine the role of material conditions—including not only the physical interface, but how the narrative and fiction of a game are expressed at the physical level—in the construction of a situated gaming activity.

While videogame machines are ludic objects designed to provide an interactive game experience, they are foremost design objects existing in a given space. In the case of arcade games, this space is the cultural ecology of game centres. Natasha Dow Schüll's work on the study of casinos and video slot machines in Los Angeles demonstrates how examining machine designs and space structure help better understand the nature and the dynamics of gambling addiction. According to Schüll, the phenomenon of shutting oneself out of reality and engaging in the obsessive play of video gambling machines, which some of the former and active heavy users of gambling machines she interviewed for her project described as the "machine zone" state of mind, should be analyzed by investigating the interrelationship between machine design and the psychic predispositions of certain individuals, rather than by establishing issues related to gambling as mainly caused by personality disorders. The design of gambling machines in the United States has evolved over the years to encourage long-winded and addictive play: "*What is this thing controlling me?* – it would appear that this 'thing' is neither fully within the person nor fully scripted by the machine, but rather, a hybrid force to which both contribute" (Schüll 232). The term "hybrid force" refers to the triggering of specific engagement patterns between users and design objects by the presence and interaction of multiple compatible agents, something akin to the concept of *affordances*.

Affordance is a psychological concept that explains how the relationship between an object and an organism can suggest, or afford, certain actions. The affordance of a certain object or environment emerges in its relationship with a perceiving subject; they are not inherent to either the object or the organism, but are generated from the simultaneous presence of both. This term was coined in 1979 by James J. Gibson, who stressed the complementarity of the perceiver and its environment (127). Gibson's discussion of affordances as perceived by animals led to the study of the multiple facets of a given environment as focal points, including medium (air), substance, surface, layout, and place (130–38). In 1988, Donald Norman further explored the concept of affordance and adapted it to design theory in *The Design of Everyday Things,* and revised it in 2013 with the notion of *perceived affordances*. Using the example of door handles or buttons, Norman explains that objects should afford a certain optimal use perceivable to the user through design. For him, the notion of affordance is akin to a design puzzle, as inventors are challenged to create objects with "fundamental properties that determine just how the thing could possibly be used" (9) that can be efficiently transmitted without relying on formal communication. Door handles, for example, should feature horizontal flat bars to signal users to push the door, and a vertical bar handle to signify pulling (10).

This "user-centred" framework has since been refined and adapted to other realities, such as the influence of the interface and form of born-digital communication platforms (Graves) and software design in order to understand how the structure of a media object itself, such as *Facebook,* can favour certain engagement behaviour for teaching and learning (Wang et al.). This dual emphasis on environment and a certain sense of object authorship, as developed by Gibson and Norman, informs our reading of arcade game machines as machines designed with an intended optimal use, and as environments whose surface and layout, most specifically, provide users with specific ludic behaviours. In the case of machine design for arcade videogame parlours, affordances might seem simplistic, but they do give insight to the potential player as to how a game might be used. The presence of a chair at an arcade machine, for example, might suggest that the game itself might require a deeper level of intellectual engagement and disposable time to fully enjoy the experience, while a game featuring a large screen and motion controls might suggest a more casual experience anchored on the notion of spectacle.

While investigating what machines afford players in terms of interactivity and fictional space is paramount in understanding use patterns of games, one of the primary features that differentiates arcade games from other types of videogames is their location in semi-public spaces in which one can witness both high and low levels of interaction between players. Whether the play activity is part of a dynamic of gregarious engagement involving friends and adversaries, or users are playing by themselves in relative intimacy, the public play activity is characterized by constant negotiation of the play activity with social and behavioural norms and some level of interpersonal interaction. Certain machines seclude their users from the crowd, while others allow observers to follow the game session perfectly. Network-connected games relying on cross-country matchups do not permit high levels of social interactions, but machines enabling local multiplayer games on the same machine might be instrumental in fostering social bonds between participants. Both machines and spaces are designed and constructed to afford certain types of social engagement patterns amongst users, which in turn affects how users engage in the play activity. This phenomenon can be linked to theories of *social affordances*.

Deriving from Gibson's original concept of affordance theory, social affordances have been at the heart of conversations within the field of ecological psychology since the 1980s (Valenti and Gold 77), and, later, in research on human-computer interaction and design (Bradner et al.). In this context, the idea of social affordance is defined as "the relationship between the properties of an object and the social characteristics of a group that enable particular kinds of interaction among members of that group" (Bradner et al. 153). From this perspective, and similarly to Norman's conceptualization, objects or software should include specific features and options that will lead a group of users to adopt optimal social actions and behaviours for the effective operation of a certain task or activity. These features do not accomplish anything by themselves, but users perceive specific contextual affordances within them, which will lead and encourage certain interpersonal actions towards the group.

From an anthropological perspective, Kaufmann and Clément re-examined the concept of social affordances and applied it to a greater discussion on the origin of human culture as influenced by the world around them (ecology), rather than the regular assumption of prioritizing an examination of how human beings influence their environment. However, as part of this discussion, they emphasize the idea that perception is "culturally hierarchized" (Kaufmann and Clément 25) meaning that "the degree of salience that social objects are endowed with is at the *heart of the process of enculturation*" (24). The perception of social affordances necessarily "involves a range of expectations, generalizations and predictions that go beyond the information 'contained' in the external environment" (9); social affordances are culturally situated phenomena that should be analyzed as such. Synthesizing both previous definitions of the term based on the theory of object design with Kaufmann and Clément's interpretation, we can perceive and design certain elements facilitating desired social affordances, but these objects must be read within a particular cultural context, and users approach these objects with pre-established expectations, generalizations and predictions.

Therefore, examining the social affordances of arcade game machines in Japanese game centres must be informed by their socioeconomic contexts and the history of interaction with the specific machine type and its design evolution. These social affordances, read within the context of the public play activity, may encourage seclusion, performance, observation, gregarious engagement, or other types of interaction patterns ranging from higher to lower degrees of engagement, which in turn influence the behaviour of other people in the space and shape how they engage with that space. While certain machines afford specific patterns of player interactions, the space and culture of the venue also influence how players approach their engagement with the game itself and with other players in the venue. A fighting game player, for example, will not approach playing in an independent venue marked as a gathering site for fighting game players in the same way as in a more anonymous commercial game centre.

This project attempts to account for the importance of social affordances in the experience of arcade playing and to place the material conditions of the playing activity at the centre of its analysis. One way to accomplish this goal is to approach arcade game machines as social "actors" that are involved in the construction of the game playing activity by enabling and shaping networks of social human-human and human-object interactions. The term originates in Bruno Latour's constructivist sociological framework of actor-network theory (ANT), which seeks to read social relations not as pre-established, hierarchized, and fixed links between exclusive human participants but as movements that are constantly transformed and reshuffled into new associations (64–65). The definition of actors in ANT extends to non-human agents in order to acknowledge their importance in the shaping of society as generators of actions and relationships between human agents. ANT places actors in "the centre of social activity" (72), acknowledging a heightened level of agency in the shaping of the social.

This framework enables us to consider arcade game machines as objects embedded with assumptions, social norms, regulatory practices, government interventions, and a specific history of arcade space interactions. In this sense, arcade game machines are particularly complex social agents holding functions that change in relationship with their direct spatial and social environment; the same machine may shape different social networks for different groups of people with different intentions. It is therefore important to read arcade game machines and their material conditions as fluctuating actors, not as fixed entities. ANT allows us to regard game machines as agents taking an active part in the production of the public gaming space rather than simply as providers of the experience.

An overview of affordance theory has uncovered an inherent tension between two elements in the study of objects. Where Gibson approached these issues from an object-oriented ontology perspective, which accounts for situational uses and ecological interactions, Norman's design-theory approach emphasizes authorship, intention behind design choices, and, broadly speaking, design and affordances as puzzles to solve in order to create optimal objects. Both approaches are valuable, and the study of arcade videogames' material conditions fall somewhere in between these two extremes. Arcade machines are human-made objects with a strong degree of authorship and an intended interaction pattern, but their function is not simply utilitarian in nature; while the game offers ways to play, the optimal interaction pattern is subjective to the user him/herself. However, one must acknowledge that without easily approachable player input, fictional space, or even social affordances appropriate for the situation, most players will not reach a sufficient level of engagement to reach the level of engaging creatively with the game. It is in these moments of emerging subversive use of a machine's design, at which point we realize that affordances are fundamentally ecologically driven and existing within the perception space between the machine and the user, that the most potentially meaningful readings of a game's text can be made.

Of course, an ecological understanding of arcade game culture necessarily involves the reading of the space of game centres themselves as an agent that both shapes and is shaped by the play activity. To that end, understanding and acknowledging the politics of space formation is essential to the full realization of this framework.

Spatiality: Rhythms and Territories

In *Videogame Spaces*, Michael Nitsche relates his experience engaging with an attraction ride based on the movie franchise *Back to the Future,* featured in Universal Studios' theme park located in Los Angeles. During the ride, Nitsche and his fellow ride participants were forced out of the futuristic DeLorean car featured in the movie through emergency exit doors. Only later did he realize that the plethora of colours and sounds that he had experienced had been activated solely to indicate that an earthquake had occurred during the ride, unbeknownst to him, as he initially thought that they were part of the attraction (Nitsche 12). In the context of this project, this anecdote emphasizes that the spatial conditions in which a given ludic activity occurs intimately affect the playing experience, mostly without the participants consciously realizing it. As part of his greater project examining the representation of space within cyberworlds, Nitsche also points at the importance of the plane of the *play space* designated as the "space in the physical world that includes the player and the gaming system" (16) within the gaming activity, but ultimately exploring this notion thoroughly was outside of the scope of his project. Following up on Nitsche's notion of the plane of the *play space*, this section examines the intellectual history behind spatiality to think of game centres as places in the city, and also as mappable *spaces* that house a variety of *places* that structure players' ludic experiences.

Many influential authors in the canon of Western critical theory have long subjected the notion of spatiality to the notion of time (Massey). Scholars associated with both structuralist and poststructuralist movements have conceptualized space as a fixed entity; for example, Lévi-Strauss confined cultural practices and sociological structures to specific times and places (Massey 37), while Laclau considered physical space tied to temporality; therefore, according to this model, its conception is characterized by a sense of hegemony that does not account for a plurality and diversity of experiences taking place within it (25, 44). A first step into reconsidering the idea of space necessarily involves breaking off from these notions and considering space and places as independent entities composed of different layers. Doreen Massey offers three proposals for an alternative study of space: conceptualizing spaces as the product of diverse interactions, as a sphere of plurality that accounts of multiple "trajectories", and as an ever-becoming process that is never entirely enclosed by its borders. These proposals build on various discourses and theories on spatiality that evolved throughout the latter half of the twentieth century.

In 1967, Michel Foucault established the foundational ideas that would eventually lead to a new intellectual movement in the study of spatiality. Foucault started by pointing out that, where the nineteenth century had been the century of history, the twentieth century would be the age of spatiality ("Des espaces autres" 46). Abandoning structuralism would make a place for a diversity of realities and the "era of simultaneities, the era of juxtaposition" ("Des espaces autres" 46) in which challenges and anxieties would emerge from our imagined relationship with space. This discussion resulted in Foucault's coining of the term *heterotopia* to designate concrete spaces that have both utilitarian and imaginary uses, such as the cemetery, to house both the body and the soul, or the theatre, juxtaposing a real place and multiple imaginary ones. This "era of simultaneities" invites us to abandon ideas of history and progress, to focus on the coexistence of multiple realities and experiences and to acknowledge the fracture of grand metanarratives into smaller ones (Lyotard) or the collapse of united spaces into separate but subordinate spheres under the pressure of late capitalism (Jameson). These ideas evolved into a broad intellectual current known as postmodernism or poststructuralism, at the centre of which the spatial turn is located.

Even as Foucault initiated the spatial turn in 1967, a group of intellectuals called the Situationist International was already articulating theoretical concepts that explored our relationship to space. Most notably, the *théorie de la dérive* adapted leftist revolutionary concepts that characterized the situationists' collective and coined the concept of *la dérive* (drift), an invitation to urban dwellers to navigate everyday space by paying more attention to its "solicitations" and "encounters" (Debord). Debord argued that urban spaces feature specific psychogeographies comprised of a mix of economic, social, geographical, and representational features organized in streams, fixed points, and swirls distributed across urban landscapes. *Dériver* is to make oneself open to these influences, and to nurture a greater synergy between the subject and its space. Debord recorded some of these experiences in a collection of maps titled *Guide Psychogéographique de Paris*, in which the districts of the city are represented as cut-out elements called ambiance units, and are linked to each other by lines called *pentes psychogéographiques* (psychogeographic slopes). This process of remapping the city emphasizes the connectivity of fixed points and ambiance within the urban landscape, all established through the empirical process of *dérive*.

In 1986, Henri Lefebvre published *La production de l'espace,* which describes space as a social product (39). For Lefebvre, space is produced by society and producing society, including hegemonic patterns, as its very platform (*La production de l'espace* 65); individual societies across history have produced their own spaces representing their directions and values and have shaped these sensibilities forward (*La production de l'espace* 40). This framework divides space into three categories: the *spatial practice* (la pratique de l'espace) associated with perceived space, the *representations of space* (représentation de l'espace) as engineered and conceived by urban planners and discourses emerging from conversation on space, and the *representational space* (l'espace représentationel) associated with space as directly experienced by the individual (*La production de l'espace* 42–43). Spaces act on both a local and global perspective; they are superimposed on and penetrate each other in a simultaneous and complementary manner (*La production de l'espace* 348). This understanding invites us to consider the possibility of reading and decoding space as a text that is engineered, lived, and critiqued, at the centre of which the body takes precedence as the focal point of the experience (*La production de l'espace* 206). This focus on the embodied experience would lead Lefebvre to fully develop the notion of rhythmanalysis as the science of living and non-living bodies (*Éléments de rythmanalyse* 13). Lefevbre defines *rhythms* as the encounter location, time, and expenditure of a certain amount of energy, all combined into patterns of repetition, interferences, beginnings, and ends (*Éléments de rythmanalyse* 26). These rhythms interact with one another and form cohesive eurhythmias, or dissonant arrhythmias (*Éléments de rythmanalyse* 26–27).

This process can be observed on both the local and global levels; contemporary media rhythms come to define contemporary urban spaces on a broader level. As global and national rhythms become increasingly part of daily life and become commonly intermeshed with local rhythms through media exposure and the broad reach of commodity circulation, the contemporary subject experiences what David Harvey calls a "time-space compression" effect (260–307), in which high-speed communication and transportation methods tend to efface physical borders and distances. Local spaces and rhythms characterized by specific cultural elements such as music, literature, architecture, or even food culture become targets of the influence of global rhythms and foreign ones that impose pressure on them and on which pressure is also exerted as a result of the development of the transnational network of goods and ideas. This is especially the case in the context of the videogame industry, which relies on the transnational circulation of its workforce and production patterns, as large studios often rely on subsidiary located in remote countries to produce games, and the industry must also adapt the content of its games to specific locales for them to successfully circulate (Carlson and Corliss; Mandiberg; Pelletier-Gagnon).

While urban planning and architecture influence some elements of rhythms, as Foucault outlines in *Discipline and Punish*, Michel de Certeau's contribution to the debate over the notion of spatiality emphasizes the role of the agents experiencing space as active negotiators and participants (xi). De Certeau's discussion on spatiality partly originates in the study of language and its daily use, which he sees as a set of basic rules that are continuously bent and negotiated by speakers. Whereas language is fundamentally a disciplinary regime for expression, language, as an applied concept, is open to the creative and subversive use, be it in colloquial or poetic use. Spatiality is described in a similar fashion, and the city walker is compared to a speaker in the ways in which he navigates the city. De Certeau expresses this through the concepts of *strategies*, the grid set up on the urban architecture's visible plane that imposes certain lines of movements, and *tactics*, city walkers' responses to these structures as they use their wits and creativity to negotiate them and create new ways to navigate the city (xviii). The project of *The Practice of Everyday Life* is mapping the resulting trajectories born from the walker's tactical negotiations of urban space, as representations of desires and interests that, while enabled by the system, are not captured or determined by them (xviii). The grid upon which the walker's experience occurs is not determined by that experience, but knowledge of both of these elements allows us to read space in its duality.

Within the broader discussion of politics and capitalism that constitute their seminal work *Mille Plateaux*, Deleuze and Guattari introduce the notion of striated (*strié*) and smooth (*lisse*) spaces to expose the dichotomy between structured and open spaces, albeit from another perspective than those of the other scholars I discuss above. Striated spaces refer to compartmentalized spaces designed for function and utility, the space of the sedentary subject in which numbers and meters are used to give meaning to, quantify, and, more broadly, code space in order to establish its structure and function (*Mille plateaux* 436–37). Smooth spaces act as the foil of this concept. They are spaces that are not counted or measured, but projected; spaces of fluctuations and change in which space is not coded, but territorialized and deterritorialized (*Mille plateaux* 436–37; 50). Smooth spaces are constantly being negotiated and transformed by the people using or traversing it. The occupants of smooth spaces bring their own structure, or territory, with them wherever they go. Deleuze and Guattari do not establish one type of space as superior or more revolutionary than others, but explain that both concepts exist in relation to one another, where the state seeks to quantify space to occupy it; the nomad, the agent of smooth space, is a creative force that subverts this structure, reinvents space, and occupies space without restructuring it. This conceptualization of spatiality emphasizes different types of spaces and different types of spatial occupancy as complementary to one another, and underscores that an investigation of a given place must account for this complementarianism according to the circulation of bodies and agents within.

Ludo-Egregore: Ludic Assemblage and Playing in Public

The phenomenon of situated gaming can be read as the amalgamation of the three main elements that, by interacting and influencing one another, define and explain the public play experience. To play an arcade game is to encounter game software that is itself attached to the material conditions of its cabinet or general interface, and that are themselves situated within a local context that influences and is influenced by a broader cultural rhythm. Each of these elements can be analyzed on its own, but a holistic view of a specific machine in relation to its cultural situatedness allows us to read it as a complete cultural text that accounts for its authorial elements, as well as for the meaning and cultural value that its community of players provide. Each game machine designed for play in public venues is a ludic assemblage that enunciates specific statements towards the use of technology, certain sociocultural discourses, and a relationship with spatiality. The combination of these elements in a particular machine, of course, exceeds the sum of their parts and allows for the emergence of a new text and a different set of ludic potential. In addition, arcade game machines' individual assemblages can also be read as a whole in the context of the self-contained place in which they are located and which itself also gives them additional layers of sociocultural meaning. In other words, although an arcade game is a ludic assemblage, it is also a part of the space's greater assemblage.

Even as we extend the notion of agency of machines themselves to the status of actors within our framework, it is important to stress that the ludic assemblages that constitute arcade cabinets remain unexploited until human agents encounter and engage with them in some fashion. It is at such moments, when the player explores the ludic potential of a game and the game configures the player, that the focus of this analysis should be located. I take a holistic approach that focuses on individual moments of situated human-machine interactions in Japanese game centres. As part of this project, I use the term *ludo-egregores* (*ludo-égrégore*) to identify and name such moments. This term refers to the abstract and ephemeral game space generated by the combined attention of agents involved in the process of ludic interactions towards a single instance of play activity. Ludo-egregores are phenomena that consider all agents, both human and non-human, engaged in the process, and result in an experience that is different than the simple sum of all the agents involved. Ludo-egregores qualify the moments shared between agents involved in the game playing activity, including the space itself, and influence the general ambiance and sociocultural function of its settings.

This concept incorporates many aspects of spatial and design theory, but takes its primary inspiration from the concept of egregore (égrégore) as outlined by French situationist Pierre Mabille in *Egrégores ou la vie des civilisations* in 1938. Mabille defines egregores as a special entity created from the encounters of many individuals around a single object or idea:

> J'appelle égrégore, mot utilisé jadis par les hermétistes, le groupe humain doté d'une personnalité différente de celle des individus qui le forment. Bien que les études sur ce sujet aient été toujours ou confuses ou tenues secrètes, je crois possible de connaître les circonstances nécessaires à leur formation. J'indique aussitôt la condition indispensable, quoique insuffisante, réside dans un choc émotif puissant. Pour employer le vocabulaire chimique, je dis que la synthèse nécessite une action énergétique intense. (Mabille 29–30)
>
> [I call egregore, a word once used by the hermetists, the human group endowed with a different personality than those of the individuals that compose it. While most work on the topic has been either confused or kept secret, I believe it is possible to understand the circumstances necessary for their formation. The indispensable condition, while not sufficient in itself, resides

in a powerful emotional shock. To borrow the vocabulary of chemistry, their synthesis requires an intense energetic action. (my trans.)]

Egregore, from the French *égrégore*, is derived from the Greek *egrēgoros,* meaning *wakeful* ("Égrégore"). Egregores emerge from the gathering of individuals that all share a common goal or object of focus; they can be described as a communion of minds coming together for intense activities such as rituals, prayers, or group therapy. Mabille borrowed the term from the esoteric tradition of hermetism,[4] but repurposed it by replacing its magical and mystic connotations to infuse it with a sense of subversive notion of the collective unconscious.[5]

Mabilles describes the object or idea at the origin of this communion of minds as an element that provides an "intense energetic action" or an intense emotional shock that provides a sense of synthesis. In this original project, the idea of egregore is used to trace the history of Western civilization, focusing on epoch-defining ideas such as, for example, the emphasis on material comfort and pragmatic considerations of power consolidation over spiritual development that characterized the Roman civilization (107). Here, the Roman egregore is said to be assembled around ideas of individual freedom, civic life, and its preservation from foreign forces rather than transcendental or metaphysical discussions. For Mabille, such historical moments in which the forces of societies are all directed toward a specific project constitute an entity that surpasses the sum of its constituents, and that becomes a driving force of its own.

Although it is possible to disagree with the applicability of this framework to the broad historical development of the Western world, this issue is beyond the scope of my discussion. However, while the former describes egregoric moments in terms of eras that may last up to hundreds of years, the moments that I want to put forward are much more restrained as they might last minutes, seconds, or even less. This project takes inspiration from Mabille's core concept, and scales its main ideas to a much smaller size to be used in conjunction with the other theoretical tool reviewed so far. Similarly to how Mabille repurposed the concept for the study of civilizations, I am also repurposing it with the goal of disentangling from spiritual or macrosocial analytic ambitions, choosing to focus instead on observations of human-machine interactions on a microscopic scale. The use of the concept of egregore is applied to discreet and reoccurring events belonging to the realm of everyday life and game play activity occurring in Japanese game centres. For an egregore to come into being, as Mabille states, a strong emotion or experience (or any kind of catalyst) is required to trigger a common direction, or what Doreen Massey calls a "trajectory", in which the focus of the members of a group is concentrated on a specific idea. In turn, this emotion transforms the group into a collective that surpasses the individual personalities and values of its individual members. The idea of ludo-egregore is an adaptation of this concept that constitutes one perspective amongst many from which to read games situated in space, such as arcade videogames, as play-related texts predominantly accessed in public and influenced by many elements, including the player, the machine, the bystanders, and the context of the play activity. At the heart of the ludo-egregore is the videogame itself, the emotions it conveys, and the cognitive trajectory it proposes to players and bystanders. I argue that, beyond the textual qualities of videogames that can be read in a restrictive fashion, arcade games are characterized by their public setting. Arcade games capture the attention of a group of people, whether directly engaged in the activity or not, who are concentrated into a single play activity, either as active participants or as observers, and influenced by the machine's social affordances.

Ludo-egregores constitute discrete moments of interaction in which different human agents' attention, afforded by specific spatial conditions, converge in the same trajectory around a communal gaming experience catalyzed by assemblages of non-human agents, resulting in a greater entity that exceeds the arithmetical sum of its constituents. The anchor point of this phenomenon is, of course, the arcade game machine, which, within the greater venue in which it is placed, creates an abstract place within a space based on the engagement of different agents. Unlike the notion of the magic circle that would isolate the play experience from outside influences, this place of engagement is not hermetic to other interactions in the space, or from elements characterizing the backgrounds of agents engaged in the activity. Similarly, this concept acknowledges the idea of gaming rhythm proposed by Apperley, inscribing the gaming activity within both a local and global rhythm. The specific case of Japanese games also enables us to consider rhythmanalysis from a national perspective as well; contemporary arcade games are often part of a specific local media environment and, from a technological perspective, a close network circuit connecting venues from across Japan that excludes other regions. Therefore, though ludo-egregores can be clearly witnessed in physical settings, they are not necessarily bound to their local limits; the concentration of different agents towards a single play activity also occurs through network connection, but the effects of this concentration are less clearly seen.

The concept of ludo-egregore strives to provide an understanding of the phenomenon of situated gaming in public settings by examining the game playing experience as the succession and superposition of discrete, ephemeral moments that, as such, are tied to our previous definition of space as plural, multilayered, and home to the simultaneous. The spaces of arcades are theatres of ludo-egregoric moments generated in relation to a specific part of a larger environment. In addition, space, taken as the place of the arcade itself, is home to a multiplicity of micro-events that, superposed, generate the global conditions of play in a given location. However, when discussing ludo-egregores as moments, the concept of spatiality, here, needs to be conjugated in complementarity with the notion of time.

Space has historically been subordinated to time in the Western intellectual tradition, and it is not the objective of this project to do the same. Game centre spaces, for example, are not tied to specific interaction patterns that characterize public play across specific time periods: for example, visiting venues of different types, such as a multi-floor complex and a local retro-style arcade, is not akin to experiencing a time travel phenomenon. Walking from a game centre multiplex built in the 2010s to a smaller, old-fashioned venue that originated in the 1970s is not the same as transitioning between gaming environments and practices belonging to different stages on a teleological evolutionary scale. Rather, both exist in simultaneity, and commonly construct expectations towards the practice of playing in public. Ludo-egregores, taken as so many moments of encounters between different agents characterized by the playing of a game, have a beginning and an end marked in time. In addition, time comes as a vector that provides additional conditions that might influence the condition of the encounter between agents, as the same space is not quite the same at noon than it is at midnight. Similar spaces provide the material for encounters and play experiences that vary in nature and intensity not only from a physical perspective but also in relation to time. Therefore, Mabille's interpretation of moments, which are rather abstract and all-encompassing, become much smaller and more precisely defined for the purposes of this project.

Ludo-egregores generated from the interactions of digital games are also characterized by software and material affordances that encourage the configuration of players' bodies in space and in relation to observers of the activity. However, this project takes the perspective that arcade machines are not ludic objects storing behaviours waiting to be unpacked, but rather are designed agents whose affordances must be understood from an ecological perspective; focusing on the relationship between the player(s) and the machine. This allows us to shed the notion of a proper engagement pattern, and to consider the mobile, fleeting, and ephemeral aspect of engagements that may potentially be of a more subversive nature. From a ludo-egregoric perspective, machines are more than just essentialist ludic apparatus, but are complex agents that might afford different uses according to different contexts. Arcade machines and their players are not tied to firm identities or optimal uses, as patterns of engagements are multiple and in constant motion.

The fundamental idea behind egregore, the notion of a communion of minds occurring between members of an audience, is not limited to the context of videogame arcades, and games are not the only objects or texts to which this definition applies. Theatre, cinema, and music performances are all events that similarly engage the focus of many participants around a performance or an object in a setting that favours such concentration. However, although arcade gaming does integrate some elements common with these forms of engagement, the egregores generated are more ephemeral and more susceptible to transformation due to the lack of official structure regimenting them. No official code of conduct is imposed on arcade players, for example, as opposed to a theatre in which spectators are not expected to move or talk, nor do they typically interact or directly influence active participants or observers during the performance. In other words, egregores occurring in videogame arcades are distinctly and inherently interactive. Indeed, the proposed concept of ludo-egregore focuses specifically on the ludic nature of the catalyst of the experience, and thus could be extended to other forms of play, whether digital or non-digital. Team sports such as ice hockey or soccer could be read through the framework of ludo-egregores, as the play activity that characterizes them is also a core component of the activity. For example, the rules of hockey provide a core system that players negotiate in relation to the space in which the activity is conducted, such as an indoor arena, an outside rink, or a backstreet, and whether the activity is being observed by other participants. However, this project uses the concept solely to unpack the phenomenon of play in the context of Japanese game centres.

This study uses the concept of ludo-egregore to examine the ramifications of the public videogaming experience in Japanese arcades as a fluid, intermittent, ephemeral, situated, and multiple phenomenon. This methodology requires examining arcade gaming beyond the abstract notion of text, in order to look for specific instances of play engagement in key spaces and at particular moments. The investigation of public gaming relies on the accumulation of such discreet moments acquired through empirical research rather than an essentialist analysis on arcade games and players as generic experiences and model players. Many ludo-egregores occur simultaneously within game centres, and certain venues will nurture certain types over others. These short-lived social formations break off and reconstitute at a regular pace for as long as some interest in the games in the venue remains.

Notes

1 Ian Bogost demonstrated how, through the interlocking of rules and fictional elements, videogames are objects embedded with meaning and ideology that can be experienced by way of interaction with their individual systems. Unit operations are understood as "modes of meaning-making that privilege discrete, disconnected actions over deterministic, progressive systems" (*Unit Operations* 3). Though he applies this approach to an array of media, Bogost's model is inspired by the process of videogame playing, in which users engage with large textual systems through discrete units of interactivity that users must learn and use to their advantage, such as exploring, aiming, and buying. Such unit operations also include fictional units of representation, such as gender, class, or the other, or theme.

2 Bogost describes procedural rhetoric as a "practice of persuading through processes in general and computational processes in particular" (*Persuasive Games* 3). It represents the idea that interactive systems should be understood as expressive mediums that convey persuasive arguments about certain topics or situations by forcing users to negotiate their navigation of the interactive text with sets of rules.

3 Csíkszentmihályi's concept of optimal experience is defined by the presence of four elements: rules that require skill acquisition, clear goals, feedback, and user control (72). These characteristics are found in many facets of daily life, from conversation with good friends at dinner parties, to experiences requiring certain types of skills, such as mountain climbing. Such activities are autotelic, in that they provide intrinsic rewards and are considered ends in themselves (67). Activities said to generate such a state of mind create their own sense of gratification rather than relying on external outcomes and rewards.

4 Hermetism refers to ancient philosophical and religious ideas associated with the Christian faith, based on the writings attributed to mystic Hermes Trismegistus, who taught contemplation for humankind to better comprehend the world and reach the status of deity. Though it was produced during the period of Antiquity, hermetism exerted influence over several significant writers during the Middle Ages and the Renaissance (Bladel; Gordon; Hanegraaff; Howatson).

5 Beyond Mabille's work, Ray Ellenwood has repurposed the term in his analysis of the Quebec-based *Automatistes* avantgarde artistic movement to emphasize on the collective nature of the realizations of this interdisciplinary group of like-minded artists, such as the *Refus Global* manifesto (XI–XIII).

Works Cited

Aarseth, Espen J. *Cybertext: Perspectives on Ergodic Literature*. Johns Hopkins UP, 1997.

Apperley, Tom. *Gaming Rhythms: Play and Counterplay from the Situated to the Global*. Institute of Network Cultures, 2010.

Bladel, Kevin van. *Hermes Trismegistus*. Edited by Michael Gagarin, Oxford UP, 2010, https://www.oxfordreference.com/display/10.1093/acref/9780195170726.001.0001/acref-9780195170726-e-581.

Bogost, Ian, Simon Ferrari, and Bobby Schweizer.

Bogost, Ian. *Persuasive Games: The Expressive Power of Videogames*. MIT P, 2007.

———. *Unit Operations: An Approach to Videogame Criticism*. MIT P, 2006.

Bogost, Ian, Simon Ferrari, and Bobby Schweizer. *Newsgames: Journalism at Play*. MIT P, 2010.

Borduas, Paul-Émile. *Refus global suivi de Commentaires sur des mots courants* [*Total Refusal Followed by Commentaries on some Frequent Words*]. 1948. Éditions Allia, 2022.

Bradner, Erin, Wendy A. Kellog, and Thomas Erickson. "The Adoption and Use of 'Babble': A Field Study of Chat in the Workplace." *ECSCW 1999: The Proceedings of the Sixth European Conference on Computer-Supported Collaborative Work*, Sept. 1999.

Carlson, Rebecca, and Jonathan Corliss. "Imagined Commodities: Videogame Localization and Mythologies of Cultural Difference." *Games and Culture*, vol. 6, no. 1, Jan. 2011, pp. 61–82.

Certeau, Michel de. *L'invention du quotidien Vol. 1, Arts de Faire* [*The Invention of the Quotidian Vol. 1, The Art of Doing*]. Union générale d'éditions, 1980.

Consalvo, Mia. "There Is No Magic Circle." *Games and Culture*, vol. 4, no. 4, 2009, pp. 408–17.

Csikszentmihalyi, Mihaly. *Flow: The Psychology of Optimal Experience*. 1st ed., Harper & Row, 1990.

Darwin 4078. Arcade videogame cabinet, Data East, 1986.

Debord, Guy-Ernest. *Guide psychogéographique de Paris. Discours sur les passions de l'amour* [*Psychogeographic Guide of Paris. Discourse on the Passions of Love*]. 1957.

———. "Théorie de la dérive [Theory of the Derive]." *Les Lèvres nues*, no. 9, 1956, http://www.larevuedesressources.org/theorie-de-la-derive,038.html.

Deleuze, Gilles, and Félix Guattari. *A Thousand Plateaus: Capitalism and Schizophrenia*. Translated by Brian Massumi, U of Minnesota P, 1987.

———. *Capitalisme et schizophrénie 2 : Mille plateaux* [*Capitalism and Schizophrenia: A Thousand Plateaus*]. Éditions de minuit, 1980.

"Égrégore [Egregore]." *Grand Dictionnaire Terminologique*, Gouvernement du Québec – Office de la langue française, 1989, https://vitrinelinguistique.oqlf.gouv.qc.ca/fiche-gdt/fiche/17563700/egregore.

Ellenwood, Ray. *Egregore: A History of the Montréal Automatist Movement*. Exile Editions, 1992.

Fernández-Vara, Clara. "Play's the Thing: A Framework to Study Videogames as Performance." in *DiGRA '09 - Proceedings of the 2009 DiGRA International Conference: Breaking New Ground: Innovation in Games, Play, Practice and Theory*, Brunel University, vol. 5, 2009.

Foucault, Michel. "Des espaces autres (conférence au Cercle d'études architecturales, 14 mars 1967) [Of Other Spaces (Conference at the Cercle of architectural studies, March 14, 1967)]." *Architecture, Mouvement, Continuité*, no. 5, 1984, pp. 46–49.

Foucault, Michel—. *Discipline and Punish: The Birth of the Prison*. 1st American ed., Pantheon Books, 1977.

Frasca, Gonzalo. "Simulation versus Narrative: Introduction to Ludology." *Video/Game/Theory*, edited by Mark J. P. Wolf and Bernard Perron, Routledge, 2003, pp. 221–235.

Gibson, James J. *The Ecological Approach to Visual Perception*. Houghton Mifflin, 1979.

Gordon, Richard L. "Hermes Trismegistus in Late Antiquity." *The Oxford Dictionary of Late Antiquity*, edited by Oliver Nicholson, Oxford UP, 2018, https://www.oxfordreference.com/display/10.1093/acref/9780198662778.001.0001/acref-9780198662778-e-2216?rskey=XSnrkk&result=1.

Gradius. Arcade videogame cabinet, Konami, 1985.

Graves, Lucas. "The Affordances of Blogging: A Case Study in Culture and Technological Effects." *Journal of Communication Inquiry*, vol. 31, no. 331, 2007, pp. 331–346.

Hanegraaff, Wouter. "Hermetism." *The Oxford Guide to the Historical Reception of Augustine*, edited by Karla Pollmann and Willemien Otten, Oxford UP, 2013, https://www.oxfordreference.com/display/10.1093/acref/9780199299164.001.0001/acref-9780199299164-e-366.

Harvey, David. *The Condition of Postmodernity: An Enquiry into the Origins of Cultural Change*. Blackwell, 1989.

Howatson, Margaret, editor. "Hermēs Trismegi'stus ('Thrice-Greatest')." *The Oxford Companion to Classical Literature*, Oxford UP, 2011, http://www.oxfordreference.com/view/10.1093/acref/9780199548545.001.0001/acref-9780199548545-e-1486.

Huizinga, Johan. *Homo ludens, essai sur la fonction sociale du jeu* [*Homo Ludens, Essay on the Social Function of Play*]. 1938. Translated by Cécile Seresia, Gallimard, 1951.

Jameson, Fredric. *Postmodernism, or The Cultural Logic of Late Capitalism*. Duke UP, 1991.

Jørgensen, Kristine. *Gameworld Interfaces*. MIT P, 2013.

Juul, Jesper. *Half-Real: Videogames Between Real Rules and Fictional Worlds*. MIT P, 2005.

Kaufmann, Laurence, and Frédéric Clément. "How Culture Comes to Mind: From Social Affordances to Cultural Analogies." *Intellectica*, vol. 2, 2007, p. 7.

Kocurek, Carly A. *Coin-Operated Americans: Rebooting Boyhood at the Videogame Arcade*. U of Minnesota P, 2015.

Kort, Yvonne A. W. de, Wijinand A. IJsselsteijn, and Brian J. Gajadhar. "People, Places, and Play: A Research Framework for Digital Game Experience in a Socio-Spatial Context" in *DiGRA '07 – Proceedings of the 2007 DiGRA International Conference: Situated Play*. The University of Tokyo, vol. 4, 2007, pp. 823–830.

Lammes, Sybille. "Approaching Game-Studies: Towards a Reflexive Methodology of Games as Situated Cultures*" in DiGRA '07 – Proceedings of the DiGRA 2007 Conference*. The University of Tokyo, vol 4. 2007, pp. 25–30.

Latour, Bruno. *Reassembling the Social: An Introduction to Actor-Network-Theory*. Oxford UP, 2005.

Lee, Ichia, Yu Chien-Yi, and Lin Holin. "Leaving a Never-Ending Game: Quitting MMORPGs and Online Gaming Addiction." *DiGRA '07 – Proceedings of the 2007 DiGRA International Conference: Situated Play*. U of Tokyo, 2007.

Lefebvre, Henri. Éléments de rythmanalyse: introduction à la connaissance des rythmes [*Elements of Rythmanalysis: Introduction to the Knowledge of Rythms*]. Syllepse, 1992.

———. *La production de l'espace* [*The Production of Space*]. Éditions Anthropos, 1974.

Lin, Holin, and Sun Chuen-Tsai. "Cash Trade within the Magic Circle: Free-to-Play Game Challenges and Massively Multiplayer Online Game Player Responses." *DiGRA '07 – Proceedings of the 2007 DiGRA International Conference: Situated Play*, U of Tokyo, 2007.

Lyotard, Jean-François. *La condition postmoderne: rapport sur le savoir* [*The Postmodern Condition: Report on Knowledge*]. Éditions de Minuit, 1979.

Mabille, Pierre. *Egrégore ou la vie des civilisations* [*Egregore or the Life of Civilizations*]. 1938. Egrégores Editions, 2005.

Mandiberg, Stephen. "Playing (with) the Trace: Localized Culture in Phoenix Wright." *Kinephanos*, vol. 5, no. 1, 2015, pp. 111–41.

Massey, Doreen B. *For Space*. SAGE, 2005.

Mäyrä, Frans. "The Contextual Game Experience: On the Socio-Cultural Contexts for Meaning in Digital Play." *DiGRA '07 – Proceedings of the 2007 DiGRA International Conference: Situated Play*, U of Tokyo, 2007.

McGregor, Leigh Georgia. "Situations of Play: Patterns of Spatial Use in Videogames." *DiGRA '07 – Proceedings of the 2007 DiGRA International Conference: Situated Play*, U of Tokyo, 2007.

Montola, Markus. "On the Edge of the Magic Circle: Understanding Role-Playing and Pervasive Games." *School of Information Science*, U of Tampere, PhD Dissertation, 2012.

Nitsche, Michael. *Videogame Spaces: Image, Play, and Structure in 3D Game Worlds*. MIT P, 2008.

Norman, Donald A. *The Design of Everyday Things*. Basic Books, 1988.

Oppitz, Michael. "Shangri-La, Le Panneau de Marque d'un Flipper. Analyse Sémiologique d'un Mythe Visuel [Shangri-La, A Pinball Machine Marquee. Semiotic Analysis of a Visual Myth]." *L'Homme*, vol. 14, no. 3–4, 1974, pp. 59–83.

Pelletier-Gagnon, Jérémie. *Videogames and Japaneseness: An Analysis of Localization and Circulation of Japanese Videogames in North America*. McGill U, MA Thesis, 2011.

Salen, Katie, and Eric Zimmerman. *The Game Design Reader: A Rules of Play Anthology*. MIT P, 2006.

Schüll, Natasha Dow. *Addiction by Design: Machine Gambling in Las Vegas*. Princeton UP, 2012.

September 12. Windows PC videogame, Powerful Robot, 2003.

Stenros, Jakko. "In Defence of a Magic Circle: The Social and Mental Boundaries of Play." *Proceedings of 2012 DiGRA Nordic*, DiGRA Digital Library, 2012.

Suits, Bernard. *The Grasshopper: Games, Life and Utopia*. 1978. Broadview P, 2005.

Taylor, Nicholas, Jennifer Jenson, and Suzanne de Castell. "Gender in Play: Mapping a Girls' Gaming Club." *DiGRA – Proceedings of the 2007 DiGRA International Conference: Situated Play*, U of Tokyo, 2007.

Valenti, Stravos S., and James M. M. Gold. "Social Affordances and Interaction I: Introduction." *Ecological Psychology*, vol. 3, no. 2, 1991, pp. 77–98.

Wang, Qiyun, Huay Lit Woo, and Choon Lang Quek. "Exploring the Affordances of Facebook for Teaching and Learning." *International Review of Contemporary Learning Research*, vol. 1, no. 1, 2012, pp. 23–31.

Xevious. Arcade videogame cabinet, Namco, 1983.

Part II

Case Studies of Play and Space in Japanese Game Centres

5 Player-*flâneurs* and Extended Spatiality

Play Between Performance and Observation in A-cho

I am dripping in sweat under my winter coat meant for North American weather. It has been a long day. The street is packed as I start the one-hour journey back to my rental apartment in eastern Kyoto. Amongst all the tourist hotspots for which Kyoto is known, Teramachi Street is perhaps busiest. The commercial street known for its myriads of souvenir shops, iconic food markets, and shrines attracts all manner of visitors due to its location at the heart of the city. This is for a good reason, as everyone wants to get some tasty treats to bring home. The evening has barely started. Through the heavy foot traffic, I notice the familiar signs of a pachinko parlour, and above it a game centre. The "A-cho" poster is significantly smaller than the "ENTERTAINMENT OMEGA" sign on the left, but advertisements for purikura machines and character good lotteries cannot be overlooked. My long overdue shower will have to be postponed, because it is time for a quick game.

As I reach the second floor, I am first attracted by the crane game machines on the right, but I remember to resist the urge to try my luck at getting one of the coveted figurines behind the glass. There is no appetizer tonight, so I can move right to the *pièce de résistance*. Rows of machines are lined up, all seemingly playing fighting games. I stand at a comfortable distance behind the first row. Someone is playing. I observe the match. How long would I last against someone of that calibre? It would surely not be long, because fighting games are not my forte. I barely understand what is happening on the screen, as I have never played any games from the *BlazBlue* series before. The learning curve in this environment seems very steep. Looking for a game better suited to my mood, I resume walking along the rows of machines.

I recognize a few other machines, but nothing strikes my fancy. Some of the standard cabinets are playing a selection of 1990s shooting games. I get the basics. I reach the first boss, but I die before I can learn his attack patterns. Game over. Perhaps it is best to head home early after all. As I ready my backpack, I hear some familiar sounds of characters punching, kicking, and vaulting around on a *Virtua Fighter 4* machine. That is a game I can play, and I am not so helpless at it either. *Virtua Fighter* is no *BlazBlue* with its complex manoeuvres and combinations; everything is contextual and feels natural. It has three buttons: one to punch, one to kick, and the last one to guard. Since no one is playing, perhaps I can get in a few practice rounds before someone challenges me. I put

DOI: 10.4324/9781003273776-7

my 50-yen coin in the slot, and select my main character, Pai Chan. Here goes nothing. I wonder how long I will last…

—

Arcade Fighters of the 1990s

The years following the reform of the Fūeihō regulations saw a dramatic change in the game centre operation and arcade videogame industries; development in game genres stalled as players gradually left arcades behind in order to enjoy the new types of story-driven games published on home videogame consoles. Arcade games were still primarily meant as single-player experiences, which did not particularly lend themselves to playing in public amongst other potentially disturbing activities. Although the impressive *taikan* game cabinets made a significant impression on players, these were designed for the larger spaces of game centres in the suburbs and could only be enjoyed by one player at a time. The arrival of the epoch-making fighting game *Street Fighter II*, and the many other arcade fighting games that found inspiration in its one-on-one competitive combat formula featuring charismatic characters, helped game centres located in urban settings attract a new category of players distinct from the ones that preceded them, inspired by the competitive aspect of the game and eager to prove their skills to one another. In many ways, the fighting game community was animated by different dynamics and thus would develop as a sort of subculture within the arcade gaming community itself. The first venue I studied for this book was a game centre called A-cho Neo Amusement Space, which made its home on Teramachi Street in Kyoto in 1997, during the heyday of the development of arcade fighting game culture, and displays spatial structure and elements that remain present in this culture to this day. My observation of A-cho addresses several key issues: the fluid nature of ludic trajectories and the simultaneity of different types of engagements, the extension of spatiality towards the virtual, as well as the dynamics of performance and observation in the context of organized events.

A-cho: Structure and Spatial Design

A-cho is located on the second and third floors of the A-break building of the commercial Teramachi Street, perhaps the busiest shopping and nightlife entertainment destination for locals and tourists visiting the cultural capital of Japan. The entrance of the famous Nishiki food market is located just a few blocks north, right next to the Nishiki-Tenmangū Shrine. The venue's building also houses a pachinko parlour, owned by the chain Entertainment Omega, on the ground floor. A-cho has two direct accesses from the street level: a one-way escalator located very close to the street level, and a stairway behind a small smoking area shared with the pachinko hall. Both entrances lead directly to the second floor of the building. Both venues share the stairway, which allows customers to walk from one venue to the other with ease. The venue is located not very far away from another prominent amusement centre complex, belonging to the Round 1 chain, on the neighbouring Kawaramachi Street, which vastly surpasses A-cho in floor space and diversity of arcade machines. Although one would expect this larger venue to completely eclipse A-cho, they both seem to serve different purposes and attract different types of crowds.

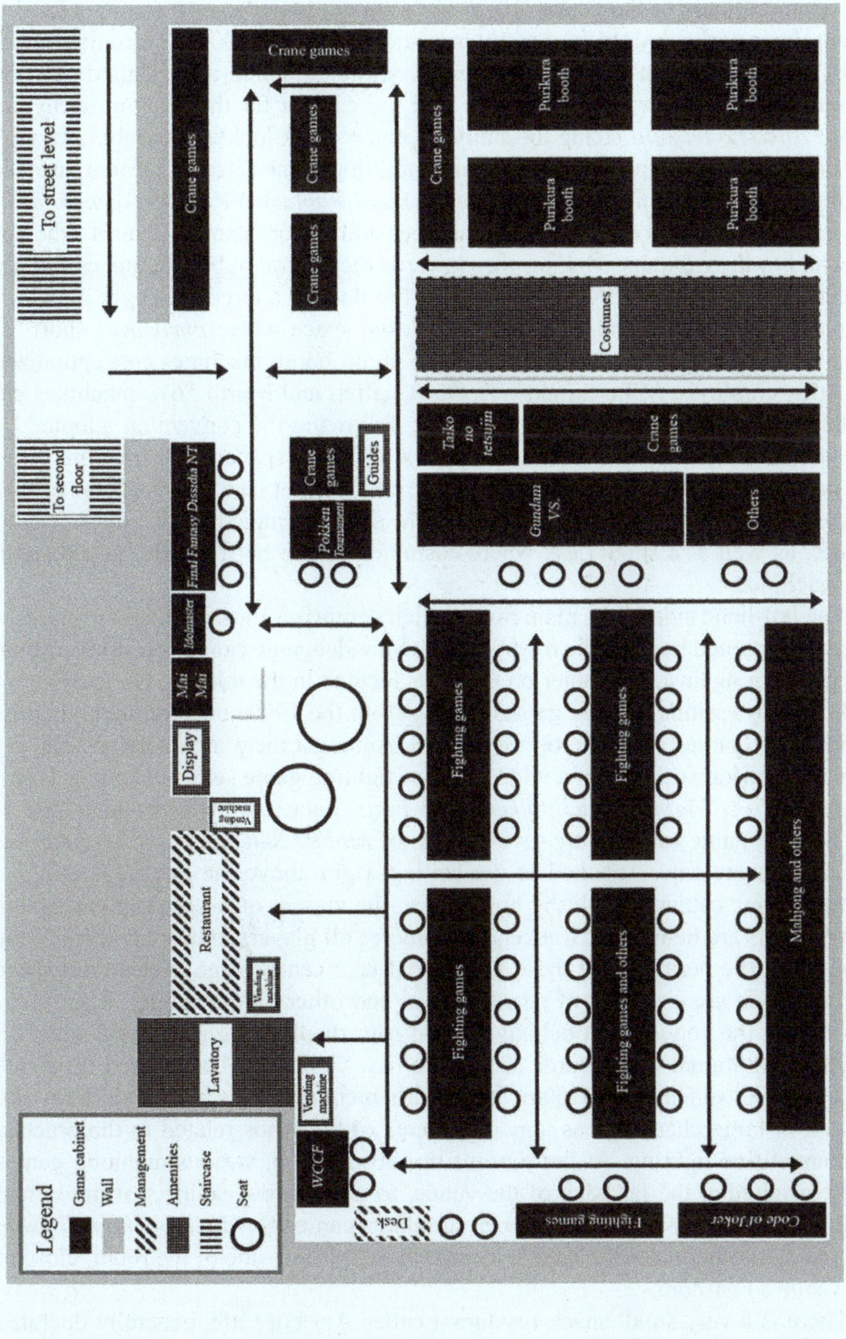

Figure 5.1 Visual representation of A-cho's first floor. Sufficient circulation space between rows of machine enables observation of play sessions, especially within the restaurant section (image by the author).

On the second floor, customers are greeted by a standard row of *gachapon* and crane game machines and, at their left, another smoking area. A board clearly states the opening hours of the venue (10:00 to 24:00 daily) and age restrictions for different times of the day (16:00 for children under 16, and 22:00 for customers under 18). A few significant machines that easily attract attention are installed near the entrance of the venue; one can easily spot the cabinet for the drumming rhythm game *Taiko no tetsujin* facing the stairway, and a quick look at the right is enough for one to notice the presence of two new fighting game releases located near the high traffic zones of the arcades: *Dissidia Final Fantasy NT* and *Pokken Tournament*. Both machines display large marquees and feature games' control schemes attached to the cabinets. Making way towards the central hub area, one can easily discern the overall structure of the venue: the floor is a large rectangle on which a crane game section and a relatively enclosed space where *purikura*—short for *Purinto kurabu*, the name of the first ludic photo booth machines conceptualized by Atlus employee Miho Sasaki in 1995 (Chalfen and Murui 56)—machines are installed on the right-hand side. The latter, following the convention adopted by the rest of the arcade operator industry, is a restricted space into which men who are not accompanied by women are not allowed to enter (see Chapter 8 for further discussion). This restriction encompasses the space occupied by the *purikura* machines, as well as a small desk where costumes can be borrowed to be used with the machines.

The left-hand side of the main floor, which comprises most of the floor space, is entirely occupied by multiple rows of sit-down videogame cabinets leaning against the walls, or against each other on the rows located in the middle. These rows are dedicated to various fighting games, dating from the 1990s onward, including the most recent games available on the market. Amongst them are machines playing copies of various titles from a wide range of fighting game series including *Virtua Fighter*, *Street Fighter*, *Darkstalkers*, and *Fatal Fury*. On the right-hand side of the fighting game cabinets are several units of *Mobile Suit Gundam: Extreme Vs.*, all in the same row. Attached to the ceiling, right above the large gathering of fighting game cabinets, a plushy brown bear, the mascot of A-cho, announces that tournaments are held every weekend and invites all players to come and enjoy the games. On the periphery of these games that take centre stage in the main space of the arcade are a variety of puzzle games and other unique games. The southern wall of the venue, right behind this last row, displays a gigantic wallpaper on which inspirational watchwords such as "a new challenger has entered the field" or "taikai ha itsudemo koko ni aru" (the tournament is always here at all times) are written in large characters as announcements of the ethos related to the practice of competitive fighting. At the time of my observation, various mahjong games were installed at the far back of the venue, as were a few cabinets of the virtual card game *Code of Joker* and soccer simulator game *World Club Championship Football*. Another smoking area is located at the far-left side of the room, close to the venue's restroom.

There is a very small snack-restaurant called Apricot Café, generally operated by a single female employee dressed in fancy clothing vaguely reminiscent of that of nineteenth-century French maids; customers can purchase drinks, snacks, various types of fried food, and lottery tickets granting them a chance to win prizes from a rotating collection generally themed around a videogame or anime. These are displayed in glass cases located on the right side of the counter. This location is also used to display a variety of pamphlets advertising local events or restaurants, game magazines or guidebooks, and also provides a space for players to write or draw in notebooks. The pamphlets themselves are used to convey information about some of the most prominent games of the venue, most often supported by a strong marketing campaign, but they also disseminate other types of information about the broader culture of the Japanese arcade world in general. Two tables and a few chairs are installed close to the coffee shop, offering a vantage point from which to observe some of the gaming activity occurring. While customers can freely observe some of the games located nearby, a network of television sets connected to a few key game cabinets constantly relay some matches played live to the entire floor. A selection of vending machines offers additional snacks, drinks, and IC cards for players to purchase. Two *Mai Mai* rhythm game units are located near the tables, and these are the only machines on the floor enclosed by a circulation strap that enforces line-ups. Behind the tables, one may notice the unique silhouette of a music group simulator game, *The Idolmaster*, which looks somewhat out of place and is hidden between two bigger units, but creates a sort of synergy, considering that most of the prizes available through the raffle are themed after this game series.

Overall, the first floor of A-cho is the busy hub of the venue, in which many people circulate between machines that, though still relegated to specific locations on the floor, all coexist within the same broad environment unified by the live transmission TV networks. The venue is designed to steer the circulation of players towards its central hub of fighting game cabinets, which offers more space to freely loiter around and to circulate between rows either vertically or horizontally. This relative potential for creative navigation of the space is not fully realized in other parts of the venue.

Facing the main entrance, another flight of stairs leads to the third floor. The upper section of the building can be accessed directly without having to walk through the machines on the other floor, which suggest that it houses games belonging to completely different genres and geared towards a different community. Before entering, one comes across another smoking area facing two cabinets of the free-to-play game *Puyopuyo!! Quest*; both cabinets and the smoking space are significantly more secluded than their equivalents on the floors below. The two cabinets are parallel to the wall, so that they are only accessible by their right-hand side, preventing other customers from peeking, while the smoking area is made up of a few tables and chairs put in between the bannister and the wall. The loud music that can be heard from the staircase signals the heavy presence of a variety of rhythm games installed throughout the floor.

Taking centre stage on this floor, a *Dance Evolution* cabinet and a dedicated dance floor section delimited by a blue strap and some blue tape glued on the floor are prominently installed in the middle of the room. This installation is certain to

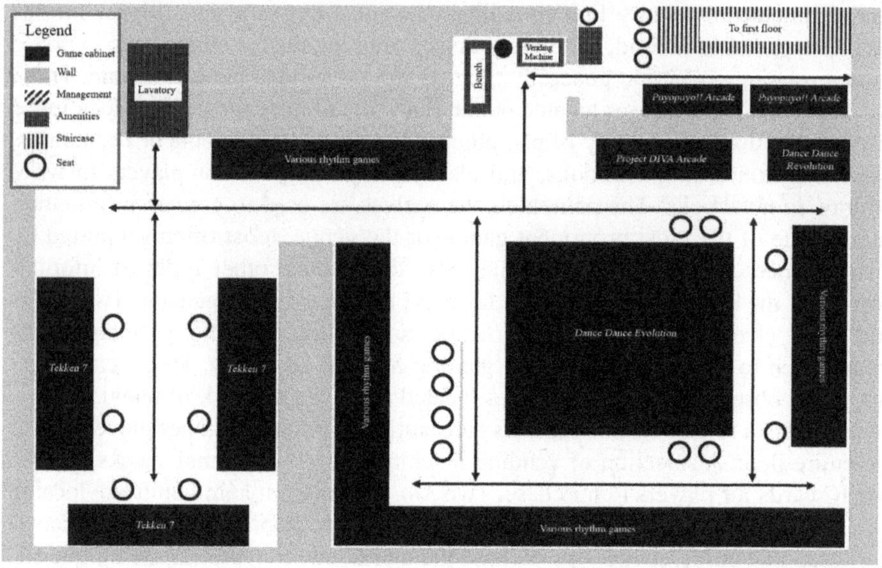

Figure 5.2 Visual representation of A-cho's second floor. Both the upper right and lower left sections provide some amount of isolation from the rest of the venue (image by the author).

automatically attract the attention of anybody wandering the floor. The machine can be seen from almost every vantage point on the floor, and thus exposes the player interacting with the machine to the gaze of every passer-by. Multiple signs and posters directly surrounding the machine prohibit customers from taking pictures or video of the installation when someone is engaged in a play session. The ambiance of the second floor is slightly different than on the first floor; the lights are dimmer, and most machines are equipped with side panels that isolate machines from each other. Many different games, such as *Museca*, *Hatsune Miku: Project DIVA Arcade*, *Dance Dance Revolution*, *Beatmania*, *Jubeat*, *Sound Voltext*, and others, all of which are variations on rhythm game conventions, can be found on this floor. Some of them are equipped with headphones to allow players to completely focus on their play session. The floor features its own managerial desk and amenities catering to general rhythm game business, such as cabinet maintenance or event management.

Additional information concerning past and upcoming tournaments, and a practice station for the *Hatsune Miku* rhythm game, are located at the right-hand side of the entrance. An additional lavatory is located in the northwest corner of the floor, facing a distinct zone secluded from the rhythm game environment dominating this floor. Inside are several *Tekken 7* cabinets separate from other fighting game cabinets on the floor below, presumably because this specific fighting game does not allow flexible local competitive play, but instead requires players to play against each other via its publisher Bandai Namco's own private network, accessible with a Banapassport IC card.

Extended Spatiality: Virtual Space and Emotional Labour

A-cho displays all the characteristics of an independently operated venue. The employees do not wear distinctive uniforms; many of the signs and pamphlets decorating the venue are in a crafty, do-it-yourself style; and, most importantly, the elaborate in-house café that also acts as a communication channel through monthly hand-written letters is a unique touch that brings a strong sense of personality and conviviality to the venue. The venue not only encourages engagement with videogames but also provides amenities that make it an informal meeting space supporting non-ludic activities. However, investigating this game centre more closely online reveals that A-cho is not, strictly speaking, an independent venue, but part of a greater corporate entity called Daiichi Bussan Ltd., an entertainment conglomerate that operates a chain of grilled chicken restaurants and a network of pachinko parlours, one which is located on the first floor of the same building. Daiichi Bussan operates exclusively in western Japan around the Kyoto area and the prefectures of Fukui, Shiga, and Ishikawa. A-cho constitutes the corporation's unique presence in the amusement business, and as such, its distinctively unique ambiance and niche game selection effectively makes the venue stand out from its much bigger competitors in the arcade operation business.

The unique atmosphere of the venue is partly generated by a sustained community-building commitment from the hosts to the player community, expressed in the organization of reoccurring events such as social gatherings and tournament play. As the central banner fixed on the ceiling of the main floor indicates, fighting game tournaments are organized every weekend. Indeed, the monthly schedule pamphlet freely available in the venue and offered in print informs customers that tournaments for at least one specific fighting game are organized most Saturdays and Sundays. A-cho also hosts other complementary events over the course of the week, such as ranking battles (*ranbato*), in which players compete over a very strict set of matches to gain ranking points and increase their overall status at the venue, and "recorded matches" or *eizōtaisenkai*. During the latter type of event, players are invited to play games on a few selected machines connected to video recording software that will record all activity on the machine from 7:00 PM until closure of the venue at 12:00 AM. On the following day, the staff saves the resulting videogame and posts it on A-cho's *YouTube* account unedited for everyone to watch. This allows players the chance of having their play session recorded so they can watch their personal highlights or study their own performances. In order to create an environment that accommodates both high-level and casual players, weekends are also designed specifically for lower-rank players of two of the most popular games played in A-cho: any of the current versions of the *BlazBlue* and *Guilty Gear* fighting games. On these days, players seeking opponents close in rank to theirs are encouraged to come and enjoy the games.[1]

Another weekly event specific to A-cho that is worthy of mention is a unique livestreamed talk radio program, "Shūen no ninnin rajio", recorded live on Wednesdays between 7:00 and 10:00 PM. At the time of my observation, the show seemed to have been in a period of transition; while in the past the host would personally choose a game, a new format was developed in which a guest could directly apply to challenge a game of their choosing as a live performance, or act as a guest to talk over the footage. The show was broadcast on the venue's local television network, Ustream, and also recorded and posted on *YouTube* for archival purposes. According to the archives posted on A-cho's website, the formula of this stream changed between 2015 and 2016, and would eventually stop altogether by the beginning of 2017. However, throughout these changes, it remains clear that these streams put forward a different game experience than those provided by ranking battles and tournaments. Indeed, the combination of the online community's involvement in the comment section of the stream and its generally highly expressive and humorous tone were meant as entertainment; the crowd would cheer the streamer as he progressively loses hope to ever finish the game as he faces very difficult and seemingly unfair challenges provided by the often obscure games put in the spotlight. The stream was, thus, very much in the same vein as *Game Center CX*, a humorous television series, produced by Fuji Television, on the theme of retrogaming.

It is important to note that all of these tournaments, competitive play sessions, and other game-related entertainment nights are centred around the fighting, puzzle, and, sometimes, quiz games located on the first floor. In addition, these games all share the common characteristic of not being configured for network play. Indeed, due to publisher constraints and operating logistics, the game centre industry tends to segregate games not by genres, but on whether or not they require access to their publisher's private game network to operate. Games available at A-cho are presented to the public on the game centre's website, and are separated into several categories: "otoge" (rhythm games), "videogames", "online games", and "prize games". "Videogames" are usually understood in the business as games that do not require an internet connection to be operated; many fighting games belong to this category, as do most retro games or games released before the 2000s. These games are compatible with most standardized cabinet types, such as the popular Sega Astrocity series. On the other hand, "online games" comprise most of the high-profile contemporary releases that rely on constant network connectivity to keep track of players' data, allow online matchmaking, update the game itself with the most current version, and integrate promotional time-limited events. These are also released along with dedicated cabinets that maximize the game's visibility. Although the genre might be similar, these games are treated differently by operators; A-cho segregates these types of machines to the second floor rather than putting them on the main floor. *Tekken 7*'s presence away from other fighting games is indicative of its function as a primarily online experience that could potentially disrupt the flow and sociability of play on the main floor. Indeed, while games belonging to the "videogame" category might be less attractive as older or less beginner-friendly titles, they require less financial commitment, can be customized to fit tournament requirements and allow greater venue versatility, since they can be more easily traded in and out of a machine in order to address players' preference.

A-cho's emphasis on communication and community building constitutes a unique approach by a corporate entity toward the game centre business that effectively erases the traces of its affiliation. This approach uses not only all of the elements mentioned above but also a strong web presence used to further reach players outside the space, and that partly relies on the grassroots labour of its employees. As mentioned above, A-cho maintains a *Ustream* account[2] and a *YouTube* channel to stream and archive tournaments and a variety of recordings from other events; it also occupies a web presence on *Twitter* with the handle "a-cho" (@acho_kyoto). This communication channel is used to relay official information about the venue, including new products, promotions, and tournament schedules and standings. An alternative *Twitter* account called "a-cho sutaffu" (@achostaff) is also operated in parallel to the official one, maintained directly by the staff of the venue. Though it retweets some of the information relayed by the official A-cho account, it is also allowed to freely retweet and comment on other tweets and publications related to gaming and transmedial culture; its tweets are also less formal in style, and often convey more light-hearted content. Overall, the coexistence of these two accounts seems to position A-cho not only as a simple arcade operator, but also as an active participant in gaming culture. Most importantly, it gives a human, more relatable touch to the operator's online presence, which thus creates a more inviting cyberspace in which players can engage, something that the venue also wants to replicate in the physical space of the arcade.

Perhaps the online component that best represents the game centre's desire to appeal in much more intimate ways to its player base is the blog maintained by the staff in charge of the café located on the first floor of the venue. In addition to a monthly printed newsletter, the *Apricot Blog,* hosted by the Japanese FC2 web platform, reaches out to A-cho's player base with regular posts about a range of different topics, including updates about staff members and their personal lives, discussion about popular smartphone games,[3] and posts about seasonal festivals and food. Both the visuals and the tone of the blog differentiate it from A-cho's *Twitter* and streaming accounts. The website is designed for comfortable reading on mobile devices, and its minimalist imagery featuring the silhouette of a waitress on top of the page and frills surrounding the posts themselves gives the website a resolutely approachable *kawaii*, or cute, aesthetic flair. The posts themselves generally consist of short sentences, punctuated by *kaomoji.*[4]

This aspect of A-cho's online presence as an extension of the imaginary space of the arcade exemplifies the integration of cyberspace into the social fabric of game centres, and its reliance on its staff's personal engagement towards their workplace and the emotional labour required to maintain these lines of communication open. Although the emergence of cellphone technologies, Web 2.0 platforms, and network connectivity on new arcade releases have somewhat affected the income and financial structure of game centres, and certain voices are starting to question the venues' capacity to attract and retain a viable customer base in physical locations, Katō warns us against quickly judging the future of game centres through the prism of technological determinism ("Online jidai no gēmu sentā" 303–05). Social media has brought a plethora of new methods allowing players to share high scores and to discuss games online, but Katō insists that these means of communication, now implemented to some degree in many venues, complement the physical experience of the arcades rather than threatening it; players are attracted to arcades not only to play but also to experience serendipitous encounters with other players, and to engage with them in a more creative way beyond the limited social functions featured on networked games and social media. A-cho's online reach, seen in its entirety, can be seen as an additional "platform" catering to players that further increases the benefits of engaging directly with the community and culture of the arcade, and prolonging the ludic engagement beyond the borders of the venue.

On another hand, as one navigates this platform, it becomes obvious that the weight of this online reach falls on the shoulders of the staff members. The existence of such a strategy is partly based on the emotional labour of young employees who are paid hourly wages, and whose engagement with these platforms must be personal, for the purpose of creating a playful and comfortable atmosphere for players. Emotional labour is a feature of occupations such as flight attendants, a type of labour that "requires one to induce or suppress feelings in order to sustain the outward countenance that produces the proper state of mind in others" and "calls for a coordination of mind and feeling, and […] draws on a source of self that we honour as deep and integral to our individuality" (Hochschild 7). The blogging component of A-cho's online presence requires female staff to demonstrate a friendly disposition while sharing personal anecdotes from their daily lives online; the cultivation of this online self is also echoed in the space of the arcade itself, where the coffee shop employees are subjected to a strict dress code, inspired by European maid outfits, and are expected to greet customers with a smile.

This situation is comparable to other types of occupations that rely on various types of emotional labour in what could be called the broader otaku market. Maid cafés, which grew in popularity in the second decade of the 2000s, are the most obvious of these venues in an entire industry that relies on young women's capacity to take on a gentle persona and make customers feel welcomed by adopting a specific speech pattern and engaging in various activities such as playing rock-paper-scissors, photo shoots, and signing autographs for customers.[5] In game centres, female employees seem to feel the pressure of emotional labour more than male employees; men typically occupy positions that require more technical knowledge, such as maintaining machines, or direct involvement in the game culture, such as tournament announcers or streamers, and fewer interactions with players directly. Apricot Café's employees do not engage in these types of activities, and, to some extent, their emotional involvement also grants them a sense of agency through the creative process of maintaining the channels of communication for which they are responsible for. However, they are tasked more directly to keep an "outward countenance" meant to make feel customers at home, and make the space homelier and more approachable, at the cost of a heavy personal engagement in their job which, as Hochschild suggests, may cause a sense of disconnection or alienation from one's self. Though a detailed examination of this phenomenon is not part of the main objectives of this project, further research on this subject is certainly warranted to unpack, for example, how employment is negotiated in game centres in terms of using gaming knowledge and practices of young staff as community-building assets to serve specific nodes of the broader gaming industry. Emphasis on the ludic qualities of the work sphere often fills the gap between the discrepancy of the value that workers operating at the most precarious level of employment bring to the industry, and their remuneration (Kirkpatrick).

Gaming Trajectories: The Ludo-egregores of Fighting Games

The space of A-cho mobilizes the outward disposition of the staff and the visual identity of the venue specifically to generate a sense of familiarity and homeliness. However, what we can call the "ludic trajectories" of the people who come to engage with the machines and with one another bring these elements to life and generate the conventions and the emerging atmosphere in which the play activity occurs and by which it is influenced. The idea of ludic trajectories implies a diversity of purpose and intentions coming from each customer visiting any game centre, which itself does not remain stable, but may evolve over the course of a visit; many people will come to engage with specific machines or social groups, while others might find satisfaction in simply observing the action, following their friends, or engaging in other types of activities. Regardless of their type of engagement, players' behaviour is modulated by the affordance of the machines present on site, the structure of the space they occupy, the social affordances generated by the design of the machines, and the behaviour exhibited by other players. However, though the potential for specific kinds of experiences is designed within the machines and structured through the layout of the space, these affordances only prompt action when perceived by human agents and, as such, are subjected to a multiplicity of agents that interpret them in different fashion depending on their ludic trajectories. This phenomenon becomes apparent when considering the spectrum of players who visit a single game centre at different times of the day, and on different days of the week. Examining and comparing different key periods of crowd attendance in A-cho indicate how the space of the arcade, which essentially stays fixed, is mobilized in different ways by its clientele, which adopts certain engagement patterns at specific moments to negotiate the venue's centralized focus on fighting games around its hub area.

As a rule of thumb, the most observable and distinctive ludic trajectories adopted by A-cho's customers are negotiated around the fighting game genre. Fighting games are played at all times in A-cho, but they can be observed primarily in the evenings, both during weekdays and weekends, and are at their strongest during and around the tournaments and the other forms of events organized by the venue. At any given time when the venue is open for business, players can be seen engaging with fighting games on an individual level without being part of a group, or necessarily playing with a human opponent. However, during weekends and most evenings, groups tend to form around the fighting game cabinets, bringing more players around the central hub of the venue, or patrons who do not directly engage with the machines themselves but watch the action unfolding either far away from or directly behind the machines or beside the player they are observing. During these more populated time windows, multiple people are seen engaging in ludic trajectories of different natures, thus negotiating the space of the venue: around the same area, some players will engage in individual play sessions and rarely engage other customers, while others engage the space in an egregious fashion, prioritizing exchanges with fellow players over engaging with the machines directly. However, these types of interactions are not fixed and customers routinely part from groups to engage in play sessions, and vice versa. Though fighting games display many characteristics that distinguish them from one another, the games shown prominently in A-cho's main area are linked by their potential to generate similar types of ludo-egregores.

From a design perspective, cabinets used for most fighting arcade videogames are similar. Sit-down cabinets, also called *han'yō kyōtai* or *standard cabinet* in Japanese, feature a large flat screen installed at a slight inclination at toward its back, thus giving a screen/controls angle that leans towards 110 degrees as opposed to the 90 degrees that would be the ideal position for the active player. The controls themselves require the player to be sitting down on the provided seat to be accessible; when the player matches his/her body position to the most optimal play configuration afforded by the machine, most of the upper portion of the play screen can be seen by passersby, and just enough of the game action can be observed by standing behind the active player and looking over his/her shoulders.

The standard format of this genre of game is a one-on-one confrontation between two adversaries, one located on the left side of the screen and the other on the right side, that lasts up to a maximum of 99 seconds, depending on the game. Rounds are very short in duration, and thus concentrate the bulk of the game experience in a focused time frame of high intensity without much downtime. Although the complete game experience also includes moments to let the tension build up and cool down before and after the matches, as well as a character and command input selection screen, it is within this short time frame that players are invited to let out their creative side and express their personality through strategies, tactics, and mastery of the controls that often require quick reflexes and strong composure. In addition to a regular set of basic character input, fighting games typically feature sets of combination moves and more or less secret commands that are specific to each character; though these commands are usually difficult to pull off in the middle of a heated match, players might be tempted to risk using them to reverse the course of a round, or simply to rouse the enthusiasm of the potential crowd watching the confrontation. Since players cannot talk to one another or otherwise use language to communicate with their opponents, the potential for significant exchange is operated through the "mind game" of expectation, subversion, and intimidation throughout the gameplay.

From a spatial perspective, A-cho's fighting game cabinet disposition within the arcade follows the traditional configuration of these machines in space, which emerged in the 1990s in parallel with the fighting game boom that hit the Japanese arcade scene at the same moment. As mentioned previously, in A-cho, fighting game cabinets that are played on a local network configuration are located in the primary hub area of the venue, organized in a few rows in which the machines are lined up against one another, but the most important aspect of this spatial configuration is the organization of the games in pairs, each pairing in a back-to-back configuration, with two machines leaning against each other's back. Game cabinets set up in pairs in this way are called *taisendai* or battle cabinets.

In the West, most competitive arcade game machines configure two sets of player controls on a single front end of the cabinet. However, the development of the culture surrounding fighting games in Japan owes much to the innovation of reconfiguring arcade cabinets to facilitate play with unknown adversaries, a practice that was popularized around the release of *Street Fighter II*. Zenji Ishii, former editor of the videogame magazine *Gamest* and famous arcade scene game critic, recalls that at the time, most players were much more comfortable playing against the artificial intelligence than against one another (*Gēmu sentā kunonikuru* 174); playing a match against a human adversary meant playing directly beside that player and potentially exposing oneself to the shame of losing the match or the equal empathetic embarrassment of winning against a weak opponent. Thus, multiplayer matches were played by people between whom a social link was already established, which inhibited the development of a safe space for players to challenge unknown opponents in public venues without having to navigate the social consequences of winning or losing. However, by changing the play configuration at the spatial level, and to some extent at the design level as well, arcade operators successfully changed the play condition of these games, which allowed the rapid development of a competitive fighting game culture that far surpassed that of the West in scale.

We can see the engagement dynamics specific to *taisendai* fighting game cabinets at play quite clearly in A-cho, in terms both of how it invites a certain type of interaction from players, and of the broader cultural milieu it takes part in creating and maintaining. During daytime and most weekdays, players who engaged with the fighting game cabinets were usually on their own and were not part of any social pre-established groups formed prior to entering the space. Couples also seldom played fighting games when they visited the arcade. Thus, for that crucial moment of the day, the *taisendai* cabinet organization, as a spatial strategy, enabled players to play against human opponents without going through the social hurdles of socially engaging with another player. The *taisendai* exude a certain form of social affordance that, at first glance, seems opposed to the purpose of playing in public, but is compatible with the range of social expectations of this specific type of space; the objects of *taisendai* hold design affordances that, when perceived by human agents, enable players to engage in a common ludic activity while retaining a very low social threshold, which is best adapted for the type of weak social engagement dynamics that the space of A-cho harbours at these times.

The resulting long-term effect of this configuration is the establishment of a space in which the communicative medium and focus of attention remains the games themselves. The *taisendai* configuration does not necessarily feature the right properties to support play by groups featuring players with already pre-established social links, who typically do not engage with players outside of their social group. The people who engaged with fighting games were more likely to approach one another during events, using the games themselves as introductory points and discussion topics, thus strengthening their belonging to a certain game genre, specific title, and even A-cho as a gathering place. It is this type of communicative practice that is often emphasized as a central point of the revival of game centre culture around the fighting game genre in the 1990s.

On the other hand, during weekends and some weekday evenings when A-cho was at its busiest, a different set of the *taisendai*'s properties took precedence in players' minds, and could be perceived at a much higher frequency. The slight inclination of the screens of these cabinets offers a great vantage point over the game's action from a relatively long distance, which, in turn, affords patrons to adopt the position of an observer over the action. In periods of low attendance, one could observe a tendency towards intimacy and reclusion from the crowd during play sessions. It was possible to observe an opening towards the greater social space of the arcade during periods of high attendance in which like-minded fighting game players gather, usually over a type of game-related evening event, and in which the properties of the screen became catalysts for much closer types of social interactions. Combined with the speed at which rounds are contested, when matches started, nearby players, whether socially related or not, were often compelled to observe the actions directly from behind the active player and engage in this activity with a sustained focus lasting at least one round. A game session was typically punctuated by breaks and moments in which tension was released, were the active player regained his composure, and observers commented on the action. The synergy between the industrial design aspect of the cabinet, the rules under which the software operated and the social climate of the space created the conditions that allowed these affordances to be perceived by the players and the public, and which then influenced both the game session and the space around it.

Figure 5.3 Venue-goers overlooking an active player at A-cho near the restaurant section. One of them observes the action on the screen from a distance, while the other engages more directly with the player, exemplifying diversity in a typical assemblage of agents (photograph by the author).

The resulting human-machine configuration that operated at the level of both the machine and its surroundings exudes a machinic assemblage that allows for different types of ludo-egregore to emerge around the broad categories of fighting games at A-cho, which all shared the same properties. These can be divided into the two broad categories described above, and they demonstrate the extent to which a single videogame object holds the potential for different sets of affordances that players perceive in different manners in different settings. This multilayered assemblage thus acts as a catalyst for the formation of ludo-egregores that are plural and ephemeral in nature, which give a sociocultural meaning to the play activity and are essential to consider as part of a holistic reading of these games played in public settings. The intense energetic action provided by the human-machine assemblage of fighting videogames is adaptable to the prevailing low-involvement social dynamics of game centres. In other words, most customers may be seen as embodying certain characteristics of the cultural figure of the *flâneur*.

Emerging in Paris at the turn of the nineteenth century, the *flâneur* has been famously described by Walter Benjamin as an individual strolling the city in a state of semi-aimlessness, an observer of the environment driven by an intoxication of the sensory stimuli provided by the endless exploration of streets, objects, people, and experiences (416–18). A product of modern life and a precursor to the contemporary figure of the tourist, the *flâneur* is particularly receptive to the rhythm of urban design and to the affordances of his surrounding environment. We might say that the figure of the contemporary arcade venue-goer, the player-*flâneur*, is akin to his/her nineteenth-century counterpart in seeking the intoxication of electronic ludic activities. The arcade-goer strolls, explores, consumes, and enjoys different ludic experiences and their ephemeral ludo-egregores. His/her initial ludic trajectory might initially be that of an observer at a safe distance, but the structure of the space allows for easy change of roles towards active engagement in play activity. He/she is the essential constitutive figure of ludic engagement in public in game centres, always participating in the construction of the ludo-egregore formed around specific games. The player is also partly staging his/her performance (*se met en scène*) for this potential observer, whether consciously or not, as the combination of players and *flâneur* forms a bond that goes beyond the simple sum of the human and non-human actors involved in the play process and influencing the player's ludic engagement. Both intimate and gregarious ludo-egregores are fundamentally the encounter of these ludic trajectories, brought together by the arcade game's machinic assemblage.

The low social engagement that characterizes the ludo-egregore of fighting arcade games also gives these entities a sense of impermanence. The escalation and release of tension that come with every round signal exit points at which observers may be prompted to distance themselves with performance to seek other activities or points of interest within the venue. This change brings forward a fundamental transformation of the play activity, be it minimal and unnoticeable, as actors involved may leave or join the abstract entity of the play session. Impermanence is the watchword of the ludo-egregores observed in A-cho's fighting game playing activity. The importance of tension brought by the software was essential to consider in the reading of ludo-egregores as the catalyst, a phenomenon that became much more obvious at specific moments of the sociocultural life of A-cho.

Event Case Study: *BlazBlue* Raking Battle on Thursday, February 25, 2016

One of the common business strategies that game centre operators use is to structure their game offering around a small selection of select titles in order to make their venue an unmissable place in which fans of a specific game are most likely to find good matchups and a community of like-minded players. A game centre that engages in this practice is often called the "holy site" (*saichi*) of a particular game, defined as a venue known for attracting high-level players of a particular game, which makes it a prime location to come practice, gather information and meet members of the community (Katō, "Online jidai no gēmu sentā" 277). Based on the floor space, visibility, and tournament focus dedicated to the specific fighting game *BlazBlue*, it is fair to say that the administration of A-cho was consciously positioning itself as the "holy site" of this game for the Kyoto region. In order to justify this status, the venue dedicated a notable amount of key weekly operating hours of high player density to structure various types of organized play around this game. In light of our previous discussion of the types of ludo-egregore generated by fighting game machines in general in A-cho, *BlazBlue*'s status as one of the highlighted games in this venue made it an effective case study to examine another form that the ludo-egregore of fighting games could take in a different context to which other games are usually not exposed in this venue. To this end, the following section focuses on a single structured game event that took place on the evening of February 25, 2016: the biweekly Kansai region ranking battle event of *BlazBlue* at A-cho.

As mentioned above, ranking battles are designed as long-term and region-specific events in which players compete with other players from the broader regional community to acquire points reflecting their skill levels, thus establishing a local ranking system that grants players a certain prestige and social capital effective at the level of the venue where these matches are played. This system also contributes into providing a dynamic scene and community surrounding the game centre in which they are played, a phenomenon that could be verified in A-cho. The venue held a singular position as sole organizer of ranking battles for the Kansai region, which does much to attract players from different cities in their venue. Three different fighting games had their own specific rankings and appropriate events at A-cho, the others being *Street Fighter IV* and *Guilty Gear*. However, *BlazBlue* held a unique position as the only game featured prominently in events during weeknights, and one of the few games around which many different kinds of events were organized regularly throughout the week. At the time of this field study, *BlazBlue: Continuum Shift* (abbreviated as BBCS on the schedule), the second game of the eponymous series, was the version installed in the *taisendai* cabinets.

Developed by Arc System Works, the *BlazBlue* game series shares many characteristics with other games made by this studio, such as the *Guilty Gear* and *Arcana Heart* series. The game features memorable and over-the-top characters and settings, each equipped with a specialized move set and special abilities that make learning each character an important aspect of improving one's ability at the game. During each round, or "rebels" according to the game's unique nomenclature, players must defeat their opponents by reducing their health gauge to zero, or by preserving more of their own health bar than their opponents by the end of the 99-second round. The game is fast-paced and features a complex command scheme reminiscent of the *Street Fighter* game series; simple combinations might only require one quarter or a half-circle joystick movement, while higher level techniques require many of these precise and quick joystick moves along with precise button combinations. Move sets are also more creative and flashier than those of more traditional fighting game formulas. The game features the older-style two-dimensional visual representation and sprite-based character art that characterized fighting game titles created during the golden years of the genre, but the unconventional move sets of *BlazBlue*'s characters clearly break from this tradition by exploring freer movements and animation style.[6]

Over the course of a match, players must manage different resources at their disposal, including the Heat Gauge, which gradually fills up with every hit taken and given. Players can then use parts of the Heat Gauge to unleash character-specific skills or wait until it reaches its maximum charge to unleash an attack devastating enough to reverse the course of the confrontation and allow them to recover from a bad start. In this specific version of *BlazBlue*, other elements, such as the Guard Primer and Break Burst systems, add more nuances to the gameplay, granting players another set of resources allowing them to either guard against some of the fiercest attacks, risking temporary immobilization in doing so, or break the guard of their opponent a limited number of times over the course of a match. These elements require players to manage many different systems over many rounds, and observers to keep track of these aspects simultaneously. These elements give the game a distinct edge and an additional excitement factor over many other classic games of the genre while still retaining key visual aspects of a highly competitive title on par with the most recognized classics of the genre on the scene. *BlazBlue* is thus a highly competitive game that requires a great deal of investment from its player to reach a high level of play, characters and an art style that can only be qualified as unhinged, dynamic action-filled gameplay and sonic presence, and a mixture of both classical and hard rock musical inspirations, all of which makes it an entertaining spectacle.[7]

The event of February 25, recorded as the 143th *BlazBlue* Kansai region ranking battle, started at around 7:00 PM, moments after the end of the preliminary warm-up session conducted by the participants. A sheet of paper indicating the flow chart of the event's participant was attached to a white board located nearby with a set of magnets. The participants' handles and bracket positions were clearly advertised throughout the event, and as matches were won and lost, names were crossed out and the bracket's direction was highlighted with a coloured permanent marker, leading to the final confrontation. From the start of the ranking battle, a staff member tasked to manage the event announced the matchups and offered lively comments on the action, using a microphone that transmitted his words to the entirety of the first floor through a network of speakers installed in the venue. In addition to this system of live commentary that added noise and excitement to the sonic atmosphere of the venue, the matches were broadcast live on the television sets scattered around the venue, enabling customers to follow the action from anywhere in the venue. Although these matches were not streamed on any of A-cho's online outlets, the entirety of the tournament, which lasted approximately two hours, was published on A-cho's *YouTube* account two months later, on April 7, 2016. A-cho's webpage aggregated videos of all events taking place in the venue, including detailed information on their results, both from specific events and the monthly rankings.[8] Although the ranking battle only took place around two sets of *taisendai* cabinets, the performance of the commentator, combined with the sonic and visual apparatus installed throughout the venue, turned the event into an imposing force that could not be ignored by other patrons.

The event itself consisted of a preliminary round involving every ranking battle participant, followed by a short tournament involving the best contestants from the qualifying rounds. On February 25, 15 participants were registered and participated in qualifying rounds, of which eight successfully entered the subsequent tournament held the same evening. This was a small sample of the 115 players registered who accumulated points between November 2015 and September 2016, but a good proportion of 52 more dedicated players accumulated a total of three points or more during the same period. By looking at the larger picture of the *BlazBlue* Kansai competitive scene, one could easily notice the domination of a specific player called Enu'o over the rest of the players involved in this scene. Enu'o, an A-cho regular, had dominated the last four *BlazBlue* ranking battle seasons by an often-outrageous margin, scoring 149 points against his closest adversary at 79 points at the end of the fifth season. Enu'o's mastery of the game established him as a formidable opponent and usually designated him as the player to beat during the event, the king of the *BlazBlue* scene. On that night, however, and much to the excitement of the crowd, another player would attain a chance at seizing his crown.

The qualification rounds were played on two different sets of *taisendai* to maintain a quick flow of the games and a single stream of matches being played at any given time and retransmitted throughout the venue. Matches consisted of a best-of-three contest, at the end of which the best eight players were granted ranking points according to their position in the final tournament or their participation in the event. Subsequently, the two highest-ranked opponents of this tournament were pitted against one another in an 11-game gauntlet-style tournament lasting around 30 minutes, the winner of which was declared grand champion of the evening. During the whole process, participant players surrounded the machines closer than they would in normal time and, as players traded their seats to other players after the end of their matches, a constant flow of players animated the area. Players interacted with one another in between matches more frequently, keeping an eye on the action from up close while commenting on it. In comparison, active participants themselves rarely acknowledged each other before and after a match. While only a handful of observers watched the action during the first rounds, over time more and more patrons gathered around the machines to observe the action that was simultaneously increasing in intensity as good players were pitted against each other and the stakes of each match became heavier. Matches themselves, with their specific rhythm of 90-second rounds marked with a distinct escalation of tension and sudden release, seemed to exert a gravitational pull over players and observers as the body mass of people surrounding the machine contracted on one another more tightly, and then dilated back into the greater space of the game centre.

As tension escalated toward the showdown, active players were seemingly becoming more nervous as more players gathered around the only set of *taisendai* still in operation for the tournament, and active players reacted much more openly to the action of the screen, often letting show clear facial signs of dissatisfaction when losing a particularly tight round. Players were also performing more than before: more care was given to a straight sitting position and players sometimes exaggerated final blows on the cabinet's control panels. At the outset of the 143rd *BlazBlue* ranking battle, Enu'o would finish in second position, next to a player called Tenchi, who had been making his way into the group of 15 best players of the Kansai region competition over the previous year.

Once the conclusion of the main event was reached, participants reshuffled in the space in preparation for the second event: an 11-round mini-tournament (*jūichi sen gachi*) pitting the two best players of the night, Tenchi and Enu'o, against one another. After enquiring as to their opponent's machine of choice, both players started the tournament. The fight was fierce and hard-fought. The tournament extended to its limits in the 11th match, in which Tenchi and Enu'o emerged victorious five times; the 11th and last match would decide the grand champion of the night. The stakes were thus much higher for this tournament, and the fewer players involved meant that the focus rested exclusively upon the two contestants, while previous ranking battle participants stayed to watch this high-level match. Observers gravitated slightly around the machines so as to give participants enough space to play comfortably, but nonetheless, they ended up surrounding the machine entirely to the point that observing became difficult. The extended presence of the same two active players also encouraged observers to stay in between matches rather than dissipating within the venue; the ludo-egregore of the event exerted a greater influence over time than in normal conditions. Both participants and observers became much more vocal match after match, reaching its final climax in uncharacteristic loud cheers and applause when the tournament reached its end. Tenchi defeated Enu'o in the last match by preventing his opponent from performing an impressive comeback with very little health left.[9] As a relative outsider, Tenchi defeated the venue's most fearsome *BlazBlue* player on his own ground. Upon this final demonstration of emotion, the group surrounding the *BlazBlue* machines rapidly dissipated into other areas of the venue, leaving the inner circle of top *BlazBlue* contestants to discuss the events of the night in a relaxed atmosphere.

A step-by-step examination of this event revealed important characteristics that defined the ludo-egregoric generation located at the crossroads of *BlazBlue* as a ludic platform, the *taisendai* as the material conditions of the play activity, and the space that brought these elements together and connected them with human agents. The distinction of organized tournaments from regular organic play during hours of operation was that, while retaining a very distinct atmosphere surrounding the machines directly, these moments seemed to translate an extension of the ludo-egregore of the specific game, that is, the entity formed by the coming togetherness of both human and non-human agents, to the whole of the venue, a phenomenon that rarely occurs without some level of structure. At this point, it may have been recognized by other patrons and engaged in from a secure social distance while still influencing the performance of the players involved. It also brought players and observers socially closer together than in regular play sessions, as the players and their bodies contracted on one another following the intensity of the matches and the stakes at hand on a longer match-to-match term involving the same players. This is also evident from the heightened sonic activity originating from the observers' and participants' emotional involvement and the clear transition towards performance and communicative play on the part of the active player who acted in full acknowledgement of the observers. This event was also a vector of solidification of the latent social links nurtured within the venue, that took on more significance from the common experience of an emotionally intense activity. *BlazBlue* can be understood as a combination of specific rules and material conditions that all act as catalysts and make players vibrate at the same frequency. Traces of these events and the social vibration that it provided are recorded and made visible on A-cho's website, on which a picture of each night's four aces is published.[10]

Conclusion: Anonymity, Familiarity, and Competition

Between its informal meeting spaces, coffee shop, competitive events, and numerous online outlets, A-cho as an example of a contemporary game centre indicates the complex dynamics of providing a spatial setting in which game activity can be fully realized. A-cho, understood as a set of spatial conditions influencing the gameplay activity taking place within, contextualizes the ludic activity and situates it at the centre of a broader narrative associated with high-level competitive play places promoted by the joint effort of the operator and the team supporting its many facets. However, this narrative, tied to the space of the venue, remains profoundly performative; to maintain this greater narrative and make this contextualization effective, the space constantly reaffirms this stance through regularly organized competitive play events that reinforce this association. The performance of smaller narratives based on the notion of competition is broadcast widely in the venue and, to a certain extent, forced onto players to consume as a condition of the space. Tenchi's victory in the *BlazBlue* ranking battle event of February 25, 2016 acted as one more brick in the wall of the venue's larger narrative and a concrete example of how, in the space of game centres, anyone has a fair chance of emerging victorious. These organized tournaments, as so many narratives of victories and defeats taken as a whole, reflect and bestow a certain significance on the hundreds of seemingly more mundane matches taking place in the same space over the course of a day, projecting them onto A-cho's performed spatial narrative. The physical layout of the venue—the rows of fighting games located in the hub area, the private network of television screens showing fighting game action, and the coffee tables located at a comfortable distance for peeking at someone's ongoing match—is mobilized to support this narrative.

This set of spatial conditions exerts a great influence in shaping the form of players' engagements towards the game. Although fighting game cabinets at A-cho afford players with different stances and methods of active or passive engagement thanks to their design, the space of the venue itself and the broader narrative that it embodies also exude social affordances that guide players' social attitude in the venue and define what players should expect to happen around them during their play session. Both the machines and the space of the arcade afford players to allow other unacquainted players to observe their play sessions without causing any disturbances and from a relatively long distance. To play at A-cho means to watch, and agree to be watched by, other *player-flâneurs* as part of their ludic engagement, a fluid performance-audience relationship that is perhaps the goal of many venue-goers' ludic trajectories. Previous fieldwork conducted in game centres on the topic of Japanese fighting game communities also evokes the idea that fighting game players, aside from being influenced unconsciously by players observing the gameplay session, also sometimes seek to directly "enthrall the audience" by taking on the role of a performer "showing off their gameplay" to an excitable crowd (Kijima 262). However, though the same set of social affordances supports this form of low-level interpersonal interactions, deeper levels of interactions are rarely seen. Indeed, as A-cho represents itself as a space of performance and observation, the structure of the venue did not, at the time, afford casual conversation between players during or after the play; players engaging the same play session were physically separated from each other by the game cabinets, and the victor is usually allowed to play an extra match at no cost. This space's non-written rule set includes the idea that talking to opponents is frowned upon. However, it is precisely this low social engagement threshold that makes possible the creation of a public space that eases player interaction through games with little at stake. It is at the intersection of these ludic trajectories afforded by space and machine design that individual ludo-egregoric moments, simultaneously taking place in space and time, are generated.

The operators of A-cho also strive to create a comfortable and familiar space that remains accessible beyond the physical boundaries of the space by reaching players through the other platforms that regiment their daily lives. Through its numerous online outlets and its staff's dedication to creating a friendly and approachable atmosphere through social media, A-cho is, in reality, composed of many virtual entry points so as to maintain close contact with its user base, thus extending the space of the venue and its imaginary online. However, the rise of social media and internet outlets as means of communication for arcade game fans does not, as one would think, undermine the value of game centre of places of exchange and communication (Katō, "Online jidai no gēmu sentā"). Rather, they provide complementary layers to the arcade experience through their narrative and communicative aspect that further contribute to defining the space and contextualizing the activity that takes place within. Thus, the material and conversation that permeate this online presence also act as additional agents influencing the ludic experience of A-cho and the ludo-egregores generated by its games.

Notes

1 On these special days, called "tai'i betsu taisen suichō DAY," some machines are reserved to players ranked in fifteenth position or less.
2 Since 2017, A-cho has also operated a *Twitch* account to relay its major tournaments.
3 Many posts about the mobile game *Shironeko purojekuto* were published in early 2016.
4 Kaomoji are suites of horizontal characters used to communicate emotions using ASCII and Shift JIS characters, similar to how emoticons do the same through vertical character positioning. They have been widely used in blog posts and private communication in Japan, and are especially popular amongst teenage girls (Karpinska et al. 68). These pre-date emoticons, which automatically translate specific characters to images, as a form of quick and image-based form of digital communication. For more information, see Giannoulis and Wilde.
5 While pertinent to the close reading of this space, the topic of maid cafés in Japan falls outside the reach of this project. For more information, see Galbraith (184–226).
6 The designs of playable characters featured in the *BlazBlue* game series appear to be inspired by archetypes found in works of Japanese animation and manga, ranging from androids, magical girls, and big-muscled swordsmen, to uncanny creatures. While the topic falls outside the reach of this project, the roster could also be examined in terms of the representation of gender stereotypes (Hutchinson, "Gender Stereotypes") and Asia in general from a Japanese perspective (Hutchinson, "Virtual Colonialism"), which may well play a part in the public performance of arcade fighting games.
7 This project's methodology prevented the acquisition of meaningful data on the important notion of player-character identification in fighting games, but Goto-Jones' and Kijima's work on the topic provides useful contextualization. In drawing parallels between fighting games and martial arts, Goto-Jones sheds light on the emotional connection between the player, the character and the joystick (the joystar), highlighting the erosion of the duality between human and technology at the heart of the practice (69–70). Kijima further articulates this in highlighting the importance of one's main character (*my-chara*) in order to express one's particular playstyle and individuality, an important element in the context where the player, in the act of playing, is thrust both into the position of performer and observer of his/her own practice (263).
8 Every year or so, A-cho published the final rankings for a set period of time as an Excel document before restarting the rankings for another "season". The document featured participants' handles, ranking points (attributed for qualification round results and final tournament position), favoured character, and "home" game centre.
9 Harper also highlights how a great fighting game match does not depend only on technical prowess or mastery but also on contextual dynamics of drama and emotions, ideally reacting to the crowd's input throughout the match (42). In this case, the stakes between the two players generated a high level of engagement and reaction from the crowd of observers, which the players timidly acknowledged.
10 The precise ranking data of the event were acquired from this specific page on A-cho's website ("Dai hyaku yonjū").

Works Cited

Arcana Heart. Arcade videogame cabinet, Examu, 2009.

Beatmania. Arcade videogame cabinet, Konami, 1997.

Benjamin, Walter. *The Arcades Project*. 1999. Edited by Rolf Tiedemann, translated by Howard Eiland and Kevin MacLaughlin, The Belknap P of Harvard UP, 2002.

BlazBlue. Arcade videogame cabinet, Arc System Works, 2008.

BlazBlue: Continuum Shift. Arcade videogame cabinet, Arc System Works, 2009.

Chalfen, Richard, and Mai Murui. "Print Club Photography in Japan: Framing Social Relationship." *Visual Studies*, vol. 16, no. 1, 2001, pp. 55–73.

Code of Joker. Arcade videogame cabinet, Sega, 2013.

"Dai hyaku yonjū mikkai kansai ranbato [143rd Kansai Ranking Battle]." *a-cho.com*, https://web.archive.org/web/20160407195707/; http://www.a-cho.com/ac/bb/20160225.html.

Dai hyaku yonjūsan kai a-cho BBCF kansai ranbato shūryōgo jūichi-sen gachi 2016. 2. 25 [*After the 143th BBCF A-cho Ranking Battle – The Eleven Matches of Importance – 2016.2.25*]. Directed by a-cho GAME, YouTube video, https://www.youtube.com/watch?v=xaahKftAfdI&list=PL6ciyIYcGWJFMSqHtS8YZkyQk_elODPSg&index=81. Accessed 8 July 2023.

Dance Dance Revolution. Arcade videogame cabinet, Konami, 1998.

Dance Evolution. Arcade videogame cabinet, Konami, 2010.

Darkstalkers. Arcade videogame cabinet, Capcom, 1994.

Dissidia Final Fantasy NT. Arcade videogame cabinet, Square Enix, 2015.

Fatal Fury. Arcade videogame cabinet, Capcom, 1991.

Galbraith, Patrick W. *Otaku and the Struggle for Imagination in Japan*. Duke UP, 2019.

Gēmu sentā shī ekkusu [*Game Center CX*], Television series, Fuji TV, 2003–2023.

Giannoulis, Elena, and Lukas R. A. Wilde, editors. *Emoticons, Kaomoji, and Emoji: The Transformation of Communication in the Digital Age*. Routledge, 2019.

Goto-Jones, Christopher S. *The Virtual Ninja Manifesto: Fighting Games, Martial Arts and Gamic Orientalism*. Rowman & Littlefield International, 2016.

Guilty Gear. Arcade videogame cabinet, Arc System Works, 1998.

Harper, Todd. *The Culture of Digital Fighting Games: Performance and Practice*. Routledge, Taylor & Francis Group, 2014.

Hatsune Miku: Project DIVA Arcade. Arcade videogame cabinet, Sega, 2010.

Hochschild, Arlie Russell. *The Managed Heart: Commercialization of Human Feeling*. U of California P, 2003.

Hutchinson, Rachael. "Gender Stereotypes in Japanese Fighting Games: Effects on Identification and Immersion." *The Journal of New Media & Culture*, vol. 10, no. 1, 2015, https://ibiblio.org/nmediac/summer2015/GenderStereotypes.htm.

———. "Virtual Colonialism: Japan's Others in Soul Calibur." *Transnational Contexts of Culture, Gender, Class, and Colonialism in Play*, edited by Alexis Pulos and S. Austin Lee, Palgrave Macmillan, 2016, pp. 155–78.

The Idolmaster. Arcade videogame cabinet, Namco, 2005.

Ishii, Zenji. *Gēmu sentā kunonikuruzu: 1972–2017* [*Game Centres Chronicles: 1972–2017*]. Standards, 2017.

Jubeat. Arcade videogame cabinet, Konami, 2008.

Karpinska, Marzena, Paula Kurzawska, and Katarzyna Rozanska. "Emoticons: Digital Lingua Franca or a Culture-Specific Product Leading to Misunderstandings?" *Emoticons, Kaomoji, and Emoji: The Transformation of Communication in the Digital Age*, edited by Elena Giannoulis and Lukas R. A. Wilde, Routledge, 2019, pp. 67–81.

Katō, Hiroyasu. "Online jidai no gēmu sentā [Game Centres in the Online Age]." *Digitaru no kiwa – jōhō to busshitsu ga majiwaru genzaichiten* [*The Digital Moment – Contemporary Mixing of Information and Materiality*], Seigakuin daigaku shuppansha, 2014, pp. 267–305.

Kijima, Yoshimasa. "The Fighting Gamer Otaku Community: What Are They 'Fighting' About." *Fandom Unbound: Otaku Culture in a Connected World*, edited by Daisuke Okabe Mizuko Ito and Izumi Tsuji, Yale UP, 2012, pp. 249–75.

Kirkpatrick, Graeme. *Computer Games and the Social Imaginary*. Polity P, 2013.

Mai Mai. Arcade videogame cabinet, Sega, 2012.

Mobile Suit Gundam: Extreme Vs. Arcade videogame cabinet, Bandai Namco, 2010.

Museca. Arcade videogame cabinet, Konami, 2015.

Pokken Tournament. Arcade videogame cabinet, Bandai Namco, 2015.
Purinto Kurabu. Photo booth cabinet, Atlus, 1995.
Puyo-Puyo Quest. Arcade videogame cabinet, Sega, 2013.
Shīa, [@S1Amk]. "Nanka Osonae Mono Shinagara Dogeiza Shiteru Raburaibā Irundakedo Wwwwwwwwwwwwwwwwwwwwwwwwwwww [Somehow, There Is a Love Liver Making an Offer Kneeling on the Ground (Laughing)]." *Twitter*, 2 Aug. 2015, https://twitter.com/S1Amk/status/627698645970714624.
Shironeko Purojekuto. Mobile device videogame, COLOPL, 2014.
Sound Voltext. Arcade videogame cabinet, Konami, 2011.
Street Fighter. Arcade videogame cabinet, Capcom, 1987.
Street Fighter II. Arcade videogame cabinet, Capcom, 1991.
Street Fighter IV. Arcade videogame cabinet, Capcom, 2008.
Taiko no tetsujin. Arcade videogame cabinet, Namco, 2001.
Tekken 7. Arcade videogame cabinet, Bandai Namco, 2015.
Virtua Fighter. Arcade videogame cabinet, Sega, 1993.
Virtua Fighter 4. Arcade videogame cabinet, Sega, 2001.
World Club Championship Football. Arcade videogame cabinet, Sega, 2002.

6 Old Surfaces, New Interfaces

Palimpsest and Territorialization in Tsujishōten

I activate the self-lock mechanism installed on the rear wheel of the bicycle provided by the apartment complex where I am staying, after parking it on the side of the street. The device does not seem to be secure, but in Kyoto, I am sure, from experience, that I will find it untouched when I head out to leave. There are few tourists around this part of the city, despite its being located so close to the city's main train station; this semi-residential area is more geared to locals' needs than to those of visitors in search of the mystic feel of the old imperial capital. The shops on the street are advertised by discoloured placards that may well have been there for decades without being replaced or repainted. The few bicycles similarly parked near the entrance of Tsujishōten, the game centre I am planning to visit today, suggest that I should not judge its popularity by this first impression.

As I step through the automatic glass door and into the venue, I am greeted by an unidentifiable ruckus that is uncharacteristic of the game centres I have visited so far. There do not seem to be that many people inside. As I quickly scan the machines in the venue, I notice that most of them are the same modern network-connected games as those in larger game centres, but the structure of the venue itself is anything but contemporary. Columns and subsections are numerous, and I find myself getting slightly lost in a space that is not much bigger than a neighbourhood family-run restaurant, due to an archaic and confusing architectural design. This combination of new machines and old space betrays the previous use of the space as a café; tables and old machines have been replaced by newer ones, but an old aura still persists. The owner is at a desk in a corner of the venue watching over a collection of snacks and drinks. I receive confirmation that this game centre has existed since the 1970s. This might the oldest game centre that I have ever visited.

I wander through the venue. The players are so close to the aisles that one cannot help but look away from the screen for a second to acknowledge my presence. I probably stand out from most of the regulars of this arcade, but perhaps they are expecting somebody. I have to squeeze my body between the old stools and the machine behind them so as not to disturb the game session. As I finally reach the far end of the venue, the source of the loud noise that hit me when I entered becomes clear: a group of players playing some old arcade game machine, who are seemingly connected to one another. I do not dare approach to confirm what game

DOI: 10.4324/9781003273776-8

they are replaying, because it would be too obvious that I would be peeking in on their game and I want to avoid causing any discomfort. That area has become their territory; judging from the food containers scattered around them, they have been there for a while and plan to remain there for longer.

—

Ekimae: Game Centres and Palimpsests

The golden years of the Japanese arcade in the late 1970s were characterized by the emergence of thousands of small venues operating on a very human scale. Most of these shops, which occupied small commercial spaces located in small to medium-rise residential areas and, perhaps more importantly, around train stations that acted as public transportation hubs, were operated directly by their owners, who could earn a living from the income that their operation provided. These convenient neighbourhood business operations located on people's daily routes could attract children on their way home from school or salarymen on their lunch breaks. For the most part, these were familiar safe spaces in which one could expect consistency; the dedicated operating staff who owned the space rarely changed, and the players were familiar faces from the neighbourhood. Unlike bigger establishments whose space is more structured around the economic roles of games, these types of game centres allow users to territorialize the space in a more intimate and personal manner. Fictional works that take place in game centres, such as the television series *No kon kiddo* (*No Continue Kid*) produced by Dai Satō, and Gichi Ōtsuka's novel *Ji endo obu arukadia* (*The End of Arcadia*), all released in the second decade of the 2000s, are fuelled by the idealization of these spaces. *Ekimae* game centres (or game centres facing train stations), as they are often called, embody Japan's nostalgia for arcade gaming and the retro games often associated with the experience.

The exodus of families to the suburbs and the emergence of big-box game centres in the 1990s drove customers away from these small and poorly lit places. Years of continuous negative press about game centres also took their toll on the imagination of the broader population and eventually dissuaded parts of the gaming population from visiting them. However, some of these arcades have found ways to remain relevant within an ever-changing urban ecosystem characterized by a relentless drive for novelty and the increasing reliability of network connectivity, which diminishes the incentive to remain loyal to a specific shop as player profiles and data have become mobile due to the invention and spread of IC cards (integrated circuit cards). Although none of them have remained exactly as they were at their zenith, their existence is a testimony to the humbler and more intimate nature of gaming in public in contemporary Japan. Transformation, erasure, and addition of new elements in the form of material conditions of public play and software are at the heart of the dynamics specific to these places. However, as games and cabinets are removed from the canvas of the game centre in favour of more up-to-date titles and machines, a certain palimpsestic presence of those that have been displaced remains, a presence that may be identified through the way players approach and interact with the new ludic assemblages populating the space.

Originally, the term *palimpsest* refers to an original script having been erased from or scraped off its surface in order to write a new text; the palimpsest is a compound of an existing text with the traces of a previous one that is still partly visible or could potentially be uncovered by technical means (Dillon 10). In 1845, Thomas De Quincey was the first major theoretician to use this term in a figurative fashion, which in turn led to the vast repurposing of this term in many other disciplines such as "architecture, geography, geology, palaeontology, glaciology, astrophysics, biochemistry, genetics, neuroscience, neurobiology, neuro-computing and information technology" (Dillon 1). The idea of the palimpsest has since become an important critical lens through which material from different fields finds a common ground of comparison, whether on a physical scale, as in architecture, or on a more theoretical level. If we consider the palimpsest on an abstract level—as the accidental inter- or transtextuality (Genette 7) of different texts, materials, or practices based on their existence, and traces of their existence, in a commonly shared support or platform in different periods of time. The practice of arcade gaming in Japan itself can be read and interpreted through the metaphor of a palimpsestuous construct. The spatial conditions of older individual venues are constantly being modified; to adapt to new machines or the ludic trajectories of their clientele, venues are restructured and often renovated, but traces often remain under the new purpose and function that the space is meant to serve.

Tsujishōten is an example of a game centre space that allows us to read the phenomenon of playing in public from a more historical point of view, and thus adopt a palimpsestic perspective on the evolution and transformation of the game centre space, which can partly be uncovered by examining the ludo-egregores generated therein. Observation data from this specific game centre also provided concrete examples of a variety of practices related to the use and appropriation of space and cabinet in the context of public play. This chapter discusses the two such practices that are most pertinent for this study: the use of cabinet space beyond that of its primary purpose as a videogame-playing device, as well as the appropriation of space by players through a process of territorializing the assemblage of the game cabinet and the space of the venue through different tactics involving objects, actions, and symbols.

Tsujishōten: Structure and Spatial Design

Established in 1978, Tsujishōten is in a two-story building on Higashi Street, just south of Kyoto Station, the main transportation hub of the city. The area surrounding the game centre consists of a mix of low-rise and medium-rise buildings evenly spread amongst residential and small commercial areas. *Tsujishōten*, which literally means "crossroad shop", is a relatively common name for stores. As its name indicates, it is located close to an intersection next to other businesses, including a small Panasonic radio shop, a barber shop, and a small udon noodle restaurant. The game centre itself is located between that restaurant and a two-story brick house.

Figure 6.1 Tsujishōten's facade on the afternoon of February 4, 2016. Surrounded by vending machines, venue-goers meet in front of the arcade. The quiet street environment enables spontaneous gatherings (photograph by the author).

Other nighttime businesses, such as a bring-your-own-drink mahjong game parlour and an izakaya bar that specializes in okonomiyaki, characterize this small-scale commercial enclave that, despite its location within walking distance from the Kyoto train station and an AEON department store, still retains the qualities and general feeling of a quiet neighbourhood.

Tsujishōten occupies the ground floor section of the two-story building that houses it. Motorcycles and bicycles belonging to customers are usually parked by the road facing the front entrance, which is itself sheltered from the sun by an umbrella roof that also protects three vending machines from the elements. A complimentary umbrella rack is also located near the main door. A few posters advertising rhythm games and a sign above the main door that is lit up at night, which reads "Video Game K.T.T.", perhaps the former name of the store, are the only signs indicating a game centre. The other windows are shut by safety fences from inside the building, preventing bystanders from peeking inside and any sort of light from entering the venue. On the door, an official sticker city indicates that the store is compliant with Kyoto city's Juvenile Health Development Cooperation Project (seishōnen kenzen ikusei kyōryoku jigyō) and reminds its clientele that people under 16 are not permitted entry past 6:00 PM, and that minors should leave the premises before 10:00 PM. The front door is electric, and it slides open upon the touch of a button located on the right-hand side.

Between February and March 2016, the period within which I observed the game centre, one could directly enter the venue through its rhythm game section before accessing a tight corridor leading to the back end of the venue. Its small size prevented any sort of two-way circulation for players. The general atmosphere of the venue was similar to that of older game centres from the 1980s; the venue was dimly lit and very cramped, machines were generally stuck into corners that are difficult to find, and the resulting corridors were difficult to navigate, only allowing one person to walk through at a time. Directly at the right-hand side of the entrance, the venue supervisor tended to administrative tasks from his/her little office and ensured that the place remained under surveillance. The surveillance shift was split between two staff members; though visitors could not see them directly while passing by, visual contact could be established easily by peeking into the office from a small entryway or over the counter.

The primary hub of rhythm game machines, which featured a large range of some of the newest network-enabled cabinets, was relatively spacious. Located at the left-hand side of the venue, the machines were laid out in a square-like space that felt separated from the venue and featured only two pathways. The shutters on the large glass seen from the outside prevented light from glaring on the screens, but also provided a sense of timelessness, as it became difficult to tell what time of day it was from the inside. A few stools in the centre of the square allowed players to sit and wait their turn, or, more commonly, wait for a friend to finish their play session. A rack with two plastic baskets also allowed users to store their valuables or clothing items while they played. The bright purple colours of the *Mai Mai* and *Jubeat* machines illuminated the space and dominated the colour scheme of this section. Like some other games in the venue, such as *Wonderland Wars* and *Border Break,* most rhythm game cabinets, and especially those of *Hatsune Miku: Project DIVA Arcade*, were equipped with self-recording devices that allow players to record their play session on a USB key to bring home, a service not typically provided by most commercial big-box game centres.

Facing the rhythm game section, the manager of the game centre would often sit in a small office to watch television and security cameras during the centre's hours of operation. A freezer, a fridge, and a collection of various brands of instant noodle packages were organized around the office. Players could buy cold drinks, frozen treats, or snacks directly from the manager; if they purchased instant ramen, the manager would invite them to wait at a cabinet where he would deliver it directly to the player after having prepared it. Such "table service" and the type of food available are unusual for this type of establishment; ice cream and drinks are usually the staples of game centres, since other food items such as instant ramen tend to leave a mess when eaten sitting down at a game cabinet used as a table. Indeed, it was not unusual to find empty ramen containers, paper towels, or chopsticks on game cabinets for relatively long periods before the manager tending the store at this particular time eventually came to remove the trash and clean the machines.

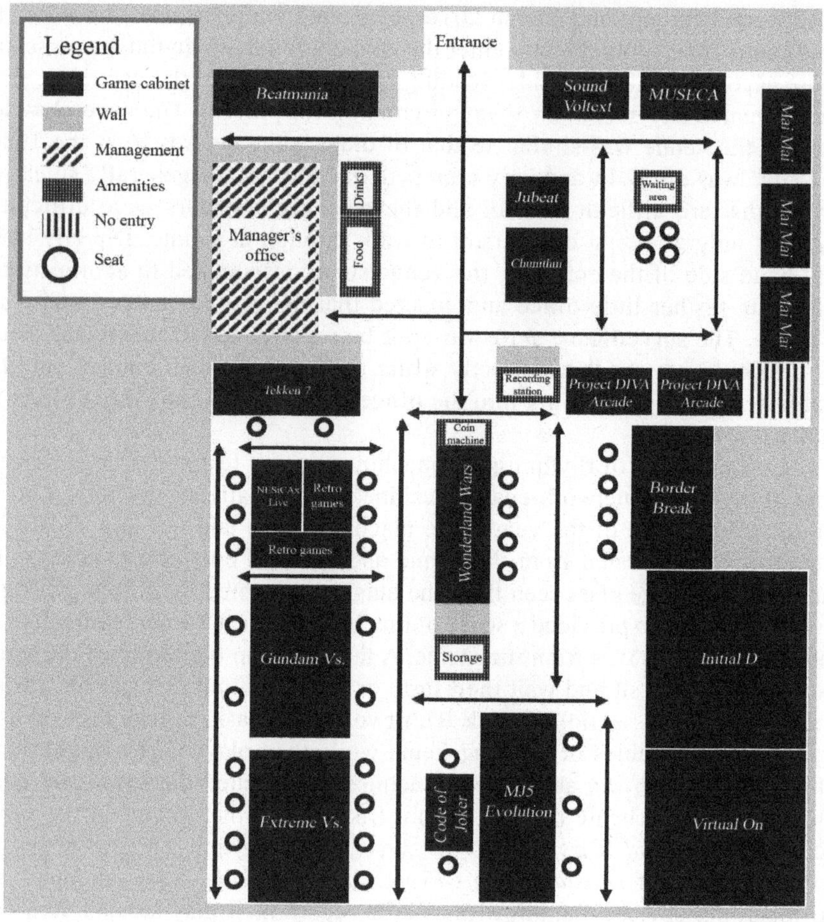

Figure 6.2 Visual representation of Tsujishōten's floor map. The design of the venue creates a few low-circulation spots, providing customers with relative intimacy during play sessions (image by the author).

The south side of the game centre, which constitutes most of the floor space of the venue, was structured by an assortment of modern and retro game machines tightly organized so as to maximize the number of machines in the space while still allowing players to walk through the venue relatively easily. The majority of the games in this section of the venue were Sega-branded products and network-connected; games such as *Wonderland Wars*, *Border Break,* and *Code of Joker* were the most contemporary machines and, given their novelty aspect, they were located near the entrance, in contact with most foot traffic in the venue. A *NesicaXLive*[1] cabinet and a *Tekken 7* machine, both offering discounted play sessions compared to other venues at 150 yen for two *NesicaXLive* credits and two *Tekken 7* credits for 100 yen, provided more traditional game styles such as fighting games and shoot'em ups; they occupied a less prestigious place, located in the eastern back end in which pathways and aisles were narrow. A mahjong game was relegated to the isolated far back end of the venue, and at the left-hand side of the back end was a collection of sit-down machines playing two variations of the team-based robot-fighting game *Gundam VS.*, based on the anime series of the same name. In total, 12 machines were dedicated to this game series, which indicated the focus of this game centre in terms of games and public. If A-cho catered to the *BlazBlue* fighting game scene, Tsujishōten relied on the *Gundam VS.* series to bring in customers. The latter machines were located in the south-east corner of the venue.

First released in 2008, *Mobile Suit Gundam: Gundam Vs. Gundam* (*Gundam Vs.* hereafter) is a multiplayer fighting game published by Branpresto that pits the most memorable robots of the eponymous anime series against each other. Players, divided into two teams, fight each other over a three-dimensional battlefield with their robot of choice; depending on their character, they can use a variety of long-range and melee weapons to take down their opponents, each time depleting the opposing team's respawn points. Each robot has an attributed respawn point value of either 1,000, 2,000, or 3,000, and upon destruction, their value is then subtracted from its team's remaining respawn point total, which is initially set at 6,000. The more powerful the robot, the more points it depletes from its own team's total when an opposing player takes it down; the team that reduces their opponent's respawn points to zero wins the battle. The original *Gundam Vs.* game, now discontinued, spanned a sequel, *Mobile Suit Gundam: Gundam Vs. Gundam NEXT* (Bandai Namco) operating on the same engine, in 2009, as well as a PlayStation Portable version in the same year. Although this relatively old game could be considered technically outdated, Tsujishōten dedicated four of its standard game cabinets to it. However, near the back end of the venue, a few additional machines with the capability of linking up to eight players in the same match operated the most up-to-date version of this successful arcade game.

With an initial version released in 2010, *Mobile Suit Gundam: Extreme Vs.* (hereafter cited as *Extreme Vs.*) effectively replaced the *Gundam Vs.* series and brought many design elements in line with the newest arcade game trends of the time, adding more content by adapting the software to allow regular updates. *Extreme Vs.* features a refined multiplayer robot-fighting experience similar to its predecessor, but implements network connectivity, high-definition graphics, an IC card system to allow players to establish a personalized profile, and a satellite-based arcade cabinet system similar to other network-based game series such as *Sengoku taisen* and *Lord of Vermillion.* A satellite cabinet system usually features four game cabinets and an additional "live monitor" cabinet that acts as a storefront for activities parallel to the game itself. Players can access replays of their previous matches, look up the global player rankings of the game, and purchase bonus and cosmetic items. The live cabinet also relays live matches within the venue, thus acting as an "attract mode" for other players within the venue who can observe the action on a dedicated screen instead of looking directly over the shoulders of players engaged with the machines. This effectively takes advantage of the game's high-quality visuals to attract observers, but also creates a certain distance between the observer and the players themselves; the matches are mediated by a different screen that makes the action more understandable for other venue-goers by presenting all active players' perspectives simultaneously, by dividing the screen into four parts rather than focusing on a single one. The live cabinet shifts focus away from players as the centre of attention by providing a different medium and, as a result, lessens the stakes for individual players to provide an embodied performance.

Tsujishōten's floor layout, however, did not allow the live monitor cabinet to be placed comfortably, and this cabinet was therefore absent from the premises. The machines that operated variations of the *Gundam Vs.* series were positioned similarly to the *taisendai* fighting cabinets, with the machines set up in two rows of six machines back to back. All types of *Gundam Vs.* machines were grouped in the south-west corner of the game centre, thus forming yet another dedicated zone for a specific genre that, due to the arrangement of the other machines, was secluded from the rest of the venue, which created a sense of isolation within the greater arcade space. Tsujishōten also used a different pricing strategy based on hourly rates to draw customers in to play these games. Indeed, for the price of 2,000 yen,[2] a group of four players could rent unrestricted access to four of the six *Extreme Vs.* machines and play as much as desired for an hour at a time. These machines required multiple players in the same space to reach their full potential, a condition that is often fulfilled in larger game centres at peak hours when people often lined up to get a chance to play the game, albeit with strangers with whom communication was at a minimum. However, Tsujishōten did not attract enough foot traffic to count on regular incentives to fill its seats. Therefore, the hourly rate ensured that a minimum of four machines would stay busy over a set period, a respectable solution despite the steep loss of revenue that it represented. A side effect of this arrangement was the joint presence of players who have already befriended one another outside the space of the arcade which, partly due to the structure of the venue, enabled them to bring and express this friendship in the space in a state of relative social isolation.

The eastern side of the venue's back end was characterized by the presence of isolated sets of machines of various genres. A few cabinets of *Sega network taisen mahjoong 5 evolution* were at the far back of the venue, just opposite two *Code of Joker* collectible virtual card game machines, while an imposing row of *Initial D* and *Cyber Trooper Virtual-On* (hereafter cited as *Virtual-On*) cabinets, respectively, a driving and robot-fighting game, occupied the far east corner. These machines were rarely used but were similarly located in a corner of the arcade that was difficult to observe from afar due to the arrangement of the machines on the floor. One had to walk close to the machines to verify whether a player was already using it or not. In order to cut the power expenses of the arcade, and potentially the amount of noise within, the *Virtual-On* cabinets were not powered on during hours of operation and were never on during the observation period. A piece of paper taped to one of the cabinets indicated that players need to directly ask the venue operator should anyone desire to pay the game in order to have the power turned on and the game activated. In this way, machine maintenance and power expenses were preserved.

These elements demonstrate how the space of the arcade supported relatively long-term engagements with the machine through hourly rates and the incentives for friends to come along and enjoy videogames together. Indeed, Tsujishōten is a meeting place for youth, a familiar spot to socialize through videogames, and an urban landmark in front of which people wait for friends to arrive. However, behind its visible structure and spatial organization is the intention of providing a comfortable and familiar space for regular commuters in order to tempt them into spending a 100 yen on a videogame experience on their way home. Game centres, at this specific moment of time usually situated between 4:00 and 7:00 PM, also provide a space for unwinding from busy work or school days before fulfilling domestic responsibilities at home. In Tsujishōten, this aspect of the space was expressed in the different types of amenities available for players: washrooms, baskets to store clothing items, including gloves, for those who play rhythm games, ashtrays, change dispensing machines, and hand towel distributors used to wash one's hands after playing. Other elements and practices that characterized Tsujishōten transcended the norms of the industry in order to create a sense of place that feels comfortable, homelike, and informal. One of the fundamental parts of this space was the wardrobe-like metallic rack located in the middle of the venue, on which a few plastic hangers were left to encourage patrons to leave their coats on the structure and their bags on one of the two shelves located at the waist and knee levels. The limited space of the venue, which also limited the number of players present in the arcade at any given time,

Figure 6.3 Storage rack filled with clothes and bags in Tsujishōten. This amenity allows players to concentrate on the games in the context of a small playing space without individualized storage (photograph by the author).

made the presence of a coat hanger viable to maximize floor space and increase the comfort of their play session, and perhaps encourage them to extend their stay.

The general state of disrepair of Tsujishōten's environment and furniture further suggested its informal approach to the relationships between players. It was not unusual to encounter a variety of trash around the machines during hours of operation, and, unlike larger establishments, not much effort was spent on hiding the numerous power and network cables of the machines from view or even keep them out of the players' way. Larger game centres tend to hide all aspects of maintenance or power management in order to retain an unhindered focus on the machines and their play opportunities. The machines here were thus not objects of an elaborate pristine or exotic *mise en scène*, but felt as though they belonged to a more regular daily experience devoid of artifice. The light bulbs on the ceiling sometimes did not work or were missing entirely, which contributed to the dim lighting of the venue. While they were sparsely used, red water buckets acted as makeshift trash and recycling bins, distributed in several corners of the venue or behind the often badly damaged seats that provided the ideal sitting position at which to play games but offer little comfort for long play sessions. The administrative office was located at the front of the venue and was not separated from the play area by a wall or a door, also suggesting the ease of communication between management and players. From the main area of the floor, one was able to see the inside of the office, including the television screen used to monitor the venue, the extensive set of keys used to access the inside of the machines, the faucet and microwave, and other documents. The operator made himself available to his clientele for help or casual conversation.

In many ways, the dynamics at play in Tsujishōten, with regard both to the play patterns of customers and to the ethos of the venue, was deeply influenced by its location and the architectural structure of the venue, which displayed toned-down elements inherited from the time when the game centre first opened its doors in the latter half of the 1970s. Tsujishōten did not house any game machines or software that could be considered "retro", such as cocktail game cabinets or games from the 1980s or earlier; despite its age, the venue did not bank on nostalgia or try to appeal to a customer base that is particularly game-savvy. The orientation of the venue was not that of a time capsule, but rather a space that housed some of the most up-to-date arcade game machines, though without the standard floor space that bigger venues have. The placement of the machines was adapted to the structure of the venue and its customer base, which in the process influenced the way in which they are played, despite being the same games usually found in standard-size corporate game centres. While the games and machines within the venue were completely different from the ones in its early days, the players' engagement with them was influenced by the venue's environmental conditions. From the dim lighting and the tight spacing between machines that allowed isolation within the venue to the direct social contact with the management and the facilitation of gregarious play dynamics with friendship established outside the bounds of the game centre, public gaming in Tsujishōten could be characterized as palimpsestuous, as a space whose previous use has been erased. The gameplay mechanics observed within could be approached as different layers, some of which could be attributed to older practices associated with arcade video gaming, but since then have been erased. In this case, the architecture of the game centre was the strongest historical link between this space and 1970s arcades, despite the absence of concrete traces of their past presence.

The space of Tsujishōten, as a palimpsest of the game-playing activity, was thus composed of different ludic trajectories than the ones characterizing other spaces such as A-cho, but this phenomenon was also diverse and different on a temporal level. The periods of activity at this specific venue also showed evidence of a thoroughly different social rhythm throughout the day, despite identical operating hours of 10:00 AM to 12:00 AM. Tsujishōten predominantly attracted foot traffic coming in and out of Kyoto station, and as a result, its player base fluctuated in relation to commute rush hours and days of the week. The different types of ludic trajectories that it attracted and the ludo-egregore created by the social affordances of the venue and the ludic qualities of the games could be recognized from the observation samples collected at different times in February 2016 and compared in order to identify the regime of machine interaction, both ludic and non-ludic, and isolate the defining traits of the ludo-egregore in Tsujishōten.

Rhythm and Fluctuations: Public Space as an Extension of Home

I conducted my research in Tsujishōten in the two weeks between February 19 and March 2, 2016, allowing for thorough observations throughout different times of the week and various hours of the day. However, weekends had to be excluded due to issues of logistics; the data gathered here are thus based on the days between Monday and Friday, which accounts for the status of the venue as part of some commuters' routines. Data gathered on the number of players in the venue and their various levels of interaction demonstrate that the game centre operated on a shifting daily rhythm; not only did the flow of customers coming to Tsujishōten fluctuate greatly during the day, but the interpersonal interactions displayed between players also changed. Studying the rhythm of the place revealed the coexistence of different modes of engagement with the machines and with the space. While some users approached the cabinet-laden space as an extension of home where one was free to relax in a familiar setting, others came in groups to make full use of the space's function as a social gathering place. In every case, however, the machines were periodically used for purposes other than ludic ones, which put this game centre in a unique position amongst the ones examined in this project. Many of the defining traits of this environment, and the most interesting for this study, were not necessarily related to videogame playing, but were instead located around it. At different times of the day, Tsujishōten embodied the paradox of enabling both collective and intimate spaces.

From 10:00 AM to the end of the afternoon, around 4:30 PM, the number of players present in Tsujishōten was very low, and the users present tended to engage with the machines on an individual level or in pairs. On March 2, 2016, the player count at 2:00 PM was four players, of whom two were engaged with the *Initial D* driving game machines with their coats hanging off the driver's seat, while two others played *Tekken 7* side-by-side, complementing their play session with snacks, drinks, and cigarettes. Later, at around 3:30 PM, the situation remained comparable, but a small group formed around the *Tekken 7* machines, watching the same players taking on one another through the game. At the same moment, other players started to occupy different parts of the space; one player enjoyed the rhythm game space, while another played against online opponents at a *Code of Joker* cabinet. An hour later, a second customer entered the rhythm game space segregated from the rest of the venue, and both players began a long multiplayer session on the rhythm game *Mai Mai*, which features a two-player mode allowing two cabinets to simultaneously play over the same song and compare their scores. The two high-school-aged boys then proceeded to enjoy the rest of the evening. The two occupied the whole rhythm game subspace and appropriated it as a sort of personal space for both of them. They made a lot of noise during and after gameplay, particularly vocal expressions of satisfaction and defeat, and also physically interacted with the space at large in typically non-conventional ways, such as performing very exuberantly before suddenly lying on the floor with both arms extended to rest, a type of behaviour that would conventionally be difficult to perform in a normal setting.

Every day from 4:30 PM onward, as the school and work day came to an end, more customers walked into the venue, and one could witness the formation of small groups of players around cabinet sets. On March 2, for example, from that time onward, all game activities occurring in the venue involved groups of two players or more that were either observing *Tekken 7* matches, playing *Mai Mai* together, or enjoying a few races of *Initial D* in networked mode. This was the busiest time for Tsujishōten observed during the field work. Despite the very tight space to which they were confined, the racing game cabinets often attracted groups of players observing the action from close up, sometimes sitting on seats and cabinets directly beside them. The layout of this section of the centre prevented casual observation of other players' play sessions from a safe interpersonal distance as in A-cho; performers and observers had to be very close to one another to allow observation and, given the social codes of game centres based on limited social interactions between strangers, this spatial disposition tended to be tailored for groups of people with previously existing social bonds. Surrounded by familiar faces, their bags scattered around the machines and casually eating bowls of instant ramen noodles, players seemed empowered and comfortable enough to be more vocal and physically demonstrative in their play style, accentuating their movements. One of the players I observed on February 25 was comfortable enough to play the game without shoes on.

In most instances, the cabinets in the venue were not used to their maximum capacity; plenty of empty space, buffer space, and unoccupied cabinets made up the usual spatial structure of the space and any game sessions. This situation also demonstrated that patrons did not use a great majority of the floor space for strictly ludic purposes, and instead of actively engaging with the machines, many players used them for other purposes than to fill their immediate needs. Many customers used the cabinets to kill time on smartphones and other handheld devices, to sit at in order to observe the play session of a neighbouring friend, or, as I observed on Friday, February 19, at 8:30 PM, even as a makeshift bed to be used for a quick nap. These types of non-ludic behaviours were more commonly found in the south-east corner of the venue, and generally involved the racing game and the *Virtual On* cabinets; the design of these machines, which feature elaborate and comfortable plastic seats that provide an additional layer of isolation due to their large edges, as well as their location in the most isolated corner of the venue, could be understood as incentives to use the cabinet in this particular way. These types of players were not economically active assets per se for the operators since they did not spend money in any of the machines of the game centre or became involved in its broader ludic activity by taking the part of the active user or the observer. Even so, these "hangers", as Samuel Tobin refers to them, were nevertheless fully constitutive elements of the social fabric of the arcade (Tobin 1).

Hangers: Non-ludic Appropriation of Space

Hangers, arcade patrons who are not playing videogames, have been part of the arcade scene in the United States since the arrival of coin-operated videogames in the 1970s. They have been defined mostly by the disciplinary regime of arcade owners and workers through various policing methods that primarily sought to manage the presence of people who did not bring in financial benefits to their operation (1–2). As Samuel Tobin points out, despite their importance in shaping the situated nature of arcade gaming, hangers have often been evicted from histories of arcade culture that prefer tales of performance and active engagement (2, 7). This is further emphasized by the instability of hanging behaviour itself, which is constantly adapting itself to the rules and affordances in specific venues, and whose negative behaviours are identified by owners and operators, never by themselves. The history of hangers in the United States illustrates not only the nature of arcades as a contested place but also the importance of tolerating certain types of hanging behaviour in order to create a sociocultural space free from exclusively economic incentives. Hangers tend to cruise from machine to machine, filling the gaps between active players, inhabiting the space's empty spots, and tactically using the space creatively for alternative purposes as they escape surveillance (Tobin 10–12). The overwhelmingly dominant responses of arcade operators to such customer practices include crackdowns, articles published in operator magazines warning of hanging behaviour, and the establishment of surveillance regimes, but as the example of Tsujishōten demonstrated, taming this disciplinary regime by restraining player agency might have helped to create a more sustainable arcade game parlour environment with different sociocultural functions, and most importantly, participating in the forms of ludo-egregores that defined the venue itself and gave meaning to the game-playing activity.

Sociological studies of game centres have examined cases of tension between operators and users linked to the game centre's ambiguous status as a privately-owned commercial space and embedded with the social functions often associated with the notion of public space. Perhaps the most significant example is Katō's discussion of the process of consensus building between different types of game centre users with regard to the use of graffiti and foul language in communication notebooks left for players to discuss game culture amongst themselves in light of their prohibition by venue operators. This phenomenon is explored through Antonio Gramsci's notion of cultural hegemony, in which the dominant strata of society impose their own rules, values, and worldviews as society's desirable status quo through consensus rather than coercion (Katō 182–220). Although this is a different phenomenon than the effect relative to the presence of hangers on the game centre space, the misuse of communication notebooks, the eventual degradation of social cohesion within the space of the arcade, and the ensuing repercussions on the financial sustainability of the venue are comparable to the disruptive behaviour of hangers in the early days of arcade culture in the United States. However, physical hanging behaviour in contemporary game centres does not seem to be frowned upon in Japan. On the contrary, some venues seem to actively encourage customers to occupy their spaces for purposes other than strict game consumption that brings tangible financial benefits, without approving of pure loitering.

In the general absence of a systemic crackdown on hanging behaviour in contemporary Japanese arcades, most large-scale game centres in urban settings provide customers with spaces and facilities that facilitate non-ludic forms of engagement. Isolated tables and stands on which communication notebooks, picture notebooks, and strategy guides are placed direct players prone to hanging behaviour to specific locations by providing the possibility of actively engaging the space of the arcade regardless of their ability to spend money for game sessions. In these contexts, however, the resulting type of engagement remains within the realm of activities from which the venue might be able to reap long-term benefits by harnessing a type of labour from these patrons. The case of Sega's game centre established in the district of Akihabara illustrates the neoliberal capture of non-ludic activities within Japanese arcades. In 2013, the multi-floor game centre complex turned one of its floor sections into an entire room filled with derivative representations of the vocaloid and rhythm game character Hatsune Miku shown wearing a variety of clothing styles (called modules). The centre invited customers to sit down at one of the many desks and provide their own illustrations of the popular character in illustration sketchbooks. Writing in communication notebooks or drawing in sketchbooks provided by the venue demonstrates tolerance of hanging behaviour in these spaces, to some extent. However, this example also shows the double-sided reasons behind welcoming non-paying customers; such installations indeed capture the creative labour of arcade-goers to feed a game franchise with content and game centre chains beyond the games themselves, as well as developing emotional connections towards specific game-related characters. As part of the process, customers could vote for which modules should be included in the then-upcoming game *Hatsune Miku: Project Diva F*, thus further encouraging players to engage with the space in a fashion that is not strictly economic.

The presence of communication notebooks or illustration sketchbooks could not be confirmed in Tsujishōten; I found no such material or method of non-ludic engagement during my field research there. However, the venue operator is very lenient towards hangers in the space for purposes other than playing videogames. The game cabinets served purposes other than ludic experiences, such as gathering places, eating surfaces, studying desks, or makeshift beds, more often than those in other venues visited. It could be argued that such repurposing of the machines originated from their intrinsic affordances that, despite being present in other venues, were perceived differently in Tsujishōten, partly influenced by the environment in which they are located and its characteristics. The appropriation of machines to realize specific ludic trajectories also reveals that the navigation of game centre spaces cannot be read in a deterministic fashion because the users make their own use of navigation tactics in a space that has been strategically structured to favour certain types of interactions.

As the structure of the game centre's space invites a familiar approach to the machines and close-knit interaction between customers, the fashion in which these affordances are perceived and acted upon need to be examined on an individual level. Users who choose and use a cabinet at which to spend time appropriate it in a much more creative and holistic fashion than those in other venues, and, to some extent, this process is like that of a complete, but temporary, colonization of a micro-public space in which users appropriate the machines for their own use by redefining their purposes.

Beyond their function as ludic objects, game cabinets in Tsujishōten could also be understood as territories within the arcade that could be and were occupied by different players or groups of players. Game cabinets, as microspaces that presented themselves as territorialized and compartmented, were more subject to territorialization, to use Deleuze and Guattari's term, by nomad player agents without reforming their initial structure; while the space of the arcade presents itself as striated, Tsujishōten's customer base turned it into an intimate place within a public setting, an extension of home.[3] The customers' use of the machines demonstrated contradictory processes of reterritorialization as they chose a cabinet and made it their own. Cabinets were often used as eating surfaces on which plastic ramen bowls, drinks, and other types of food are consumed, and the remains could often be witnessed by subsequent occupants, as trash was rarely thrown in the provided trash cans and, unlike in more orderly spaces such as restaurants and cafés, no waiting staff came to maintain the machines.

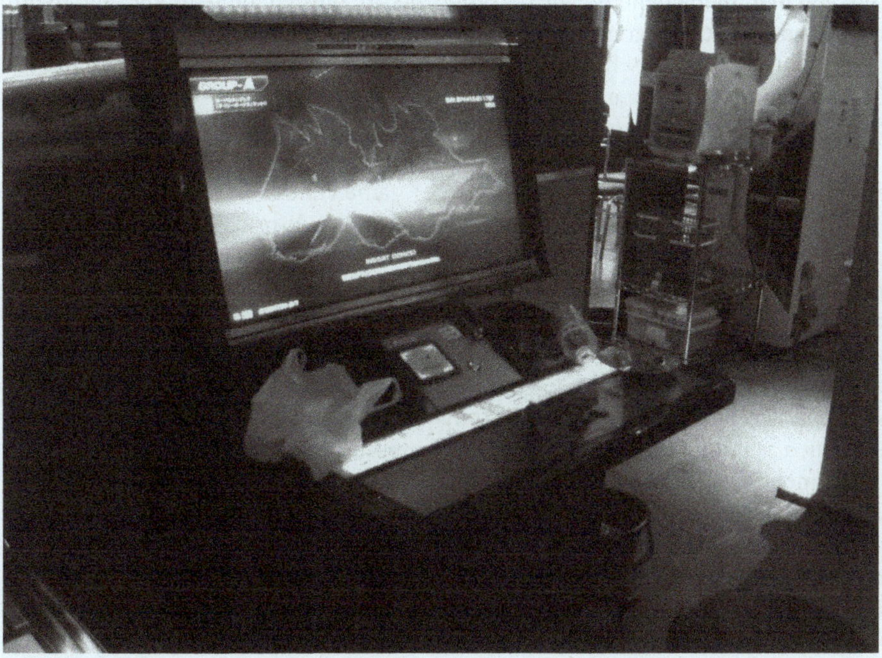

Figure 6.4 Traces of previous occupation at a *Tekken 7* cabinet, as evidenced by an empty water bottle, pack of cigarettes and plastic bag. A player has recently appropriated the space of this cabinet (photograph by the author).

Rejuvenation: Cellphone Use in Tsujishōten

The space of arcade cabinets was settled by users in a variety of other ways, all linked by the common notion of homeliness and a general direction towards an intimate and separate space within the public space. They were used as coat hangers, observation spaces, makeshift beds, and, potentially, other functions that I did not observe during this study. Though these appropriations of arcade cabinets were totalizing, they remained temporary, and as soon as customers quit, they usually left little trace of these specific types of previous occupation. Yet, the use of game cabinets as places at which one sits to use smartphones stood out as the most fully realized embodiment of this phenomenon.

The arrival and proliferation of smartphones and other personal devices in the very fabric of the public setting has been associated with the privatization of public space and even criticized as capitulation to the demands of neoliberal capitalism and the individualization of society. However, de Souza e Silva and Frith have instead argued that the use of these types of new technology constitutes "a physical instantiation of the constantly negotiated understanding of how public and private are related" as they make "their socially negotiated nature" (52) visible. Similarly, Sheller and Urry debunk the common notion of the purity of public spaces and the idea that the privatization of the public sphere equates to a loss of democratic control and the erosion of social life (109). Instead, they emphasize that the private and the public are not consensually differentiated concepts within the academic literature and that, fundamentally, the two concepts are blurred, fluid, mobile and hybrid rather than static and zoned. Similar places fulfil a mixture of purposes and host a variety of activities, what Sheller and Urry call the private-in-public life (110). The automobile, for example, comes to represent the mobility of these spheres and their interpenetration as one drives on a public road to a place akin to a dwelling.

Through the repurposing of cabinet space, players and users of Tsujishōten made visible the fluid and hybrid nature of game centres as spaces that could be read through Sheller and Urry's concept of the public-in-private. Their use of space also debunked the apparent contradiction between the existence of intimate homely play space within a public venue open to interventions by other people, a fundamental part of the act of playing in public. Game cabinets, in this context, were complementary devices of daily life that, like the automobile, provided ways to experience the public within a personal subspace; they were fluid spaces whose vocation is always in the process of transformation and hybridization due to their existence as public devices to be used as temporary personal territories.

As mentioned above, the use of mobile screens within arcades and at game machines adds another layer of individual isolation within a public setting. The use of portable screens and devices as complementary to the arcade game's own screen is not benign in our reading of arcade space; while gaming might function as escapism by immersion into a ludic activity, the public setting of arcade games always involves performance and the tacit agreement to being observed by the other users of the space. Using cellphones as communication devices and also, most interestingly, as ludic devices in this space can be seen as a way to reconnect with an entirely private space. The micro-space of the smartphone does not exclusively belong to the realm of the private space; overlooking a neighbour's smartphone screen is frowned upon despite the heavy use of smartphones in public settings such as on commuter trains, where people are usually standing very close to one another.[4] The use of smartphones in this context, far from constituting a paradox or a form of invasion by the private and individual sphere within the arcades, makes the perpetual negotiation between the private and the public visible, and illuminates the intimacy and performance that surround the act of playing on an arcade cabinet. It also demonstrates the multiple layers and functions of arcade cabinets within a single space as time passes.

Cabinets constantly switch from being settled to supporting an intimate play space through the colonization of its surface by some players' personal objects such as drinks, food, cellphones, or bags, to being used more openly for public observation or for gregarious play forms by groups of people. The use of cellphones during downtime, in between play sessions, or as brief private moments of escapism that allow moments of rejuvenation before re-engaging the public reflects this phenomenon, and the hanging behaviour that it generates is as much a staple of game centre life as game playing itself. Indeed, Tsujishōten, with its notable instances of individual hanging behaviour, was the game centre within which the most visual contact and verbal communication between customers occurred, and the only venue in which players attempted communication with me as an observer.

Gregarious Gameplay and Homely Space through *Extreme Vs.*: February 19 and 25, 2016

Tsuijshōten's distinctive trait, as compared to other game centres, was the sonic presence of players in its space, and nowhere was this presence more prominent and significant than around the *Extreme Vs.* cabinets during the times that this set of machines was rented on an hourly basis. While the other cabinets and games are each repurposed by different types of players in ways that demonstrated the influence of the space on how the cabinets' affordances were perceived, Tsujishōten positioned *Extreme Vs.* as the game centre's primary feature title, both by providing game sessions at a cheaper price than its competition and by structuring its play space in a more intimate fashion in an isolated corner of the venue, which afforded a type of interaction and, ultimately, a game experience of a different nature. Therefore, examining the activity surrounding these game cabinets revealed some of the defining characteristics of this space with regard to its territorialization by groups of players engaged in the same multiplayer game session. Over the course of the period of my field study, this group of cabinets was rented and used by groups of players at two different occasions during the evening of Friday, February 19 and the late afternoon of Thursday, February 25. My observation of both of these play sessions allowed me to identify the users' tactics for turning the row of game machines into a more intimate and homely space while simultaneously influencing the play sessions conducted and the broader atmosphere of the venue, as well as to witness the process of negotiating the presence and space appropriation by other game users in the venue.

During both play sessions I observed, the *Extreme Vs.* machines were being used at their maximum capacity, with each cabinet being played by one user. On February 19, however, the group of active players was surrounded by a handful of game observers belonging to the same social group. As a result, the concentration of people around the cabinets was exceptionally high and the space of circulation between the rows of machines became very tight and impractical, which limited access to the area. On the afternoon of February 25, at the time when high schoolers usually commuted home, the group playing *Extreme Vs.* was not playing under the same conditions of spectatorship; no observing users were present during their play session as all players present were focused on the action of their own cabinet. However, due to the time of day, Tsujishōten was comparatively busier than in my other case study, as most of the cabinets were occupied by active users, up to the *Tekken 7* cabinet, which, unusually, was being used by two players at the same time. This situation was much different than that of February 19, as the space of the arcade was more populated and, as a result, more public. However, players used different tactics to compensate and delimit their own private space from the rest of the arcade. One of the more visible of these tactics was to use the cabinets directly surrounding theirs as coat hangers by placing their winter coats and jackets on the seats or play surface of the cabinets to reterritorialize the space and create a boundary that is both symbolic and practical in order to mark the isolated nature of their

Figure 6.5 The *Gundam Vs.* section of the arcade, tucked away in a corner at the bottom of the venue. Groups of players are isolated from the rest of the venue due to the cabinet placement design (photograph by the author).

space. As a result, the machines directly besides the *Gundam Vs.* cabinets remained unoccupied by other players. Other players at the *Initial D* cabinets positioned their school bags around the cabinets in a similar fashion. Still others consumed food and tobacco at the cabinets and left traces of their passage on them, also reinforcing their marking of the space. Such behaviour seems to be more pronounced during the evening; for instance, on February 19, more users were seen using the game cabinets for purposes other than strictly ludic ones, mainly as spaces providing solitary intimate shelter at which they could relax and unwind.

How *Extreme Vs.* is played in Tsujishōten owes much to the gregarious context imposed on the game by its hourly rental dynamic and the fact that friends belonging to social groups previously formed outside of the space of the arcade are generally engaging in a form of friendly competition with their peers. This phenomenon was an important factor that explained the differences between the more open and expressive playing attitude of these players and, for example, users competing with fellow players in competitive events in which the outcomes of matches carry higher stakes. *Extreme Vs.* is a relatively simple game that is easy for new players to learn, thanks to a simple command scheme of a directional joystick and four buttons used during gameplay; it is also immediately recognizable and engaging for most people with a minimal knowledge of the *Mobile Suit Gundam* anime series. The instinctive nature of the command scheme maximizes the enjoyment of the game beyond the satisfaction of technical prowess, and directs it toward the fun of playing as the beloved gigantic robots that are the staple of the series and performing attacks and movements with weapons and special powers taken from its large repertoire. Thus, while some aspects of the game can lend themselves to high-level competitive play, *Extreme Vs.* is a very approachable game for casual players or fans of the series. This aspect, coupled with the game structure's heavy emphasis on local multiplayer as its primary play mode, encourages non-expert players to choose the game both as a ludic and social platform.

The structure of the game and its ludic context within local multiplayer game sessions conducted by players belonging to the same social circle had reverberating effects on the degree of expression active players demonstrated during gameplay. In both play sessions I observed, players engaged with the machines and with the spectating players who were focused on the action on the screen. They also voiced their appreciation, surprise, or frustration towards the state of the game with a striking degree of openness and spontaneity seldom seen in play sessions conducted in other game centres. Groups typically consisting of four to six people could yell enthusiastically when reacting to game situations either for themselves or directing their reactions to other players. Laughs of enjoyment and shouts of frustration also punctuated play sessions and dominated the sonic space of the venue as they are clearly heard by customers in the rest of the venue, thus becoming an integral part of the ludic experience. A great deal of emphasis was put on the multiplayer aspect of the game and its two-versus-two match structure encouraged players to catch their opponents off-guard whilst they are busy attacking another player. Taking advantage of a player's blind spots to inflict heavy damage on their robot is an effective in-game strategy, but in the context of a multiplayer game session in

Tsujishōten, it also surprised players who could then directly address complaints and taunts to the opposing player who used this sneaky manoeuvre. In addition, for their voices to reach the other side of the row of arcade cabinets where the opposing players are sitting, and to make their voices heard over the cacophonic soundscape resulting from the combined sound effects of all the arcade machines in the venue and the *Gundam Vs.* cabinets in particular, players often spoke louder than necessary in normal situations and occasionally attempted to make eye contact directly with their opponents by leaning towards the side of the cabinet.

By repurposing the ludic assemblage of the games to allow them to realize a specific ludic trajectory characterized by a search for an isolated and intimate play setting, players negotiating the process of playing *Extreme Vs.* with friends occupied the sonic space of the arcade, thereby enforcing a separation between their group and the rest of the venue. Speaking loudly and yelling without restraint contributed, beyond communicative functions, to isolate the group and reinforce the notion of intimacy within the public venue in a way that is similar to the physical occupation of the cabinets and the space surrounding them as noted earlier. These actions also exhibited the desire to overcome the design of the *taisendai* cabinet in which the game was played; in other words, to close the distance between the two players playing at opposing ends of the two-cabinet assemblage that normally encourages multiplayer matches between two players who are not acquainted with each other. While the design of the cabinets makes it more difficult to play in a more gregarious manner, the tactics used by players in Tsujishōten over the course of the rental of these machines demonstrated how their function is revealed in their empirical and contextual use. Designed affordances within game cabinets do not determine their use, and the optimal use of the cabinets themselves is often ignored or subverted by players in order to adapt the cabinets and the space to their ludic trajectories.

Examining the group of game cabinets that constituted the *Extreme Vs.* corner of Tsujishōten and their users revealed how a type of play structure established in the venue allows users to negotiate specific ludic trajectories and engage in a specific part of the space, which they delimited and settled temporarily. The resulting phenomenon was the formation of an arcade play experience, both for active and spectating users, that is different from the competitive, observational, and generally anonymous experience between users of fighting games as observed in A-cho. Rather, in this case, the dynamic of hourly machine rentals and the structure of the venue, allowing users to turn parts of the game centre into a more intimate play space, all combined into a ludic assemblage that generated a ludo-egregore based on semi-private gregarious play experience. Space appropriation, such as the use of the machines as personal places and the level at which vocal and sonic expression was conducted without regard to its impact on the atmosphere of the venue, allowed players gathering around these machines to use the space and the cabinets as extensions of a homely setting. The users created a symbolic distance between their play activity and the rest of the venue, and, as a result, their play activity was less influenced by bypassers, of which there are very few due to the limitations imposed on player circulation within the arcade, than by members of the group engaged in the same game. This influence on the play activity was limited not only by the direct in-game scenarios and players' responses to them but also by the social bonds established outside the arcades in normal daily life. *Extreme Vs.*, in its contextualized setting in Tsujishōten, was a ludic assemblage whose social circles are as much part of the gameplay experience as its software, material conditions, and spatial design of the venue.

Due to their popularity, *Extreme Vs.* games were readily available in many of the other arcades studied as part of this project. However, in the vast majority of these other contexts, the ludo-egregore generated as part of the holistic game experience with its active players and potential observers remained identical to those of many other games and spaces. The case of Tsujishōten demonstrated the principle of variable geometry that governs the network of game centres in Japan, where similar games are assembled with different materials and spatial conditions, but which occupy different functions in accordance to their relationship with other extra-gamic elements that form the ludo-egregore in which they take part.

Conclusion: Space and Cabinets as Palimpsests within the Intimate Play Space

From its opening in 1978 until 2016 when the field study was conducted, Tsujishōten has stood as an example of a game centre that has undergone many changes in order to adapt to trends and the evolution of the material conditions of arcade gaming throughout the past four decades. The space that must have housed cocktail cabinets for early hits such as *Space Invaders* and other shooting games has had to let go of old cabinets and games to welcome more technically advanced games in order. At the same time, such changes were also enacted in tandem with the gradual transformation of the public playing these games. However, while the games change, my investigation demonstrates that links can be established throughout the time of the arcade's existence through the ludic trajectories of its clientele, which has found ways to negotiate the evolution of these material conditions within the space of Tsujishōten. Many palimpsestic traces of the old architectural structure and spatial organization of the game centre could be seen from the subsequent layers of modern elements, and could also be found within the ludic trajectories of users in the space itself, in which a majority of its public negotiated a gregarious play experience that primarily emulated a certain culture of public gaming that is no longer supported by the game centre operation industry due to the corporate turn of the industry, and also in the ludo-egregore generated around the contemporary machines installed in the space. Although traces of the fishpond that was once featured in Shibuya Kaikan Monaco could still be witnessed through the remains of its architecture before its closure in 2013, and with it a remnant of the extravagance associated to pre-1990s Japanese urban entertainment, the decrepit benches of Tsujishōten, seemingly unchanged since the 1970s, acted as traces reminding us of the place's previous existence as an invader house. Another palimpsestic trace could be observed in the large glass windows in front of the venue, which now remain shut at all times; it would be safe to infer from these that Tsujishōten was once a coffee house that offered customers a view of the street facing the venue.

As newer machines enter game centres and erase the presence of others over the years, traces of previous forms of gameplay can be witnessed in the software and cabinet design of newer machines and the sociocultural practices and architectural elements that permeate the space. Some game experiences are the result of intended combined gameplay innovations and ludo-egregoric formations over many years, while others are more accidental, such as that between *Extreme Vs.* game cabinets and the gregarious space of the venue marked by previous gameplay experiences housed in the space. Uncovering the ludic archaeology behind the ludo-egregore formed by the *Extreme Vs.* machines in Tsujishōten would require investigating the traces of previous gameplay forms and gaming cultures that originally characterized it.

Thus, the case study of Tsujishōten uncovered the importance of adopting a historical perspective of the study of public forms of digital gaming. It revealed the phenomenon of user territorialization of the cabinet space, and challenged the notion of affordances determining the forms of gameplay made possible by ludic assemblages. Although game cabinets hold certain affordances that facilitate a certain type of play, they do not impede alternative and creative ways to repurpose the machines to fit the ludic, or non-ludic, trajectories of users. To play in public is first to occupy a territory, and always to negotiate one's position in the liminal space between the private sphere and one's exposure to the public.

Notes

1 *NESiCAxLive* is a subscription service platform used by venue operators to provide access to games via digital distribution. Launched by Taito in 2010, a second version, the *NESiCAxLive 2*, was released in 2017 with added online play functionalities.

2 The hourly rate seemed to vary depending on the season and the release of game updates, reaching up to 2,500 yen.

3 Here, I conceive of the game centre, and of the space of the play cabinet as its subset, as a smooth space, associated with the figure of the nomad who occupies and reterritorialize it through means of tactics and signs (Deleuze and Guattari 592-593). What is at stake here is the notion that public videogame arcade play is made possible through its potential for appropriating the assemblage of the game cabinet via territorialization tactics, which, in the case of Tsujishōten, are made concrete by objects such as trash and clothes. This association between the space of the game cabinet to that of home in this context is particularly significant as assemblages, ludic or otherwise, are, as stated by Deleuze and Guattari, first and foremost tied to territory, in which appropriation comes to define the assemblage itself (629).

4 The existence and well-spread circulation of privacy screen protectors for smartphones that prevent bystanders from seeing the screen from an angle suggest that a significant proportion of cellphone users are mindful of letting other people look at their phone activity in public. This also reinforces the idea that the space of the smartphone constitutes an abstract private domain.

Works Cited

BlazBlue. Arcade videogame cabinet, Arc System Works, 2008.

Border Break. Arcade videogame cabinet, Sega, 2009.

Code of Joker. Arcade videogame cabinet, Sega, 2013.

Cyber Trooper Virtual-On. Arcade videogame cabinet, Sega, 1995.

Deleuze, Gilles, and Félix Guattari. *Capitalisme et schizophrénie 2 : Mille plateaux* [*Capitalism and Schizophrenia 2: A Thousand Plateaus*]. Éditions de minuit, 1980.

Dillon, Sarah. *The Palimpsest: Literature, Criticism, Theory*. Continuum, 2007.

Genette, Gérard. *Palimpsestes: la littérature au second degré* [*Palimpsests: Literature in the Second Degree*]. Seuil, 1982.

Hatsune Miku: Project DIVA Arcade. Arcade videogame cabinet, Sega, 2010.

Hatsune Miku: Project Diva F. PlayStation 3 videogame, Sega, 2013.

Initial D. Arcade videogame cabinet, Sega, 2002.

Jubeat. Arcade videogame cabinet, Konami, 2008.

Katō, Hiroyasu. *Gēmu sentā bunkaron: media shakai no comyunikēshon* [*Theory of Game Centre Culture: Communication in the Media Society*]. Shinsensha, 2011.

Lord of Vermillion. Arcade videogame cabinet, Sega, 2008.

Mai Mai. Arcade videogame cabinet, Sega, 2012.

Mobile Suit Gundam: Extreme Vs. Arcade videogame cabinet, Bandai Namco, 2010.

Mobile Suit Gundam: Gundam Vs. Gundam. Arcade videogame cabinet, Branpresto, 2008.

Mobile Suit Gundam: Gundam Vs. Gundam NEXT. Arcade videogame cabinet, Bandai Namco, 2009.

Ōtsuka, Gichi. *Ji endo obu arukadia ekisutora bājon* [*The End of Arcadia Extra Version*]. bootleg! Books, 2016.

Satō, Dai. *No kon kiddo: bokura no gēmushi* [*No Continue Kid: Our Game History*]. Television series, TV Tokyo, 2013.

Sega network taisen mahjoong 5 evolution. Arcade videogame cabinet, Sega, 2013.

Sengoku taisen. Arcade videogame cabinet, Sega, 2010.

Sheller, Mimi, and John Urry. "Mobile Transformations of 'Public' and 'Private' Life." *Theory, Culture & Society*, vol. 20, no. 3, 2003, pp. 107–25.

Souza e Silva, Adriana de, and Jordan Frith. *Mobile Interfaces in Public Spaces: Locational Privacy, Control, and Urban Sociability*. Routledge, 2012.

Steinberg, Marc. *Anime's Media Mix: Franchising Toys and Characters in Japan*. U of Minnesota P, 2012.

Tekken 7. Arcade videogame cabinet, Bandai Namco, 2015.

Tobin, Samuel. "Hanging in the Video Arcade." *Journal of Game Criticism*, vol. 3, no. Bonus Issue A, 2016, pp. 1–17.

Tomino, Yoshiyuki. *Kidō senshi gandamu*. Television animation series, Nippon Sunrise, 1980–1979.

Wonderland Wars. Arcade videogame cabinet, Sega, 2015.

7 Media Mixes and the National Network

Compartmentalizing Play in Sega Ikebukuro GIGO

The commuter train's doors open. As I step onto the platform, I put my backpack on. It is much heavier than when I left this morning, full of notes and printouts from old Japanese videogame magazines acquired from the collection of the National Diet Library. After a whole day locked up and surrounded by old books and magazines and hours of research and photocopying, I am looking forward to a nice change of pace. I walk down the stairs of the platform and reach the Southern exit archway; Meiji Street facing the Ikebukuro Central Station is packed in the rush hour of the evening commute. The place will probably be packed tonight as well. I make my way down Ikebukuro 60 Street to reach the district's biggest game centre, GIGO Ikebukuro.

The Sega sign can be seen from a long distance before I reach the premises. The loud music, the sales pitch performed on the street by employees using megaphones, and the crane games installed outside call for everyone's attention. I am in Tokyo for only a month to conduct archival research at the National Diet Library and engage in some additional field study. I choose to live in the Ikebukuro neighbourhood for convenience's sake, and also to be as close as possible to a game centre such as this one: big, loud, and crowded, very different from the others covered in my field study. I walk by and visit the place many times a day, but despite that burgeoning familiarity, I still get lost inside on occasion, due to the confusing layout of the first two floors and the standardization of the others. The place is a maze, and the ever-changing rows of crane games often compromise my bearings. I often find it easier to gain proper orientation by paying attention to the music and ambient sounds of the venue rather than by looking at the map at the escalators, which all look the same.

The place is indeed packed, but I manage to make my way upstairs to the card game section. Ikebukuro GIGO features the latest arcade games and sometimes also games that are undergoing the "location test" phase of development, in which data are acquired to help the studio fine-tune the game before their official release throughout the country. Such games are frequently in high demand, however, and it is often necessary to line up before getting to try these hot titles. The game I am looking for today, *Kidō senshi gandamu: U.C. Card Builder*, the latest trading card arcade game featuring an impressive flat reader panel/high resolution screen hybrid device, should be located on the fifth floor. There is one machine available.

DOI: 10.4324/9781003273776-9

Blindly rummaging through the printout copies overflowing from my backpack for my cards that I carried the whole day with me in preparation for that moment, I sit down on the bench to get ready to play.

—

Media Convergence in Game Centres: The Anime Media Mix and Videogames

The examples of A-cho and Tsujishōten have shown that the ever-increasing cost of operating venues, frequent releases of new games, and implementation of network connectivity to the vast majority of newly released machines in the 2010s all placed tremendous pressure on small-scale game centres to target a more specific clientele and create a sense of uniqueness for their space in order to stay afloat financially. Over the years, game development companies have successfully influenced the business to their advantage and made arcade operators dependent on developers by charging an ongoing subscription fee in order to receive the latest updates online, allow multiplayer game sessions, and, in the case of trading card arcade games, buy booster pack boxes printed by the manufacturer on a regular basis.

The arcade game manufacturing and development landscape has also become more concentrated since the 1980s due to bankruptcies, fusions, and acquisitions; a handful of giants such as Sega (now Sega SAMMY Holdings, a company that operates in the complementary businesses of arcade gaming and pachinko machines), Taito (a property of Square Enix since 2005), and Bandai Namco (through a fusion between Namco and the toy-maker and media property owner Bandai in 2006) have consolidated dominant positions in the business. All three conglomerates, in addition to game publisher Capcom, also operate their own game centre chains in different forms that are flexible enough to allow for the operation of different types of public gaming experiences.[1] Operating amusement spaces directly allows these companies closer contact with their user base, and, more importantly, creates the conditions to generate spaces saturated with products and imagery related to the products co-developed and marketed by parent companies or other company branches while also establishing complete control over how these games are accessed by the public, allowing for a standardization of game centre experiences across the country. Such establishments, beyond their function as game centres, also become one of the many types of space embodying the convergence of advertisement and media that, in the Japanese context, is best described as the media mix system.

The first decade of the 2000s was characterized by the rapid development of a new paradigm of content creation in the mass culture of the Western world, called media convergence. Henry Jenkins has described this tendency as a phenomenon that has developed around three axes: "the flow of content across multiple media platforms, the cooperation between multiple media industries, and the migratory behaviour of media audiences who will go almost anywhere in search of the kinds of entertainment experiences they want" (2). The idea of media convergence has been used to discuss and conceptualize recent developments in content creation spread over different platforms, mainly due to the rise of digital content, media platforms, and the participatory web. Videogames, as a new interactive media platform, have been taking part in the spread of media franchises simultaneously with their advent as mass culture entertainment objects in the 1980s. While not the first company to publish licensed videogames based on a media franchise, Atari, having been acquired by Warner Brothers in 1976, fully embraced the idea of extending the experience of the movies into games, from the release of *Shark Jaws* in 1975 to that of *E.T.* in 1982, with various degrees of success (Montfort and Bogost 125–27).

Media convergence in Japan, however, has been subject to different types of influences that can be traced back to the idea of media mix, a term that, most commonly, refers to the phenomenon of "circulation of characters and narratives across media types" (Steinberg 135). The origin of the term *media mix* itself is often credited to Japanese book publisher Kadokawa (now Kadokawa Dwango) as referring to a business strategy aiming to distribute the company's content through a diversity of media platforms so as to maximize its penetration rate within the media ecology. This was a reinvention of the concept that emerged in the 1950s as more of a strategy to advertise products through a variety of media such as television, print advertisements, or billboards. The idea that Steinberg describes as the marketing media mix answers to different dynamics than the principle of the anime media mix, in which the object of consumption is the diversity of media itself: "the translation or deployment of a single work, character, or narrative world across numerous mediums or platforms (also known as repurposing) and the synergetic use of multiple media works to sell other such works within the same franchise or group" (Steinberg 142). Thus, within the anime media mix, which takes its name from the tremendous importance of the popular character Tetsuwan Atomu (Mighty Atom or Astro Boy) in its initial development, the primary consumer appeal of a marketed object becomes the characters or worldview bound to them through these characters. Although it predates the emergence of interactive digital entertainment, the videogame industry has quickly been introduced into media mix strategies to provide new directions for the dissemination of narratives and fictional worlds.

Lupin III (*Rupan sansei*), released by Taito for the arcade market in 1980, was the first Japanese videogame based on a pre-existing work of popular fiction. The game is structured around single-screen mazes and features the eponymous character conducting robberies, as the player must successfully navigate a recurring stage to steal money from a bank while avoiding policemen and watchdogs. The game was punctuated by a variety of cutscenes narrating the success of the theft or the protagonist's arrest. However, taken out of its context and material conditions, one would be hard-pressed to identify the game as belonging to the *Lupin III* franchise, since all references to its universe, except for the title screen, were located on the game cabinet itself via cabinet overlays and stickers, and in its pamphlets and other advertising materials. Thus, approaching the game as a text building on the *Lupin III* narrative world was dependent on its holistic experience in the space of the arcade. With the emergence of sprite technology and the more complex visual representation of characters that it allowed, game characters would become more recognizable across multiple media, while other characters from the manga and animation industry would better integrate digital entertainment. The 1983 arcade game *Xevious* stands out as a precursor of this trend with the first example of a game novelization, and *Madara,* a Kadokawa media mix product, was one of the first media franchises to be developed simultaneously for different media from the ground up, specifically, serialized manga, home console videogames, animation, and other printed publications (Steinberg, "8-Bit Manga" 42).

Thus, in addition to the well-known industrial links between the videogame industry and the production of other forms of popular culture (Aoyama and Izushi 424), there is also a significant link between arcade game development, game centre operation, the broader manga and animation industry and the publishing industry based on the interpenetration of characters and worldview that circulate freely between different media. This integration is twofold: game software and the spatial conditions of arcade gaming operators provide a new space in which the anime media mix can operate and deploy its world-building enterprise, and the space is also used to direct attention of customers towards certain tangible products located outside of the space. These constitute dynamics that have yet to be explored within this project, but that profoundly influence the space and the gaming experiences they generate in the majority of game centres operated by major game manufacturers in Japan. Thanks to its location at the epicentre of Japan's media ecology, Tokyo and the game centres located in its main cultural hubs constitute the ideal case study to examine this phenomenon. In parallel to this issue, the case study of Sega Ikebukuro GIGO also helps us reflect on other spatial effects emerging from the consolidation of game centres within the cultural industry, including spatial structure as a vector of unification and compartmentalization of ludic trajectories, the reproducing of cultural interfaces embedded in the materiality of cabinet design interfaces, as well as issues related to the interconnection of Japanese videogame arcades as national networks.

Ikebukuro: Otome Road and the Character Market

The city of Tokyo boasts many districts, each cultivating its own uniqueness that often fulfils a specific set of functions: Jimbōchō, for example, is the mecca of second-hand book shops, and Shimokitazawa is home to urban vanguard youth culture. Fans of electronics, videogames, and derivative products of the anime and manga industry are also provided with an urban enclave in the district of Akihabara, in which retro-style arcades and modern game centre chains face one another over Chūō Street and the back streets around the Electric Town exit of the main train station. Over the years, Akihabara evolved from the prime electronic appliance retailer hub in the 1970s to the epicentre of the home computer culture in the 1980s and, eventually, the garage kit hotspot in the following decade, a vocation that would pave the way for the district's further evolution towards mass entertainment and consumerism. Today, drawing from all of these influences, shops in Akihabara now specialize in goods aimed at male media fanatics, and businesses catering to the so-called otaku market. Though Akihabara is usually the preferred location for studying the influence of otaku media and the reach of cultural productions associated with them for obvious reasons, the preferred large-scale game centre I examine here as a case study representative of mainstream venues embodying all the connections between the game centre industry and the broader media ecology is located in Ikebukuro, the other heavily mass-media-influenced district of Tokyo.

One could argue that Ikebukuro is the original otaku-oriented district of Tokyo. The presence of shops catering to fans of visual media in the district dates to the 1980s, while their presence would reach critical mass a decade later in Akihabara (Morikawa 139). Akihabara's rise to prominence as the otaku media district is linked to the presence of electronic and personal computer hobbyist stores in the district, which has traditionally been strongly associated with hobbyist products targeted to a male demographic, and also in no small part due to the government backing it received in the 2000s to act as the storefront of the "cool Japan" campaign aiming to turn local popular culture into a tourist attraction.[2] As a result, by the beginning of the twenty-first century, Tokyo's popular culture-related districts have come to be divided according to gender identities; male consumers migrated to Akihabara, while female consumers gathered around Ikebukuro. In the relative absence of the opposite sex, Ikebukuro's media-space development was overwhelmingly influenced by female-oriented imagery and products (Morikawa 141). Shops along the aptly-named Otome Road mainly stock manga, dōjinshi, and anime goods catering mainly to a female demographic, while certain stores house cafés and cosplay floors restricted to female customers, where males are not allowed unaccompanied. This interest in catering to female-oriented commercial interests is not limited to shops dealing in popular-culture-derived goods but also pervade many of the other stores and venues surrounding Ikebukuro's main shopping area located east of the train station, between Sunshine Street and Green Street, including Sega's franchise game centre Ikebukuro GIGO.

Sega Ikebukuro GIGO (henceforth Ikebukuro GIGO) opened on Ikebukuro 60 Street in July 1993, in a period when many developers built large-scale venues that implemented the then-popular keywords of upsizing (*ōgataka*), gentrification (*kōkyūka*), and vertical integration (*fukugōka*) (Nobuoka et al. 30–36) in the wake of the burst of the economic bubble. Over the course of a few years, large entertainment complexes were built. Many of these integrated entertainment forms could retain users for a long period of time thanks to activities that were associated with premium pricing ranges unlike those of traditional videogames, which had been confined to the psychological price ceiling of either 50 or 100 yen for a play session since the 1970s. Ikebukuro GIGO was the biggest game centre of its time. It housed game machines and various entertainment facilities that included, amongst other things, karaoke booths, crane games, a casino, and a personal fortune-telling space, all on specific floors dedicated to each of these activities (33). The history of this game centre closely follows the transformation of the whole industry throughout the 1990s and 2000s; crane games experienced a period of renewed effervescence since their emergence in the 1960s with the arrival of bigger see-through cabinets displaying their offerings of goods and stuffed dolls based on popular characters (Katō, "Online jidai no gēmu sentā" 273), and, amongst other things, the development of *purikura* machines changed the demographic of game centres significantly as the number of female users rose sharply. In addition, the machines themselves grew bigger and, considering the example of *taikan* cabinets, necessitated wider spaces to accommodate their large size. Over time, shifting customer demands and incentives on profitability led Sega to review and bring changes to its games, service offerings and floor configuration.

Ikebukuro GIGO is located at the heart of pedestrian traffic in the district on the cross road of Ikebukuro 60 Street and an unnamed backstreet that marks the beginning of the dense commercial area leading up to the Ikebukuro train station, which, with its many connections to city and suburban lines, is one of the busiest transportation hubs of Tokyo. In 2016, the game centre was directly surrounded by establishments owned by the two other major arcade operating chains, Round 1 and Matahari Entertainment, the latter operating an arcade called Saint-Tropez that burst with a sense of exoticism and originality. A plethora of restaurants, nightlife entertainment venues, and cultural-product shops establish the area as a prime destination for leisure and shopping, where customers are likely to be tempted to enter a game centre on a casual level or as part of a group night out. However, the distinguishing factor of Ikebukuro is its emphasis on cultural products and derivative goods featuring young boys and male characters who are part of media mix franchises that are primarily aimed at female popular-culture consumers. To stay relevant in this specific local cultural environment, national chain operators must tailor their offerings to customers' interests, a strategy that Sega adopted not only in its game offering but also in the atmosphere and rhythm it tries to nurture within and around the premises of Ikebukuro GIGO.

The building housing Ikebukuro GIGO is a massive eight-story structure painted in bright red and adorned by the famous blue and white Sega company logo. The building is illuminated from all sides with beams directing upward that, during nighttime, lights up the various advertisement billboards; in the spring of 2016, these billboards were advertising two different anime series. The building is girdled by an impressive LED multicoloured display that constantly changes in colour and tone from left to right as if the panel was itself moving. This display constitutes the neighbourhood's most impressive use of light to attract the attention of pedestrians. A Bakudanyaki takoyaki stand is also located on the right-hand side of the central door of the venue. During the time of my field study in March of 2016, the stand was running a collaboration with TV Tokyo in order to sell goods branded after the *Osomatsu-san* anime series, which started airing in 2015, with the purchase of snack squid balls. During the time of the promotion between March 12 and April 3, dozens of customers were lining up to get their hands on the tasty treat, and one of the six exclusive keychain designs sold for 1,250 yen as part of the collaboration, thus generating much pedestrian presence directly surrounding the venue. Later, these same customers would most likely gather around the famous owl sculpture in the nearby Naka-Ikebukuro Park, the traditional gathering point for fans of pop culture to trade such collectible anime goods that one can acquire in the many dedicated stores in the districts, and to share their passion for their favourite anime characters.

Figure 7.1 Entrance to Ikebukuro GIGO. Prize machines are located outside the venue so as to attract passersby while a display advertising the *Osomatsu-san* collaboration has been placed by the sidewalk, contributing to the media mix visual presence of the district (photograph by the author).

Time-limited promotions that include character tie-in goods are not rare in this district, and Ikebukuro GIGO acts as a hub for many of these promotions. Perhaps the most notable of the many promotions put in place during the period of my field study was Sega's collaboration with game developer Bandai Namco to dedicate space and sell derivative products related to the *Idolish7* mobile phone game released in 2015. The *Idolish7* media mix is distributed amongst many media such as games, novels, music albums, and animated series, involving different companies such as the publisher Hakusensha and the Troyca animation studio. *Idolish7* is not based on a fictional storyline, but is primarily a collection of attractive characters organized around the idea of rival idol singers' groups. Each has a distinct and well-defined personality and character traits, including motivations, favourite food, musical style, and birthday. Posters depicting each fictional male idol character were lined up on the side of the street to attract customers, while another poster advertised the exclusive goods that were put on sale on the seventh floor of the game centre for a limited time starting on Sunday, March 26, 2016.

The direct surroundings of Ikebukuro GIGO can thus be interpreted as an advertisement space that promotes different types of products and services, all referring specifically to the broader pop culture character market that defines Ikebukuro and its main tourist attraction Otome Road. Some posters and signs are meant to promote different shows or movies to be watched on television or in theatres, thus the strategy of using different types of media to advertise the consumption of a single product according to traditional notions of a business media mix. However, the type of commercial activity occurring around and within Ikebukuro GIGO also transcends simple advertisements for a single product and, particularly in the case of *Idolish7*, rather became the product itself, akin to Steinberg's notion of the anime media mix. Rather than seeing the products sold in and around game centres are advertisements for a main product, they should be seen as "fragments" (Otsuka and Steinberg 106) that, combined, construct a "worldview" (109) or "system" (109) that is being commercialized, in reference to Eiji Otsuka's notion of narrative consumption. As Otsuka suggests, what is being commercialized in the media mix of *Idolish7* is not "an individual drama or thing but the system itself" (109). In this case, all the seemingly derivative products sold in the vicinity of game centres and elsewhere constitute fragments that enrich its system, and which can be then repurposed creatively by consumers to create their own stories.

Already, looking at the surroundings of the game centre, ties between the broader media ecology of popular culture, and most specifically the media mix properties that find a natural home within Ikebukuro, become obvious, foreshadowing the even greater presence of such products within the venue itself.[3] However, to fully grasp the importance of the anime media mix within the rhythm of this game centre, one must examine how the venue, from both its spatial and ludic perspectives, captures the potential of this system by providing additional narrative fragments to be not only acquired but also embodied.

Ikebukuro GIGO: Structure and Spatial Design

I—Media Mix Space

To this point, much of the discussion on game centres has been tackled from the perspective of space as a perceived and lived phenomenon, or, to refer to Lefebvre's original triad, the spatial practices and representational spaces.[4] However, to investigate one venue from Sega's game centre chain is also to consider space as a carefully conceived and constructed phenomenon that combines both conviviality and profit maximization. A company such as Sega has access to the financial capital necessary to build a commercial location that implements large-scale spatial strategies to direct customer movement and expose them to key aspects of the space to maximize profits, and to design sub-places used as enclaves for different subcultures and demographics. Space thus conceived as a created spatial representation sees its interpretation enforced to potential consumers in the form of a navigational map indicating, floor by floor, where each type of ludic activity takes place in the venue, and suggesting a disciplinary regime characterized by, amongst other things, unequivocally gendered spatial statements and a tendency towards compartmentalizing different types of gameplay. More obviously than the two venues examined so far, Ikebukuro GIGO's space of representation, as identified in Lefebvre's three-pronged spatial model, was the most apparent and worthy of consideration.

Figure 7.2 Ikebukuro GIGO's building map showing all eight floors alongside the games or services that they feature. The right-hand side of the description boxes indicate each floor's policy regarding smoking as well as the restroom availability for either male or female (photograph by the author).

Ikebukuro GIGO is composed of eight floors, ranging from the basement floor (B1F) to the highest numbered floor (7F). A map of these floors was displayed near the main entrance of the venue on the corner of Sunshine Street and the unnamed south side street. Each floor was coloured differently and was associated with a specific game genre, along with a short list of titles showcasing the most popular games available on the floor. Customers wanting to play a specific game need only follow the indications and reach the specified floor to reach the desired machine. Although smoking is generally allowed in game centres, Ikebukuro GIGO restricted the consumption of tobacco to all but the three floors located in the middle of the venue (3F to 5F), the floors with the highest concentration of medal games and videogames. In addition, the map also indicated that each floor features a washroom either for males, females, or both genders. The gender distribution of the washrooms, either for both genders or one, also indicated where the ludic trajectories of specific demographics are expected to lead them within the vicinity of the venue. It further created, from an architectural perspective, a gendered interpretation of the public gaming experience by making certain amenities available in some locations only for a certain demographic.

The first three floors of the centre (B1F to F2) constituted the general space in which machines and cabinets meant to attract regular pedestrians are located.

In our case, this was represented by a collection of various prize game cabinets that overflow on the sidewalk next to the arcade, containing a wide range of products such as plush dolls, everyday items, and, most importantly, Disney-branded goods, as specified on the map. These machines are meant to be consumed impulsively and to draw in customers who would not necessarily be interested in playing videogames *per se*, but whose familiarity with the brand or fictional universe of these goods might tempt them into taking a look, trying some of the machines, and generating revenue. A different map was provided to indicate where goods related to specific games or animation series are located on these floors, and are thus organized thematically. The other floors of the venue could be directly reached before first walking through the many rows of machines in the space; the escalator usually located near the outside wall was absent on the first floor and customers must reach a staircase located at the back of the venue to reach other floors. This is also true for the basement floor designated as the Bandai Namco Collaboration Room, in which special events and product lotteries were held. The Ichiban Takarakuji service is a lottery system common across large-scale game centres, that fulfils a role similar to that of crane game cabinets. For a small fee, customers may draw one ticket from a box at random and choose one of the assigned prize categories that are written on it. Each lottery is tied to a specific game, anime, or manga universe and the goods range from simple buttons to large-scale figurines. Though the lottery is more expensive than crane games, it provides an alternative for obtaining a product from a coveted series without relying on machine manipulation skills and diminishing player frustration.

Figure 7.3 In a corner of the venue, a large poster of *Idolish7* character Yotsuba Tamaki is put on the wall in anticipation of his birthday on April 1. Many wishes have been written and put on the poster, which can be interpreted as traces of a significant communal engagement towards the character and the franchise performed through the space of the game centre (photograph by the author).

During the time of my field study, the basement space was used to celebrate the birthday of one of the singer characters from the *Idolish7* universe. Fans of the series were invited to wish the character a happy birthday by writing a short comment on a piece of Post-it paper that they could then stick on a giant poster on the wall. The event attracted many fans of the series who took the time to proceed to the basement level of the building to send their best wishes. Many messages were posted over the weekend when the event was taking place, almost filling the wall to its capacity.

While these types of collaborative events are only hosted in some of the game centres located in the most important urban circulation hubs, their presence is nevertheless meaningful as not only do they bestow an alternative sense of spatiality on media mix properties to which customers can gather, but their presence in a space marked by a strong ludic aspect, interactivity, and carefree attitude encourages users to engage the property through sets of predetermined gestures providing a heightened sense of proximity with the characters. Despite its strong anchor in the world of screens and representation, the anime media mix is characterized by different implementations of spatiality in its ecosystem. In 1961, famous manga artist Osamu Tezuka signed on to finance what would become the first long-form animated series to be ever shown in Japan: *Tetsuwan Atomu* (*Astro Boy*). However, in order to convince TV stations to finance the project and undercut potential competition from other studios, Tezuka reportedly sold each episode of the show for about one-fifth less than what its actual production cost (Steinberg 39). As a result of this financing scheme, or what has been known since then as "Tezuka's curse", Steinberg points out that anime became dependent on a wider business strategy to seek revenues, including licensing, sponsorship, and merchandising (qtd. in Denison 79).

Many of the shops surrounding Ikebukuro GIGO, such as *Animate*, *Gamer*, and *Mandarake* (specializing in second-hand goods), take part in the business of selling anime-related merchandise, an intrinsic and essential part of the anime media mix. These shops embody a type of spatiality oriented towards the media mix in regards to how goods are displayed and how the architecture is structured for a certain type of merchandise consumption patterns. They also contribute to the spatial construction of Ikebukuro, and more specifically Otome Road, thanks to their multiple locations in the area. Other types of space also constitute the primarily spatial aspect of the media mix, such as temporary themed cafés and bars combining eating experiences with representational aspects of specific franchises, or the gigantic fan conference, Comic Market, held twice a year in Odaiba, at which fans are invited to consume and trade dōjinshi, or fan-made magazines, depicting their favourite characters in alternative non-canonical situations.

Game centres, however, allow the anime media mix system to perform a complementary type of spatial embodiment different from a strictly economic activity; whereas Steinberg described *Tetsuwan Atomu* stickers as media mix platforms marked by mobility (Steinberg, *Anime's Media Mix* 79), it should be noted that game centres, as media platforms, are marked by a specific embodiment of spatiality that allow the property developers to generate a playful type of interactive engagement. As associating the image of *Tetsuwan Atomu* and the materiality of the sticker objects leads to their "mutual transformation" into a "media-commodity" (89) granting the character a physically mobile aspect and simultaneously turning the sticker into a communicational object, the phenomenon of introducing playful interactive activities based on media mix franchises mutually transform the franchise and the space. The connection between consumers and characters takes a deeper turn while the space of the arcade becomes an event landmark for a specific franchise. Following Steinberg's original idea, the phenomenon of the introduction of space-based playful activities related to media mix franchises, could be called a ludic media space, which in turn becomes a significant part of the game centre's ludo-egregore.

The *Idolish7* character's birthday celebration spatial setup as an ongoing event in Ikebukuro's media space is an example of a space-oriented practice that remains exclusive to certain high-profile venues, but the gestures that they prompt players into performing in public are significant characteristics of their rhythm and of the discourse that characterize Japanese arcades in general. Other venues have been shown to house other types of similar playful devices inviting customers to interact with elements of a given medium through specific sets of gestures to be performed in the context of a community event. One such installation made the news across the world in 2015 when a Sega game centre in the Osaka region set up a space of worship for customers to perform *dogeza* (ceremonial bowing) in front of representations of individual characters forming the cast of the *Love Live!* media mix property managed by ASCII Media Works (Ashcraft).[5] The reports of the installation received puzzled responses from the general Western gaming public after being featured on the popular blog *Kotaku* and other web publications using the same photograph posted on Twitter (Shīa). The practice was often read as an example of problematic fan activities that supposedly indicated their difficulty separating fiction and reality; however, taking into consideration the setting of the activity within the ludic space of game centres, it is important to consider the playful mindset that accompanies these semi-ritual gestures, similarly to the case witnessed in Ikebukuro GIGO. Players know full well that worshipping fictional idols is ridiculous, just as much as sending birthday wishes to a non-existing male idol singer is, but the gesture, the character, and the setting mutually transform one another as aspects of a communicational practice in which all of these elements bring oneself closer to the product, the social sphere of the arcade, and its fraternal spirit.[6] As a result, the game centre is not only a play space for the enjoyment of videogames but, considering Lefebvre's emphasis on social practice in the definition of space, is also another organ of the media mix in which a property can be consumed differently.

Floors B1 through F2 also had an added distinction; as the only locations in which music could be clearly heard through the speakers of the venue, they had a different sonic ambiance from the rest of the floors. The sonic space of every floor of the venue was different from the others. On the upper floor, music was essentially absent, so that the noise of the machines mingles with other sounds such as tapping noises and cacophonic music on the fourth floor and fighting screams on the fifth. Conversely, the first floors helped to ease customers in while establishing both an exciting atmosphere that encouraged carefree ludic interaction with the machines, and a continuity with the cultural activities occurring outside of the venue. On March 27, 2016, the music could be heard from the street level at a distance from the venue itself; the voice of a staff member announcing daily discounts and the new crane game items to be acquired was mixed with a string of loud energetic music that would catch the attention of any passersby. The songs featured a few different male voices relaying one another in each tune, a format similar to that of the idol boy band featured in the event space of the venue. On the basement floor, the same type of music could be heard, but without the voice of the announcer, the songs themselves wholly enveloped the sonic space of the room, as if the songs were the primary events themselves and not merely accompanying the pictures of male idols on the wall. On the second floor, a mixture of songs featuring both male and female singers was played, but even though no sonic hindrance was consciously organized here, noise coming from customers talking and machines being played slightly overpowered the music.

The entry-level floors of the game centre constituted a visual cacophony of different sounds, machines, products, and references to multiple anime and manga franchises, so that the senses of passersby could become overwhelmed. Music, in this context, provided a unifying ground to the spatial experience, and gave the space more cohesion not only in terms of the *flâneur* experience of casually walking and investigating the space but also in connection to the media mix franchises that characterized it. Japanese ambient media scholar Paul Roquet notes that ambient music serves as an "organizing horizon" that is "effective because it rests just outside conscious attention, providing the sense of cohesion without claiming it more directly" (52). Thus, the use of music, and especially the idol group music that is itself represented in the venue, serves as an agent of spatial cohesion, which is more important at the entry level of the venue than on the upper portion. It provides a "horizon" of stability and security in a space that is often changing in terms of structure as machines are constantly changing and being displaced, thus creating a more inviting ambiance for customers leading to a more carefree experience. In a similar fashion to the role of music in group-based fitness activities as a catalyzing agent providing a common rhythm that mediates the participants with their surroundings, thus providing a sense of community (DeNora, qtd. in Roquet 54), fictional idol anime music attuned users to a sense of fraternity experienced in the space to the sounds of a media mix franchise. It brought stability to the relationship between space, the users and the other people in the venue while setting the tone for the interactive experiences available in the venue, as well as the types of ludo-egregore generated as part of their consumption. The sonic aspects of media properties contextualized in space, similarly to their use in commercial venues and others, unified the space and the experience, a phenomenon not observed in other venues studied.

Ikebukuro GIGO: Structure and Spatial Design II—Gendered Ludic Spaces

The space's multi-floor structural design emphasized the compartmentalization of experiences as types of games, and types of players, were segregated from one another in order to group them into expected areas of interest. Large-scale locations commonly use this practice to maximize floor space and enforce paths of circulation; to access the upper floors that house the most popular games, one must walk past all the others, thus putting players in contact with a vast diversity of machines. However, Ikebukuro GIGO used this characteristic to mark floors and certain games and types of entertainment activities with a specific gender presence, which is itself reflected by the types of machines present on each specific floor.

A large selection of fighting games, network-connected games and shooting games were housed on floors 4 and 5; taken together, these two floors featured most of the games available for play in the venue. This selection included well-known games such as the *Gundam Vs.* series, and other competitive fighting games, trading card arcade games, team-based battle area games such as *Wonderland Wars* and traditional skill games such as darts. These two floors were also markedly noisier than other floors thanks to the combination of sounds of all types of machines being played or in demonstration mode, and the smell of tobacco was very noticeable since this is one of the only floors on which customers are allowed to smoke while playing. The types of experiences provided on these floors thus catered more to fans with a sustained interest in arcade videogames in general, as most of the games required a great deal of time to acquire the skills necessary to be competitive, or to acquire resources such as trading cards in a collection mindset. Interestingly, these were the only floors whose restrooms are available to men only, forcing women to migrate to different floors on which restrooms for women are available, should they need to use them.

The displacement of female restrooms could be partly explained by the need to maximize the use of the multi-floor complex's limited space; however, the choice of these floors, seen in conjunction with the presence of certain games, suggested and contributed to the enforcement of a primarily male presence in specific areas of the game centre, to the detriment of a more gender-fluid public. The operators of the venue spatially represented these floors as male-specific floors, which itself had repercussions on floors as representational spaces, or the space as directly perceived by players. These elements, taken together, enforced a male gender hegemony in precise locations of the venues and in the accessibility of certain game genres. Although these measures did not enforce the absence of women on these floors directly, the lack of amenities did seem to send an indirect message about the degree of inclusivity expected in the player base of some of these games and reinforce the association between the more traditional "hard-core" ethos of videogame arcades and masculinity.

This kind of implicit gender-specific orientation could also be identified on other floors, though in different degrees and for different reasons. Floor 3, for example, seemed to be similarly gender-tagged, but in a fashion that encourages female presence; amenities on this floor were reserved for female use only. Whereas most competitive videogames were located on the previously introduced floors, the third floor is dedicated to very different genres and types of machines such as medal games, including pachinko and pachislot, a type of gambling machine that uses coins with no monetary value, as well as a large selection of rhythm game genres. All these machines provided what are widely considered casual experiences that, though players approach them with much dedication, were not subject to the dynamics of multiplayer competition. Rather, players approached these games at their own pace, which could be slow or reach very high levels of proficiency. The presence of these types of games, all of which feature colourful and stylish cabinet designs, suggested the opposite type of gender bias to that on the male-dominated floors and promoted game experiences that are expected of female users.

The early days of arcade gaming in Japan were vastly dominated by male players during the 1970s and 1980s, both in terms of physical presence in game centres and in media representation. It is most notably with the release of an arcade version of *Tetris* in 1988 (Amyūzumento sōgō kenkyūjo 139) and the development of other puzzle games such as *Puyo Puyo* and *Columns* during the following decade that the presence of women would become more important, and thus essential for arcade game developers to consider in the development of new products and venues. The implementation of multi-floor complexes and bright-lit spaces featuring prize games and medal gambling machines, as countermeasures to the *invader house* image of game centres as sites of delinquency and insecurity, helped arcades become more acceptable, even trendy, venues suitable for spending evenings with friends with a more diverse player base than previously ("Gēmu sentā nante mō iwanai"). In the middle of the 1990s, the emergence of purikura photo booths and rhythm games, both more closely marketed to the female demographic, would solidify a regular female presence in game centres; surveys conducted by the Japan Productivity Center indicate that between 1987 and 1993, the percentage of women frequenting game centres rose from 7 to 23 percent (qtd. in Katō, *Gēmu sentā bunkaron* 312). By 2008, surveys indicate that, until they reach 29 years of age, women slightly outnumbered men in game centres (qtd. in Katō, *Gēmu sentā bunkaron* 314), thus influencing the structure of the games developed for arcades. Rhythm games such as *Mai Mai* clearly target women customers with the use of women in advertising and with multiplayer and Web 2.0 social features integrated within the cabinets. Even though women now account for a much broader demographic of arcade customers, the space of the arcade itself often embodies a gender bias in its representational space, as men and women are led towards different types of games separated into different micro-spaces.

Two other floors made up the upper portion of the game centre. Floor 7 was a café in which customers of all genders can socialize around drinks and sweets while participating in one of the special events organized similarly to that of the basement space, while floor 6 represented another take on the same gender issues discussed in this section. Indeed, this location, in which the popular *purikura* machines were located, was a micro-space that enforced another version of gender segregation, albeit a stricter one. Given the significant presence of women on Otome Road and the direct surroundings of the arcade, operators of the game centre have naturally emphasized these machines by dedicating the entire floor to them and to the appropriate atmosphere and ludic disposition for their enjoyment. This floor offered a variety of photo booth machines and an outfit-rental corner allowing clients to cosplay in extravagant outfits or as their favourite characters. The choice of dedicating a floor to this activity and separating it from the venue thus allowed the necessary isolation for small groups to fraternize and effectively play at taking pictures but also to regulate the entry into the space itself and maintain its status as what we could call a safe space. The floor was indeed restricted to female customers only, and men could enter only if accompanied by a woman.

Such pre-emptive measures have been taken by most establishments at the beginning of the 2000s when game centres were criticized as platforms enabling activities related to compensated dating or promiscuous sexual encounters between clients and older men who would come to game centres and peruse the pictures put on public boards, on which phone numbers were written (Chalfen and Murui 64). Under the guise of creating a safe space for women to enjoy the machines without the involvement of third parties, men were gradually forbidden entry to these spaces, chairs were removed to prevent customers from occupying the space for too long, and the types of pictures and comments put on public boards were managed more closely (Katō, *Gēmu sentā bunkaron* 318–27). Although the floor is designed around the idea of creating a space in which women would feel comfortable playing, the spatial organization around *purikura* corners also clearly enforces control over how the machines are used, and over socialization around the activity of the photo shoot and the degree of circulation of the pictures themselves. What is at stake with the regimentation of *purikura* corners and the gender segregation that characterizes this regimentation is, to some extent, regulation of women's bodies and what they can do with them. The activities occurring around the use of *purikura* machines have been interpreted in terms of sociocultural discourses and moral anxieties existing outside the boundaries of game centres, and measures taken to change customer behaviour have also brought game centre activities in line with broader social norms.

The display of pictures and their trade outside the venue is a fundamental part of the appeal of *purikura* machines, and the devices and processes providing the pictures turn the photoshoot into a ludic activity of its own that is fundamentally different from regular photography. According to Katō, traditional analogue film-based photography was primarily used for recording memories (*omoide*) of the present: pictures taken at a party or of one's children are normally meant to record the moments as they happen for further consultation in the future (*Gēmu sentā bunkaron* 273). However, the pictures resulting from a *purikura* session, usually small shots printed on a single piece of paper that can be cut with scissors and exchanged with friends, are geared towards the past rather than the present: their function is to confirm the status of the bond (*kizuna kakunin*) between the viewer and the photographed subject (Katō, *Gēmu sentā bunkaron* 273–78). Rather than a spontaneous act meant to capture ephemeral moments of daily life, *purikura* picture shooting is a planned activity, as indicated by the planning of the space and of the machines, such as the selection of costumes and accessories, the poses that the software suggests taking, and the important addition of images and scribbles (*rakugaki*) on a digital panel in the final steps of the process. In addition to simply capturing the fun and sharing the enjoyment of a night out, *purikura* is an activity meant to offer a testimony of a bond shared between two or more people. It is a particularly popular activity for female users of game centres who have defined most of the practices and culture around these machines, but is not limited to this demographic.

However, as with all other gaming and non-gaming activities taking place within the highly structured context of the venue, the culture of *purikura* is dependent on the context of the arcade and on the broader media ecology within which these activities take place. The space of Ikebukuro GIGO is replete with references to outside social discourses and media properties, and their influence can be felt strongly within. Though crane games and the event space are themselves platforms that make aspects of media mix franchises playable, *purikura* space, with its references to standards of beauty conveyed by advertisement space and other media, allows customers to embody and perform these standards in a playful manner. From the imagery that envelops the game to the aura of cuteness (*kawaisa*) or elegance embodied by fashion models, the outside appearance of the machines ties the experience with a certain conformist interpretation of the female aesthetic ideal as represented broadly in Japanese society. The photoshoot experience itself is formalized, much like that of a professional photo shoot; as the subjects position themselves in front of the camera, a screen in the booth will suggest standard poses to be taken by the users, though these suggestions can be ignored. The software thus assumes the roles of both the camera device and the photo shoot director. The experience reaches its completion after the post-processing stage, as the pictures are automatically altered with an algorithm that increases eye size and produces a blemish effect on skin, effectively turning the subjects whiter in the photographs. All of these elements further connect the experience to outside standards of beauty, bringing users closer to the ideals conveyed daily in popular media, albeit in a mode of co-production whose final results might reinforce or subvert those norms.

In this designed and dedicated space, machines and games are elements meant to connect players to other media objects located outside the physical space of the venue. However, they also provide experiences that, on their own, suggest that they are not only supporting the consumption of a specific media object, but are also the main components, or organs, of the media mix complex. At the same time, this experience, more than those of the other venues discussed here, imposes a more defined rhythm on users. Even as the compartmentalization of the venue segregates certain experiences and media spaces from one another, machines and software also support a certain individualization of public play and the interchangeability of venues in favour of emphasis on a national network.

Shakōbako as a Cultural Interface in Hatsune Miku: Project DIVA Arcade, April 2016 Case Study

Much of Ikebukuro GIGO's floor space was devoted to amusement machines of all kinds as opposed to simply videogame machines, though at least three of the floors were used exclusively to host digital games and to create a specific ludic atmosphere around those games. As stated above, game machines were roughly divided by genres and types of experiences across floors; competitive fighting games were all located on floor 5 while rhythm games were conveniently all set up together on floor 3. This organizational method maximized certain types of ambient sounds that contributed to the creation of a sonic space and visual ambiance compatible with certain types of expected gameplay and ludo-egregore.

As one entered the floor dedicated to fighting games, one was automatically enveloped in the cacophonic atmosphere of characters yelling in different ways depending on whether they are on the giving or receiving end of a blow, which inspired and mentally prepared players to take part in the action. However, beyond such considerations of genre or sonic presence, another characteristic of the games in this venue was their enabling of public observation, while other machines instead created conditions for user isolation within the public setting of game centres and thus a more intimate play space that defied the conditions of the venue. This strategy provided a ludic space and a ludo-egregore that, in the context of Ikebukuro as a broad Otaku urban media space providing a porous frontier between the private and the public, was more centred on the self than on interpersonal play experiences. In Ikebukuro GIGO, *Hatsune Miku: Project DIVA Arcade* (henceforth *Project DIVA Arcade*) exemplified how the space and material conditions of games in the venue were designed for this purpose. When considered in relation to a historiography of the development of player-seclusion devices in arcades since the 1970s, this case study allows us to uncover an important element of what constitutes game centres' cultural interface, a concept that partially addresses the reasons for the viability of arcades in contemporary Japanese urban culture.

Developed by Sega and released for arcades in 2010, *Project DIVA Arcade* is the arcade port of the eponymous rhythm game series that embodies the Hatsune Miku and, perhaps more accurately, the broader media mix property system encompassing vocaloid products. Like many other media mix properties, the game is at the centre of a media content creation system that involves a variety of companies and stakeholders. Vocaloids are voice-synthesizing software products developed and marketed by the Japanese company Crypton Future Media, based on a technology developed by the musical instrument manufacturer Yamaha. In 2007, Crypton Future Media released the flagship version of what would become a long-lasting series of different software. Hatsune Miku (meaning "first sound of the future") was released as software with a specific voice tone attached to a specific character with a basic image and bodily characteristics of the singer. The company marketed the character without any restrictions as to the use of its image, and the character was quickly adopted by users to create songs coupled with illustrations on online video-sharing platforms (Coundry 63).

Though Hatsune Miku was not the first vocaloid to hit the market, it was the first software program, and character, to be intentionally developed and sold with the persona of a specific character in mind. Hatsune Miku was quickly adopted by users who disseminated her persona in fan-made songs and music videos, while Crypton Future Media further made effort to promote the character in sponsorships and live concerts while supporting grassroots multimedia productions in which she was featured. The *Project DIVA* rhythm game series, first developed on mobile game consoles, features songs and character customization elements taken from fan-produced content. The arcade version of the game, which boasts large-size colour buttons to press in accordance with the flow of the music while vocaloid characters perform in the background, reuse these same assets, but adds an online functionality so that players can keep track of how well they perform on each song regardless of the game cabinet they use. The Sega online service also ensures that a steady flow of content, most often originating from fan-produced content published on the Internet but also licensed from diverse sources, is added to the game's library to create a dynamic product that evolves along with content creation across the Japanese media environment.[7]

As a popular game, *Project DIVA Arcade* is available in most arcades and, in each case, the cabinet is featured with a standard side panel on the left side of the screen. This part of the machine's design could be overlooked due to its size and secondary function as a board to advertise promotions and current campaigns; however, its primary function as a machine divider in a context in which cabinets are tightly set up one next to the other offers a symbolic separation between users focused into their own play sessions. These panels are often featured on game cabinets that require a certain degree of isolation from other customers in the context of the arcade. However, in the case of *Project DIVA Arcade* as I observed at Ikebukuro GIGO over the course of April 2016, these panels were not enough to ensure player isolation. Additional panels that were the height of the game consoles were installed between most rhythm games on the third floor, and between each of this specific game's cabinets. This arrangement created small cubicles accessible from the front, which provided effective isolation from the user's direct neighbour's play session. The customization of side panels through the vertical extension in the context of Ikebukuro GIGO signified both the space's emphasis on individual experiences and the evolution of an interface design element that was initially conceived as a player-conceived grassroots device but was eventually integrated and applied to mainstream cabinet design as a constitutive part of the game centre cabinet's cultural interface.

Figure 7.4 *Project DIVA Arcade* cabinets and side panels as seen on April 7, 2016. Cabinets are placed side-by-side, separated by two layers of side panels: a small one made of glossy paper advertising special offers and features of the game, and a larger one akin to an office workstation cubicle. Both provide intimacy and isolation from the rest of the venue (photograph by the author).

Though integrated side panels are a relatively recent addition to the standards of contemporary game design cabinets, the idea of creating a portable enclosure device for arcade cabinets during play sessions was developed in parallel to the formation of an arcade gaming culture in the 1980s. As some of the game-dedicated *kissaten* coffee shops became the first full-fledged *invader houses* and, later, game centres, some users began to take games more seriously. High-score-seeking game enthusiasts called *scorelers* sought to perfect their skills, develop new techniques, and find more information that could allow them to reach the highest scores possible on the machines and write their initials on the scoreboards (Ishii, *Gēmu sentā kunonikuru* 160). A certain ethos of gaming performance that guided the most dedicated player base inspired them to maximize the playing conditions that they needed to negotiate. For example, horizontal cocktail cabinets and ambient lights, particularly ceiling lights, tended to produce a glaring effect on the screen, which made the action difficult to see despite the low level of artificial light provided in the venues (Ishii, "Personal interview"). In addition, one could easily be distracted by other players' activities in the venue. For games whose high scores were tied to the discovery of secrets, such as *Tower of Druaga*, players were also encouraged to hide the action on the screen from other players to keep an edge over the competition (Ishii, *Ishii zenji wo ishi ni!* 7).

At some point in the 1980s, a convergence between users and venue operators led to the popularization of *shakōbako* (also called *shakō bokkusu,* meaning *shading box*), a generic name for any type of enclosing device usually made of discarded cardboard boxes or any other type of discarded material on which a hole was carved in one of its sides. Users would put the box bottom-up on cocktail cabinets and face the carved side. The machine, with the box on top of its screen component, would thus be shaded from the ambient light and provide users with a much clearer image of the screen. Players effectively changed the material conditions of the game and the space of the arcade with a device that complemented the cabinet. Over the years, *shakōbako* became staples of arcade gaming; the device became a standard piece of equipment provided by operators themselves, and different variations made out of new materials such as plastic would appear. On rare occasions, manufacturers released cocktail table-style cabinets that themselves integrated the *shakōbako* design element with the addition of a plastic enclosure protecting the screen from light. The do-it-yourself solution to screen glare would become a standard in arcade game operations and is still associated with the image and practice of cocktail cabinets.

The introduction of *shakōbako* to videogame arcades was primarily to provide a solution to the problem of screen glaring by guarding the arcade monitors against ambient light, but it also created an alternative way to engage the games. By using a *shakōbako,* players were negotiating the social conditions of the practice of gaming in public by creating a barrier between them and the game activity, making it physically difficult for other users to observe a user's game session and also signalling that such players did not want to be disturbed. These elements can be said to have contributed to the evolution of arcade game culture in Japan towards normalizing the formation of micro-intimate play spaces within public venues. However, as new types of machines entered the market and cocktail cabinets were discarded in favour of machines providing bigger screens set at an upward angle to prevent screen glaring, the physical device of *shakōbako* was no longer needed or compatible with the new design. Even so, the desirability of a more intimate and individualized play space during play sessions in arcades that the device initiated as a collateral influence endured. In other words, although they had been discarded, *shakōbako* still exercised an influence in the conception of arcade gaming activity. The abstract concept allowing the confinement of the play experience between the user and the machine, guarding it from outside disruption and, to some extent, maximizing game immersion still endured in the culture of arcades.

The gradual disappearance of the versatile cocktail cabinet design over the course of the 1980s allowed for the emergence of other types of cabinets that, in an attempt to turn game sessions into all-encompassing sensory experiences, employed unique designs and output methods tailor-made for a single game that sometimes reiterated the notion of enclosing the players from the space surrounding the cabinet. Sega's 1979 racing game *Monaco GP*, predecessor to 1981 *Turbo* and the *Pole Position* series from 1982 onward, was released at the time of this transition, with three different cabinet types including a cocktail cabinet version integrating an inclined screen, and a sit-down version roughly replicating the design of a Formula One race car cockpit. While not essential for playing, the cockpit of the deluxe version of the cabinet also partially secluded players and the screen, which could only be seen from the sides of the cabinets. This was an innovation over previous electronic and electromechanical racing games previously released by Sega, that would become standard for future racing games for many years, and would also provide inspiration for the creation of the *taikan* game genre that made the company famous in the 1980s (*Kaette kita meisaku gēmu* 20).

Another example of a similar design sensibility for the cabinet enclosing players from the venue can be found in Bandai Namco's 2006 *Kidō senshi gundamu: senjō no kizuna* (henceforth *Senjō no kizuna*). This game, which sold over a thousand sets, each including four interconnected machines and a satellite cabinet, over the first three years of its release was conceptualized as early as 1999 as an answer to an increasingly hostile market for game centres in light of the rapid improvements in home consoles allowing them to deliver technologically impressive experiences similar to those of games in game centres ("Taikan gēmuki" 159–60). The main attraction of *Senjō no kizuna* was its impressive set of egg-shaped cabinets called P.O.D., the first commercial product adaptation of the O.R.B.S. technology developed in-house by Namco's research and development team. Players would step into the machine through a door on the left-hand side, and sit down in front of a dome-like screen displaying the game's action from a projector located behind the seat. The cabinet also included a unique control system made of buttons and levers through which the player engaged in futuristic robotic combat. Though the game used its complete immersion and haptic system to infuse a sense of uniqueness to make arcade machines competitive in the face of an evolving digital entertainment market, the complete player seclusion that it provides seemed like an extension of the idea of *shakōbako* brought to its extreme. Players entered a game device that separates them from the visual, sonic, and, to some extent, olfactory fields of the venue.

Other games also relied more profoundly on the integration of such player-enclosing devices to simply generate the proper conditions to enable players to engage the experience it provides. The date-simulation game *Love Plus Arcade* developed by Konami based on the popular handheld dating game series *Love Plus* invited players to go on dates with a virtual girl to do various types of activities. At any time during the play session, users could take snapshots of the vertically-oriented screen that could then be printed at the cabinet, providing a picture memento of the character and the virtual date. Due to the very intimate nature of the gameplay, which was mostly in the form of conversation between the player character and whose goal was to make the date enjoyable for the virtual girl, the game was equipped with larger side panels that enclosed the entire side of the machine so as to prevent other users from observing the play session from the sides at all. As an attempt to replicate the concepts used for handheld machines that encourage more intimate experiences, these side panels not only prevented noise and distraction but also guaranteed a maximal degree of player privacy.

While the act of engaging arcade videogames occurs primarily in public venues, Japanese game centres and the arcade industry have developed a sensibility for the creation of material conditions that enable isolation and intimacy in their play space. *Shakōbako*, sliders, cockpits, dome-like cabinets, and Ikebukuro GIGO's *Project DIVA Arcade*'s additional cubicle office-inspired cabinet setup structure are among the elements of arcade game design that have come to represent what we could call the Japanese arcade game cultural interface, which acts as an umbrella for arcade games' individual interface. Lev Manovich coined the term *cultural interface* to discuss, in the context of computer and digital interfaces, the integration of the language of different cultural forms that we now commonly call new media. Through "the ways in which computers present and allow us to interact with cultural data" (Manovich 71), human-computer interfaces integrate information in culturally relevant and accessible ways. For Manovich, new media interfaces are essentially aesthetic objects (Galloway 8) integrating conventions, formats and metaphors developed in other media to present relevant information. Manovich identified cinema, the printed word, and the general-purpose human-computer interface, through the metaphor of the desktop, as major influences that, in various forms, contribute to the formation of a language specific to new media platforms.

Manovich's concept examined the nature of new media interfaces by focusing on the direct interface of computers and software, including their code and material conditions such as the screen. As products of new media, arcade games and cabinets also integrate most of Manovich's insights about the integration of conventions of cinema and the printed word in the design of interactive digital games designed for game centres, but this case study suggests that the notion of the interface in a videogame arcade outreaches the boundaries of the screen towards its more general machinic assemblage, which itself includes non-digital elements such as the player-enclosing elements identified above that are commonly found in different forms in the design of many arcade cabinets across decades and genres. It can be said that the cultural interface of Japanese video gaming includes the enclosure device as a metaphor of the notion of a private room to make its interface accessible and organize its experience. Thus, the interface of most arcade games present in Japanese game centres includes side panels, sliders, and other enclosing devices, which are as much part of the content of the game experience or diegesis as their buttons, levers, and other control mechanisms.

The metaphor of the private room has been used in efforts to interpret some of the aspects of Japanese urban life influenced by new media, especially the spaces of Akihabara and Ikebukuro. Morikawa invokes the examples of the presence of display case spaces rented by figurine collectors to proudly show their collections, and the overflow of anime and manga-related advertisements and products available in these spaces, to liken parts of these public districts to private rooms:

> Businessmen gather in office districts because of their social status and roles. The takenoko-zoku were performers using Harajuku as their stage; they did not continue acting out their roles once they went home. The phenomenon in Akihabara, by contrast, represents the extension of private into public spaces, personal rooms into cities. (154)

In essence, the private space of otaku and media fanatics' bedrooms can be said to be echoed in these specific urban public spaces, of which Ikebukuro GIGO is not only part but also a central gathering point. The private, or the personal room, is echoed in Ikebukuro not only with regard to the abundance of media-related objects and images displayed inside but also because otaku do not take on particular social roles akin to salarymen or takenoko-zoku members when navigating their attributed social space.

Private rooms enable people to decorate a space with items toward which they might feel affinity, such as posters or models of favourite characters of media mix products, but are also spaces of isolation and privacy in which one would feel at ease and comfortable engaging in solitary activities such as playing videogames. This aspect was reflected in the use of the extended sliders located on each side of the *Project DIVA Arcade* cabinets in Ikebukuro GIGO. The use of the office cubicle side panels extended the realm of the private in the public space of the arcade and provided an arcade gaming experience characterized by effectively isolating players from the machines and players in its direct vicinity to create a play space devoid of visual and sonic input from the rest of the venue. Player isolation was thus an essential component of the ludo-egregore of the venue, as users were less exposed to public observation while engaging with the machines. Ikebukuro GIGO emphasized an element of the cultural interface of arcade games, the *shakōbako* enclosing device, to generate ludo-egegora characterized by an underscoring of player privacy in which interpersonal interactions are minimal despite being in a crowded public space.

The case study of *Project DIVA Arcade*'s cabinet set up in this venue demonstrates how negotiation between the private and the public in arcades can lean toward securing more private individual play spaces while demonstrating the nature of arcade game machines as assemblages. However, this particularity must be contextualized in the broader media environment that Ikebukuro GIGO itself echoes and to which it contributes to support the existence of the spatial organs of the media mix. In the context of player isolation and individualized play spaces in a public setting, the network that connects these products is important in an investigation of the ludo-egregore of these games. This also demonstrates that arcade games are historically layered design objects that take inspiration from the material conditions of older games, repurposing and reassembling them to create experiences that both draw on the old and reach for the new.

National Networks: Play, the Public Sphere, and Communication in the Connected Media Mix

This examination of the ludic space of Ikebukuro GIGO points to a key aspect of the great majority of the commercial sphere of arcade game playing in large urban centres in Japan. Whereas user proximity and interactions characterized much of the ludo-egregore generated in the spaces of A-cho and Tsujishōten, the social space of Ikebukuro GIGO was limited and structured by a series of elements not only meant to maximize players' immersion but also acting as constraints on the development of gregarious play activity and culture. In game centres, the spatial organ of the media mix, users are encouraged to interact with characters, worlds, and icons in the media mix and the broader Japanese media ecology. Interactions with fellow players remain heavily influenced by the cultural interface of the arcade machine and mediated through specific commands online. With fewer direct interpersonal interactions taking place within this space, the social imaginary becomes more closely related to what the software and cabinet design bring forward, as well as the media environment of the arcade and its industry. We may call this arrangement of geographically and corporately exclusive interconnections of machines and arcades *national networks* managed jointly by manufacturers and operators. These networks enable these agents to control access to games, enforce certain types of operational strategies, and mediate communication occurring between players, influencing the rhythm of play, the flow of ludic trajectories, and the formation of ludo-egregores.

Activities with a high potential for socialization, such as videogame playing within the context of Japanese arcades, take place in locations whose value is determined by their perception by a majority of people; arcades are as much imagined spaces as physical ones. Media take on critical roles in the shaping the function of, and value associated with, these imagined spaces and, consequently, influence the interactions between people within and outside of these spaces on a broader level. Habermas noted that in the eighteenth century, the space of coffee houses was instrumental in creating the conditions for the emergence of democratic life and a public sphere, described as a space of discussion of public affairs without regards to social status or position (Habermas 27). The development and the increased reach of printing technology were also crucial to the formation of this movement (Habermas 21) and would later come to provide material for discussion between the educated strata of society of different origins, thus establishing the basis of a community based around the discussion of public affairs.

Benedict Anderson also points out the capacity of media to form its public into an imagined community, best exemplified by the importance of printing technology and its democratization in Europe, as the fast production rate of printing machines, distribution strategies using commercial networks, and use of vernacular language converged to form a common national consciousness (37–44). This capacity of media to form a public by affecting the social imaginary has also been criticized by Marxist theorists, especially Adorno, who characterizes the media industry of the twentieth century as manipulating and homogenizing its public by disseminating the elite's ideology within the cultural fabric by emphasizing distraction rather than self-reflection (György 74). From democracy to social control, over the centuries specific spaces have been venues for the dissemination of certain media forms that carry with them the potential to transform the social imagination.

The twenty-first century, however, has witnessed the emergence of interactive media as a dominant media form that permeates life in the spaces of both work and entertainment; the dynamics that characterize new media influence the contemporary social imaginary in different ways than their forebears did. According to Kirkpatrick, interactive media, and videogames in particular, create their own social imaginary and socialization space mediated by interface and content directed by mercantile interest that comes in opposition to democratic ideals. Unlike the more passive reception pattern of traditional media, users become co-producers of interactive content due to the increased commitment that software demands from them, and are thus exposed to mediation and ideologies in different ways:

> the positive work of games and gamers in fashioning new social spaces becomes more of a source of concern because, rather than being spaces of deliberation and choice compatible with the democratic ideal of citizenship, the new spaces they open up in our experience may actually be opening to more profound kinds of manipulation and social control. (Kirkpatrick 21)

The forms of manipulation and social control to which Kirkpatrick alludes concerns, amongst other things, the blurring of the line between play and work in the digital sphere, in which capturing gamers' labour force under the guise of play is increasingly present on platforms and products dependent on dynamics of user-generated content, such as the practice of *modding* (124–25), or the structure of data, game economy, and social capital in MMORPGs such as *World of Warcraft* to allow players to attain any objective if they spend enough time performing mundane and repetitive tasks to improve their avatars' skill sets (157).

A similar phenomenon could be observed in the design of network-enabled Japanese arcade games that primarily populate large-scale game centres such as Ikebukuro GIGO, and also those that reward attention paid to the online economy and social interaction of games online, thus diminishing the incentive to give games a certain added value based on their local play space. In other words, both participants and observers of the play activity are displaced from the direct space of the venue towards the virtual space of the game software, which involves computer mediation through the interface of the machines and the games. While communication between players who interact online through arcade machines is possible, the nature of arcades as public platforms that generate revenue through play sessions whose duration is controlled through gameplay interfaces usually does not allow the development of strong and persistent social contacts or encounters. Rather, ephemeral contacts that pair players through a randomized algorithm determine social encounters, and a set of mediated communicative gestures and predetermined sentences ensures that all contact remains quick, minimal, and devoid of toxicity.

This was the case for the MOBA game *Wonderland Wars,* whose interface allowed a team of three players to send a variety of cheering messages and context-sensitive directional cues to help players plan and establish a strategy within a match. In addition, during and at the end of each match, the users were invited to send congratulatory messages by clicking the "Nice!" button and a selected player's avatar; giving and receiving such messages were rewarded with additional participation points that grant players additional resources and *kyasuto*, or characters, to play. This regime of player interaction mediation embeds certain values in such communicative acts and ensures that encounters between players remain cordial and sustainable within the game environment, but at the cost of meaningful communication. What is at stake in the jump from arcade space to the virtual space as the main social platform in public play is thus the instrumentalization of player interaction by game manufacturers through such in-game functions that mediate social encounters.

The network environment of contemporary arcade games also enforces a geographically strict environment in which players exclusively from within Japan, due to the cost of operating the game centre's network, can play within these virtual spaces. Within this system, when paired with another player, the system also indicates the region of Japan, and specifically the game centre, in which his/her opponent or teammate is playing, effectively re-entering the social imaginary of the play activity and the sense of gaming community towards the pre-established model of the nation. Specific games also remediate player location data through the fiction of the game itself. For example, the 2011 strategy game *Sengoku taisen,* which takes place in the warring state period, pits two players against one another with the goal of invading the opponent's castle using cards that they manipulate on a flat reader panel; as they move the cards, their characters move on screen and perform various types of attacks and manoeuvres. The game integrates a player location identification system displaying the locations of opposing players, and also marking that space through its appropriate historical location from the warring states period, identifying Tokyo as Edo, for instance, and other regions with their respective feudal domains. In this case, the fiction of the game reflects the conditions of the national networks of game centres and software manufacturers.

The ludic activity here was effectively displaced towards the online virtual space, and also towards a historical geography that focuses on the social imaginary of Japan as a contemporary national construct acting as a continuation of previous sociopolitical organizations that ignores surrounding countries. This in turn echoed the independence of the Japanese arcade game industry from the rest of the world's digital entertainment business. By focusing on Japan as the sole extent of the game network covered by the arcade industry, encounters with the Other are prevented, much like how focusing the social imaginary of arcade games towards virtual worlds increases the gap between the users directly within a venue. Arcade game manufacturers that operate this network also exert an increasing amount of control over the fashion in which their games are played; network-connected games automatically shut down at midnight in accordance with the government's *fūeihō* regulations effective across Japan and restrict player access when too little operation time is left before all venues shut down for the night on a national level. This makes clandestine operations and the playing of contemporary arcade games outside of the framework of the law very difficult, relegating off-the-grid arcade gaming activities to older machines.

However, the social control of the contemporary arcade machine manufacturers, as with any type of digital media, also has its limits; the types of interactions made possible by contemporary arcade game playing are not necessarily determined by the intended functions designed into the material conditions of the machine. Rather, as stated before, these methods of interaction are born from the encounters of players, ludic trajectories, and the many affordances, both functional and social, that can be perceived from the machines' design. Though arcades often embody the most commercial facet of the Japanese media environment, game centres are also creative grounds not only for the development of new technology but also in the practice and use of digital entertainment technology in a public setting.

For example, *Sengoku taisen* was made for a solitary play style involving the player, the card collection, and interaction with other players in different venues through the network connection, but over the course of my observations, I noticed many instances of subversive use of its optimal play conditions. Most notably, on many occasions and in different game centres throughout Japan, one may witness the game being played in tandem, with two players sitting beside one another at the machine and sharing control over the different cards played on the flat reader panel. The bench provided by the game manufacturer was large enough to cover the entire play field of the machine, which also allowed two players to sit close to one another with easy access to either the left- or right-hand side of the cabinet. In addition, splitting control of the cards in play did allow more complex operations to be performed, but required more communication to coordinate movements, effectively turning the game into a more challenging team-based experience requiring a high level of involved sociability. Although *Sengoku Taisen* did implement design elements directing the optimal play experience towards solitary play, the ludic trajectory of players seeking an experience suited for such an involved notion of cooperative play sometimes perceives the affordances of machines differently, in a way that manufacturers or operators did not necessarily predict or encourage. Ultimately, as such counterintuitive gaming tactics would suggest in a place such as Ikebukuro GIGO, the definition of the game experience attached to a specific title remains strongly performative rather than associated with a pre-defined essence of the game as based on the authorial input of its designers.

Conclusion: Together in the Networks

Ikebukuro GIGO as a ludic space situated at the convergence of players' ludic trajectories and the material conditions of the machines could be said to be located somewhere between the interests of the media ecology of Japan, including the commercial imperatives of the media mix and manufacturers' national networks that control the flow of the game and mediate its interactions, and a site of playful creative potential in which players often subversively operated the machines to produce alternative play patterns. To play in public is also to negotiate the type of experience sought between the optimal conditions provided by the machines, and other types of experiences that push the boundaries of what types of ludic engagements are possible in public settings. From this perspective, Ikebukuro GIGO, despite the commercial imperatives that its architectural structure suggests, was also a site of experimentation in which new forms of engagement were developed and, eventually, could fuel the imagination of game manufacturers to then be reintegrated into the design of other products.

However, the relation between the player, the game, and the observers in the context of a play space designed to emphasize player isolation, and the displacement of the social ludic engagement online, were defining elements of the ludo-egregore generated in Ikebukuro GIGO that I could observe. The playing experience here was more closed off from the influence of other players observing a game session than in other locations. This is not to say that sharing the screen with a stranger is not possible in this context, but that the material conditions of the venue do not afford it. Here, the side panels as a cultural interface turn the player toward the private experience and, as a result, play as performance is intended only for the active user, as well as fellow participants connected to the network. This type of installation allowed the intrinsic ludic invitation proposed by the game's software, and its mediated social structure in the case of online games, to be the main object of focus.

The ludo-egregore generated by these types of experiences was thus located on a broader plane than in the other spaces investigated in this study: the sense of unity generated between players, machine, and software here was shared predominantly online, where all human actors involved are necessary active players. Though the latter took active parts in shaping the nature of the shared experience, non-human actors such as the software interface of the game and its built-in socialization mediation interface in particular perhaps influenced and contributed in standardizing the experience more than the players themselves. Thus, the form of ludo-egregore, which we may qualify as virtual if not imagined, generated within these conditions extended beyond the physicality of the play space to involve other agents located in different similarly organized play spaces throughout Japan, which, as a result, could be said to further associate this activity with the nation as a collection of individuals interacting through the same ludic platforms simultaneously.

Notes

1 As mentioned in Chapter 3, Sega no longer operates a videogame arcade division since 2022.

2 Douglas McGray first discussed the export of popular culture now commonly understood to fall under the umbrella of "cool Japan" as the country's "gross national cool". See his 2009 article for more detail.

3 As the central hub of female-oriented pop culture in Tokyo, Ikebukuro warrants its own discussion, but such prospect falls outside the scope of this study. For a gendered perspective on Otome-road pedestrian culture, see Ernest dit Alban.

4 See Chapter 4 of this book for further detail on Lefebvre's spatial triad.

5 While certain representations of the *Love Live!* franchise such as the animation series of the same name can be traced back to a single studio, the multimedia project's stakeholders are numerous, including Kadokawa, ASCII Mediaworks and Bandai Namco.
6 Expanding on Joleen Bloom's notion of the "dynamic game character" which is defined as a predominantly player-constructed phenomenon requiring the active input of player (199), one might associate these practice of pretend-worshipping, alongside the birthday celebration event, as arcade-specific instances of this process of active input which then feed the construction of the character and enrich the game experience.
7 See Coundry for more detail on the role of the Hatsune Miku franchise in the development of the "social energy that arise from" people's "collective engagements" through Japanese animation (2).

Works Cited

Amyūzumento sōgō kenkyūjo, editor. *Amyūzumento* [*Amusement*]. Sangakusha, 2014.

Anderson, Benedict. *Imagined Communities: Reflections on the Origin and Spread of Nationalism*. 1983. Verso, 2006.

Aoyama, Yuko, and Hiro Izushi. "Hardware Gimmick or Cultural Innovation? Technological, Cultural, and Social Foundations of the Japanese Video Game Industry." *Research Policy*, vol. 32, 2003, pp. 423–44.

Ashcraft, Brian. "Arcade Creates Area for Worshipping Anime Girls." *Kotaku*, 4 Aug. 2015, https://kotaku.com/arcade-creates-area-for-worshipping-anime-girls-1721945977.

Bessho, Makoto, director. *Idolish7*. Troyca Studio, 2015.

Blom, Joleen. *The Dynamic Game Character: Definition, Construction, and Challenges in a Character Ecology*. U of Copenhagen, PhD Dissertation, 2020.

Chalfen, Richard, and Mai Murui. "Print Club Photography in Japan: Framing Social Relationship." *Visual Studies*, vol. 16, no. 1, 2001, pp. 55–73.

Columns. Arcade videogame cabinet, Sega, 1989.

Coundry, Ian. *The Soul of Anime: Collaborative Creativity and Japan's Media Success Story*. Duke UP, 2013.

Denison, Rayna. *Anime: A Critical Introduction*. Bloomsbury Academic, 2015.

Ernest dit Alban, Edmond. *Le recyclage comme moteur de la fabrique de l'espace social (et piéton) du sanctuaire féminin otaku d'Otome-Road à Ikebukuro* [*Recycling as the Driving Force of the Formation of Social (and Pedestrian) Space in the Feminine Sanctuary of Otome-road in Ikebukuro*], *Tokyo*. Concordia U, PhD Dissertation, 2019.

E.T.: The Extra-Terrestrial. Atari 2600 videogame, Atari, 1982.

Fujita, Yoichi, director. *Osomatsu-san*. Studio Pierro, 2015.

Galloway, Alexander R. *The Interface Effect*. Polity P, 2012.

"Gēmu sentā nante mō iwanai - amyūzumento supēsu ni henshin! [Don't Say Game Centres Anymore. They Turned into Amusement Spaces!]." *Mainichi shinbun*, Evening edition, 3 Apr. 1991, p. 5.

György, Markus. "Adorno and Mass Culture: Autonomous Art against the Culture Industry." *Thesis Eleven*, vol. 86, no. 1, 2006, pp. 67–89.

Habermas, Jürgen. *The Structural Transformation of the Public Sphere: An Inquiry into a Category of Bourgeois Society*. Translated by Thomas Burger and Frederick Lawrence, MIT P, 1991.

Hatsune Miku: Project DIVA Arcade. Arcade videogame cabinet, Sega, 2010.

Idolish7. Mobile device videogame, Bandai Namco, 2015.

Ishii, Zenji. *Gēmu sentā kunonikuruzu: 1972–2017* [*Game Centres Chronicles: 1972–2017*]. Standards, 2017.

———. *Ishii zenji wo ishi ni! Moto gēmesuto henshū-chō koramushū* [*Ishii Zenji Going Left! Columns Articles Collection by the Former Gamest Magazine Editor*]. Hobby Japan, 2015.

———. *Personal Interview*, 4 Apr. 2016.

Jenkins, Henry. *Convergence Culture: Where Old and New Media Collide*. New York UP, 2006.

Katō, Hiroyasu. *Gēmu sentā bunkaron: media shakai no comyunikēshon* [*Theory of Game Centre Culture: Communication in the Media Society*]. Shinsensha, 2011.

———. "Online jidai no gēmu sentā [Game Centres in the Online Age]." *Digitaru no kiwa* – jōhō to busshitsu ga majiwaru genzaichiten [*The Digital Moment – Contemporary Mixing of Information and Materiality*], Seigakuin daigaku shuppansha, 2014, pp. 267–305.

Kidō senshi gandamu: senjō no kizuna. Bandai Namco, Arcade videogame cabinet, 2006.

Kidō senshi gandamu: U.C. Card Builder. Sega, Arcade videogame cabinet, 2016.

Kirkpatrick, Graeme. *Computer Games and the Social Imaginary*. Polity P, 2013.

Lefebvre, Henri. *La Production de l'espace* [*The Production of Space*]. Éditions Anthropos, 1974.

Love Plus. Nintendo DS videogame, Konami, 2009.

Love Plus Arcade. Arcade videogame cabinet, Konami, 2011.

Lupin III. Arcade videogame cabinet, Taito, 1980.

Madara. Family Computer videogame, Konami, 1990.

Mai Mai. Arcade videogame cabinet, Sega, 2012.

Manovich, Lev. *The Language of New Media*. MIT P, 2002.

McGray, Douglas. "Japan's Gross National Cool." *Foreign Policy*, 2002, pp. 44–54.

Mobile Suit Gundam: Gundam Vs. Gundam. Arcade videogame cabinet, Branpresto, 2008.

Monaco GP. Arcade videogame cabinet, Sega, 1979.

Montfort, Nick, and Ian Bogost. *Racing the Beam: The Atari Video Computer System*. MIT P, 2009.

Morikawa, Kaichiro. "Otaku and the City: The Rebirth of Akihabara." *Fandom Unbound: Otaku Culture in a Connected World*, edited by Daisuke Okabe, Mizuko Ito and Izumi Tsuji, Yale UP, 2012, pp. 133–57.

Nobuoka, Yoshikuni, Kazuo Kobayashi, Atsushi Hosokawa, and Yūji Hayami. *Kore kara no gēmu sentā keiei* [*The Future of Game Centre Management*]. Edited by Yūichi Tadano, Keiei Jōhō Shuppansha, 1994.

Otsuka, Eiji, and Marc Steinberg. "World and Variation: The Reproduction and Consumption of Narrative." *Mecademia: Franthropologies*, translated by Marc Steinberg, vol. 5, U of Minnesota P, 2010, pp. 99–117.

Pole Position. Arcade videogame cabinet, Sega, 1982.

Puyo Puyo. Arcade videogame cabinet, Compile, 1991.

Roquet, Paul. *Ambient Media: Japanese Atmospheres of Self*. U of Minnesota P, 2016.

Sengoku taisen. Arcade videogame cabinet, Sega, 2010.

Shark Jaws. Arcade videogame cabinet, Atari, Inc, 1975.

Steinberg, Marc. "8-Bit Manga: Kadokawa's Madara, or, The Gameic Media Mix." *Kinephanos*, vol. 5, no. 1, 2015, pp. 40–52.

———. *Anime's Media Mix: Franchising Toys and Characters in Japan*. U of Minnesota P, 2012.

"Taikan gēmuki Kidō senshi gandamu senjō no kizuna no kaihatsu – dai ikkai – Yoru na yoru na yakuin ōsetu ni shinobikomu [The Development of the Taikan Video Game Kidō senshi gandamu: senjō no kizuna – Part 1 – Sneaking into the Executive Officials' Office Night after Night]." *Nikkei Electronics*, 21 Sept. 2009, pp. 158–61.

Takahiko, Kyōgoku, director. *Love Live!* Sunrise, 2012.

Takashi, Gomikawa, editor. *Kaette kita meisaku gēmu 1978~1987* [*The Returning Masterpiece Games*]. Riido, 1995.
Tetris. Arcade videogame cabinet, Sega, 1988.
Tezuka, Osamu. *Tetsuwan Atomu*. Mushi Production, 1963–1966.
Tower of Druaga, The. Arcade videogame cabinet, Namco, 1984.
Turbo. Arcade videogame cabinet, Sega, 1981.
Wonderland Wars. Arcade videogame cabinet, Sega, 2015.
World of Warcraft. Personal computer videogame, Blizzard Entertainment, 2004.
Xevious. Arcade videogame cabinet, Namco, 1983.

8 Conclusion

Game Centres and Videogame Arcade Play as a Rupture of the Quotidian

Ludo-egregore: A Model for Situated Gaming

This project has investigated and contributed to defining the history and culture of Japanese game centres in an urban context, and from a theoretical perspective, the situatedness of public gaming. The three case studies that comprise the bulk of this project provide insight into the nature of Japanese game centres as diversified cultural sites of research marked by both the broader culture of Japan as a society and by practices, material conditions, strategies used by industries, and tactics borrowed by players and passersby, which, taken as a whole, constitute a subculture of arcade gaming specific to the sites examined. The study examines the contextualization and situatedness of games, demonstrating their importance in the definition of games as sets of circumstances and textual qualities. In light of these developments, this project proposes a new perspective from which the study of games played predominantly in public settings may be examined to understand their dynamics.

The model of a ludo-egregoric analysis—that is, an investigation that focuses on gaming as a shared common engagement between human and non-human agents, both active and passive—cannot be rendered with a simple and straightforward analytical workflow. Guides introducing the steps and elements to examine as part of a field study of public gaming are also well-nigh impossible. Nevertheless, this perspective is essential to understand the microscopic aspect of situated gaming in public locations, as it reveals how machines, cultures, and publics interact with one another, which is essential to the study of play itself. While the examination of gaming rhythms allows one to connect local dynamics with broader global cultural, technological, and sociological moments, the ludo-egregore catalyzed by games allows one to link the affordances of gaming in its materiality, the social interactions it generates and by which it is influenced, and the immediate spatial context that structures the activity. At the heart of this method centred around the idea of ludo-egregores is the objective of dividing the public play phenomenon in terms of individual moments situated in both space and time, which then emphasizes the plurality, simultaneity, and ephemerality of experiences that contribute to defining, on a performative level, the phenomenon of playing games in public.

DOI: 10.4324/9781003273776-10

Just as this project has attempted to argue that the study of videogame arcades cannot be dissociated from the situated conditions in which they operate, it is challenging to provide guidelines for the use of ludo-egregore as an analytical model in a vacuum, as it is deeply dependent on context. Nevertheless, and despite this shortcoming, in its emphasis on the microscopic and the ephemeral, I believe it is useful as an additional lens for scholars through which to examine play in public in many different types of situations. Similarly to the data acquisition method that marks this project, the idea of ludo-egregore encourages keen and distanced observations of the flow of circulation of people, which may well apply to the examination of the increasing number of digital interactive installations made to inform, entertain, or connect people in cities' public squares. Amongst the multiplicity and simultaneity of interactions, it identifies videogames and digital interactive texts as catalysts through which contraction and dissipation of energy from a variety of agents assemble and territorialize space through objects and signs, which may underscore observations of videogame arcades, game parlours, and eSports arenas in many contexts across the world. Tracing these agents and their trajectories, human or otherwise, may help name and reveal the dynamics that explain the pertinence of these institutions and the values associated with them.

For similar reasons, it was not the original intent of this project to situate and apply this model to game centres and amusement centres in a historical perspective, but one may be tempted to draw a few conclusions from the elements underlined throughout the project, more specifically how play is harnessed to communicate ideas in public settings. If colonial imagery and the ideology justifying the domination of East Asia by Japan as an imperial entity permeated the devices that populated early forms of amusement centres—ironically, before the material reality of the war in the Pacific theatre caused their disappearance—on rooftops and spring resorts in the 1920s, and, similarly, the newly emerging logic of consumer societies had a profound influence on the types of public amusement found in Japanese cities such as in medal game parlours in the 1970s, what type of ideologies do game centres embody? How do they, as ludic spaces that showcase a will to provide a sense of place located beyond the bounds of everyday life, translate or subvert the socio-political realities of contemporary Japan? The emergence of individuality-driven *kissaten* coffee houses in the 1970s, strongly associated with the videogame boom led by *Space Invaders* during the same period due to the introduction of cocktail table game cabinets, provides a clear narrative of the influence of space-related narratives and the introduction of computers as entertainment devices. However, we find no compelling overarching narratives that link social trends to the types of games present in game centres. Game centres are now as numerous and diversified as the games produced for them.

Case Studies as Snapshots

The three examples of game centres studied in this project provide clues of significant importance as to which broad tendencies characterize game centres. All the venues examined here, and particularly A-cho, demonstrated the marked presence of a specific subculture existing thanks to the establishment of norms, practices, and a certain ethos related to public gaming itself, linked to a specific genre of games. These sets of values, whether they are implicitly followed or, as in certain cases, more explicitly suggested, heavily influenced the ludic disposition players adopt towards games, the space, and its social climate. These all contributed to the generation of types of ludo-egregores in which the player/observer relationship, based on the idea of performance and competition, as evident in our examination of the *BlazBlue: Continuum Shift* Ranking Battle tournament, was emphasized the most.

The case of Tsujishōten, however, reminds us that game centres also act as familiar third spaces in which elements of interpersonal interactions and the nurturing of a sense of community are underscored. As demonstrated by the analysis of the *Mobile Suit Gundam: Extreme Vs.* play session, this space, and presumably others similar to it, were gathering places for small groups of players who firmly occupied a play space that remained set apart from the rest of the venue. Through a combination of spatial tactics and use of the cabinets, they formed an intimate bubble within a technically public sphere where they nevertheless freely express themselves. This indicates that game centres, despite their profoundly public nature, are also repurposed in other ways. They allow citizens to reconnect with the self outside formal structures, such as work, school, or facility life, that often impose duties or responsibilities. This emphasizes another aspect of game machines beyond their prescribed ludic functions; cabinets are perceived according to their most basic uses as glorified benches or makeshift beds that, unlike public parks, offer privacy and intimacy. Sleeping or eating snacks at isolated machines can be described as different types of the same broad trajectory, known as hanging behaviour, in which citizens populate the space of arcades for reasons other than engaging in a preconfigured ludic activity.

The case study of the Sega Ikebukuro GIGO game centre showed another side of game-centre culture in Japan and allowed this project to touch upon the issues of broader scope in relation to the rhythm of Ikebukuro as a district, Tokyo as a city, and Japan, along with its vast entertainment industry, as a media ecology with national borders. Game centres are also major centres of media convergence for many popular industries, most notably the animation, manga, and game industries. The space of game centres acts as one of the many types of spaces in which the Japanese media mix can be disseminated in a more situated fashion; the space becomes a gathering site in which specific gestures acquire meaning and grant a certain degree of cultural capital for those who perform those gestures.[1] Game centres are spaces that call for a ludic disposition from their participants, and their spaces provide symbolic meanings to certain actions that would, in other contexts, seem out of place. The games themselves also provide alternative sites in which further narrative fragments of a fictional world can be consumed. On the other hand, the ludo-egregore of GIGO Ikebukuro was marked by a pronounced importance of player isolation, as evidenced in our analysis of the cabinet of *Hatsune Miku: Project DIVA Arcade*, more specifically its side panels which effectively cut off the player from his/her surrounding environment, but which can also be read as a cultural interface with a specific history tied to the space of the game centre. The primary method of interaction between players was displaced online on the national network that connects venues throughout the country. Thus, the appropriate metaphor to discuss similar places is more closely related to the image of one's bedroom, in which collections of images and figurines produced by the media mix frame a more physically isolated activity that nevertheless provides connection with other people through specific products. The structure of the space itself imposes a specific configuration of public gaming influencing gender presence, machine use, and play on the axis of gregariousness.

Game Centres in Daily Life: Ruptures of the Quotidian and Commercial Spaces

Although the multitude of game centres in Japan cannot be reduced to a single form or function, on a broad scale, we can safely identify characteristics that are common at least to all the case studies explored in this project. Indeed, if games and play provide their users with a sense of temporary escape from real life thanks to alternative rule-based environments and fictional worlds, game centres, as sites collecting many games and other devices and installations to be used in a ludic fashion, similarly provide respites from, and ruptures in, the rhythms of everyday life. When entering a game centre in the middle of walking through a densely crowded downtown area or simply commuting home, one notices how these spaces, through their architectural structure and machine installation, invite us to adopt a ludic mindset. Elements such as dimmed lights, bombastic soundscapes, and, often, the smell of cigarettes are all different from other standards common to other urban establishments and signal the quasi-otherworldly nature that game centre operators want to project. From the rooftop amusement centres developed in the 1920s to the contemporary game-centre chains that comprise most of the urban scene, operators always ensured that the spaces they built were unconventional and gave the impression of stepping into a different world.

Paradoxically, however, while these spaces are designed to provide a sense of rupture from normal life, they are increasingly connecting their players to the broader media environment that permeates daily life. Players are thus more connected than ever to products, images, franchises, and the nation itself through the network of game centres distributed around the country and in which venues serve as nodes. This system is emancipating, as it allows players to play beyond the rhythm of the venue or city where they play, but it is also limiting, most notably in terms of disconnection with the local game culture and practices and bordering the gameplay experience to the nation. Images and ideas that permeate the urban environment are also present in game centres.

Each venue is different from others, but one common thread can be located on the axis of performance/intimacy, in which each venue negotiates both tendencies in ways that distinguish them from others. On one end, the assemblage of certain game centres favours the generation of ludo-egregores based on performance and spectatorship, in which players stage their play activity and themselves in public for the attention of an audience. Various devices, such as specific machine types and television screens distributed across venues, allow these dynamics to reach the entire venue at any given time, and thus enforce this specific ethos of gaming. Others, however, favour a structure in which players can more easily feel secluded from observers and fellow players. *Shakōbako* and their subsequent transformation into side panels for more contemporary machines are devices and materials that enable the generation of intimate ludo-egregores, thus allowing certain types of play and engagement patterns despite their public settings.

In other words, operators use two main metaphors to convey a sense of play within game centres. On one end, some game centres are treated as *arenas* in which players engage in the ludic activity, knowing full well that they are providing a show for observers that themselves influence players through their observation. On the other end of the spectrum, other venues convey the image of game centres as otaku *bedrooms* in which one can safely be surrounded by familiar fan images and objects ranging from anime series to videogame characters. It is also a metaphor for the intimate and the secure, as the panels between some machines and the seclusion of others offer a distinct sense of privacy akin to one's own home.

However, given the historical reach of this project, it would not be correct to assume that game centres and other public amusement spaces in Japan show evolution, at least not in the sense of stages of technological and sociopolitical conditions making previous ones obsolete. On the contrary, in contemporary urban spaces in Japan, multiple forms of game centres coexist, from the small neighbourhood store to the big national chain and everything in between. Amusement spaces providing prize-based games still thrive, and in every major city, one can still find small-scale game centres offering primarily off-line play experiences. Different forms of play engagement also coexist within a single venue. New types of spaces and ludo-egregores do not erase previous ones, but rather add to the mosaic of public gaming offerings.

Perhaps, at this point, it is relevant to revisit one of the most persistent questions surrounding Japanese videogame arcades. Why, despite the emergence of more convenient play devices ranging from the powerful home console to the practical handheld machine, do game centres still exist in Japan? Why do people still want to visit these public places to play games that, in many cases, are available on other platforms? To refer to a question asked previously in this project, what are people looking for in game centres? These questions have been raised in Japan since the 1980s, and their endurance is a testimony to the complex answer they warrant. There is no single answer that can address the myriad functions of these spaces, but considering the case studies examined here, we can provide at least a partial interpretation.

Perhaps what explains the success of game centres in Japan and their continued relevance is that they negotiate the balance between strategies of operators and tactics employed by players to navigate the space. Despite the clear economic incentives of game centres as income-generating businesses, these spaces remain flexible in allowing users nurturing a variety of ludic trajectories to realize their objectives in different ways, even ways that could be considered subversive. Beyond issues related to profitability and return on investments, operators are creating spaces that can be inhabited and that users feel free to call their own. Even though game centres are undeniably part of a larger economic network that pushes forward economic and emotional investment in cultural products and commodities from their customers, they also provide a structure and framework that are, in large part, permissive, and that allow individuals or groups to appropriate them and call them their own in various ways.

Games are catalysts for the emergence of a spirit of community based on play, but it is the joint assemblage of the cabinets and the space as interpreted by active and non-active users that come to fully realize the play activity in ways that are not possible in other contexts. Perhaps it is toward the diversity of the play experiences that involve interactions between players, observers, game software, cabinet design, and overall space structure—a concept that we call ludo-egregore—that we must direct our gazes in order to understand the dynamics of game centres. As this investigation demonstrates, the broad question of what functions game centres fulfil in urban Japan should be answered by a micro-investigation of how the dynamics of interaction of the games they house play out on an empirical level.

Further Research: Preservation and Heterotopias

Even as the main axis of analysis extracted by the case studies observed in this project identified the intimacy/performance concept as central, this idea might certainly not be the only one worthy of attention. A project of this scope is bound to encounter certain practical limitations that prevent the exploration of important aspects, sites, and practices that would benefit our general understanding of Japanese game centres and of situated gaming in general. As a final comment, I will here suggest a few paths for further investigations that touch upon issues that, throughout this project, have emerged as relevant elements connected to the fundamental aspects of research on public gaming and Japanese cultural studies.

Perhaps the most self-evident aspect of this study is the need for further research on the dynamics of arcade gaming on a historical level. As previously noted, game centres and arcade videogame parlours are public spaces that change at very high speeds; in the case of Japan, older venues are also closing their doors while others open up shop. These transformations carry with them important spatial and sociopolitical structures informing the play dynamics and ludic rhythms of these spaces, and thus make analysis difficult, especially for venues that ceased to exist decades ago. However, a historical perspective on the development of game centres' play dynamics remains essential to understand current practices and spaces. Thus, the challenge becomes one of retrieving information of specific locations based on second-hand material and oral histories to inform our understanding of these places. This would necessarily involve efforts to reconsider game preservation practices and methodologies beyond games as playable programs and cabinets as material conditions of the play activity to include space from the point of view of architecture, and its multiplicity and simultaneity based on various first-hand accounts and second-hand material.

Although this project sheds light on situated gaming as an all-pervasive phenomenon, too little has been said about game cabinets and software in relation to their effects on the body itself. Arcade machines and software often feature input methods that require players to enact gestures and body movements that are rarely seen in traditional videogame design but are also unconventional to perform in public spaces. The rhythm game *Chunithm*, for example, mimics the often-flamboyant style of professional pianists performing on stage, such as lifting both hands in the air before hitting specific keys. The game thus captures an element relative to performance and repurposes it to its system so that points are granted when the movement is performed properly. Bringing light to the importance of re-entering our understanding of arcade games in situated context thus allows us to refocus on the body on a holistic level in relation to the play activity and in relation to the space in which it takes place.

A last point of interest to which further research should be directed concerns, not strictly the empirical analysis of game centres, but rather the study of their representations in different media and examining their effects on arcades as imaginary constructs and urban heterotopias.[2] The focus of this project is the co-presence of users, machines, software, and space, but one cannot undervalue the importance of the perception of the social and ludic frames of game centres through their representations and discourses that, over the years, have come to constitute a body of literature in themselves. Game centres are represented profusely in, as one would expect, manga, animation, and videogames themselves, but more recent works of cinema, television drama, and even literature invoke the images of game centres and project onto them certain ideas, expectations, and feelings that, inevitably, frame the public's perception of these spaces, and thus potentially influence how people approach and inhabit them daily. For certain communities and individuals, game centres have an imaginary use tainted by these representations that are as important as their actual uses. Uncovering these heterotopias in fiction and literature will enable us to nurture a broader understanding of the multiple meanings of playing in public.

Notes

1 The term *cultural capital* is used in accordance with Pierre Bourdieu's model. In the context of the worshipping practice presented in Chapter 8, this term refers more specifically to its institutionalized form insofar as we can consider photographic evidence of the tongue-in-cheek ritual being performed and recorded to prove, through performance, one's dedication, and credentials, towards the fandom associated with the franchise (5). However, many more applications can be identified, such as incorporated cultural capital in the case of gaming prowess being honed through training and practice in arcades, as well as, increasingly, the acquisition of goods such as prizes or collectible cards from a specific game cabinet as a form of objectified cultural capital. The former is closely related to what Mia Consalvo has called gaming capital, which refers to the knowledge, skills, and experience of a videogame player (4).

2 Tracing back to Michel Foucault's original work, heterotopias are physical spaces defined by their strong association with the collective imaginary where culture is "represented, contested and subverted" (17). These include sites dedicated to worship and

the sacred, such as churches or temples; sites dedicated to memory, such as cemeteries; or places for the arts, such as theatres. As these places transcend their physical presence and functions to address imaginary archetypes that are constantly being negotiated, perhaps we can consider the game centre as one such heterotopia upon which values related to videogame culture are being represented and subverted.

Works Cited

BlazBlue: Continuum Shift. Arcade videogame cabinet, Arc System Works, 2009.

Bourdieu, Pierre. "Les trois états du capital culturel [The Three States of Cultural Capital]." *Actes de la Recherche en Sciences Sociales*, vol. 30, no. 1, 1979, pp. 3–6.

Chunithm. Arcade videogame cabinet, Sega, 2015.

Consalvo, Mia. *Cheating: Gaining Advantage in Videogames*. MIT P, 2007.

Foucault, Michel. "Des espaces autres (conférence au Cercle d'études architecturales, 14 mars 1967) [Of Other Spaces (Conference at the Cercle of architectural studies, March 14, 1967)]." *Architecture, Mouvement, Continuité*, no. 5, 1984, pp. 46–49.

Hatsune Miku: Project DIVA Arcade. Arcade videogame cabinet, Sega, 2010.

Mobile Suit Gundam: Extreme Vs. Arcade videogame cabinet, Bandai Namco, 2010.

Index

Note: *Italic* page numbers refer to figures and page numbers followed by "n" denote endnotes.